T0407031

American Popular Music in Britain's Raj

Eastman Studies in Music

Ralph P. Locke, Senior Editor
Eastman School of Music

Additional Titles of Interest

The Gamelan Digul and the Prison-Camp Musician Who Built It:
An Australian Link with the Indonesian Revolution
Margaret J. Kartomi

Good Music for a Free People: The Germania Musical Society in Nineteenth-Century America
Nancy Newman

John Kirkpatrick, American Music, and the Printed Page
Drew Massey

Musical Creativity in Twentieth-Century China:
Abing, His Music, and Its Changing Meanings
Jonathan P. J. Stock

Music and Musical Composition at the American Academy in Rome
Edited by Martin Brody

"The Music of American Folk Song" and Selected Other Writings on American Folk Music
Ruth Crawford Seeger
Edited by Larry Polansky

The Music of the Moravian Church in America
Edited by Nola Reed Knouse

Ruth Crawford Seeger's Worlds:
Innovation and Tradition in Twentieth-Century American Music
Edited by Ray Allen and Ellie M. Hisama

"Wanderjahre of a Revolutionist" and Other Essays on American Music
Arthur Farwell
Edited by Thomas Stoner

The Whistling Blackbird: Essays and Talks on New Music
Robert Morris

A complete list of titles in the Eastman Studies in Music series
may be found on our website, www.urpress.com.

American Popular Music
in Britain's Raj

Bradley G. Shope

UNIVERSITY OF ROCHESTER PRESS

The University of Rochester Press gratefully acknowledges generous support from the AMS 75 PAYS Endowment of the American Musicological Society, funded in part by the National Endowment for the Humanities and the Andrew W. Mellon Foundation.

First published 2016

University of Rochester Press
668 Mt. Hope Avenue, Rochester, NY 14620, USA
www.urpress.com
and Boydell & Brewer Limited
PO Box 9, Woodbridge, Suffolk IP12 3DF, UK
www.boydellandbrewer.com

ISBN-13: 978-1-58046-548-9
ISSN: 1071-9989

Library of Congress Cataloging-in-Publication Data

Names: Shope, Bradley, author.
    Title: American popular music in Britain's Raj / Bradley G. Shope.
    Other titles: Eastman studies in music ; v. 131.
    Description: Rochester, NY : University of Rochester Press, 2016. | "2016 | Series: Eastman studies in music, ISSN 1071-9989 ; v. 131
        Identifiers: LCCN 2015036869 | ISBN 9781580465489 (hardcover : alkaline paper)
        Subjects: LCSH: Popular music—India—History and criticism. | Popular music—United States—History and criticism. | Popular music—India—American influences. | African American musicians—India.
        Classification: LCC ML3502.I4 S56 2016 | DDC 781.640973/0954—dc23 LC record available at http://lccn.loc.gov/2015036869

A catalogue record for this title is available from the British Library.

This publication is printed on acid-free paper.
Printed in the United States of America.

Contents

Figures

Acknowledgments

Sharad Nagar in Lucknow facilitated my initial field research. His help with my exploratory work was especially essential to developing a preliminary network of interviewees throughout India, and his devotion to reading and writing were immensely inspirational. I am deeply grateful for his many invitations to me to stay in his home. The hospitality of A. P. Seth in Gomti Nagar was unending. Anup Basu at the Indian Council for Cultural Relations (ICCR) in Lucknow facilitated introductions to a number of people helpful to my research. The Mumbai office of the ICCR assisted in finding housing through the University of Bombay. Purnima Mehta of the American Institute of Indian Studies (AIIS) was especially helpful with my work in Delhi. I am grateful for two Research Enhancement Grants from Texas A&M in Corpus Christi. Grants from the AIIS and the Foreign Language Enhancement Program of the Committee on Institutional Cooperation were also crucial to my research.

I am most especially devoted to all the people who took the time to speak with me about their lives as young men and women in the 1930s and 1940s in India. My conversations with guitarist James "Jumbo" Perry unfolded into a lasting friendship that I will always treasure. I also thank Nawab Jafar Mir Abdullah, Ram Advani, Barbara Antunis, Peter Antunis Jr., Louis Banks, Francis Braganza, Ronny Bush, Rakesh Chandra, Shubha Chaudhuri, Micky Correa, Tehrim Das, Sheila D'Costa, Betty Dignum, George Figg, Narendra Gambhir, Anthony Gideon, Satish Grover, Noreen Hansen, Jackie Joachim, K. N. Kacker, Tuku Khan, Carlton Kitto, Susheel Kurien, Carlyle McFarland, Dorothy McFarland, Anto Menezes, K. D. R. Pande, Carlton Ram, John Raphael, Rubin Ribeiro, B. D. Sanwal, Captain Ram Singh, Sister Elizabeth, Sister Saline, and Sharad Thadani, many of whom I quote in this book.

I thank the faculty and staff in the Department of Music at Texas A&M in Corpus Christi. Morag Walsh and others at the Chicago Public Library were supportive of my requests to make copies of the materials of the Roy G. Butler Collection of the Visual and Performing Arts Division. Christine

Correa in Brooklyn was highly accommodating to my requests to review and document the personal collection of her father Micky Correa. She went out of her way to ensure that I had access to this valuable collection. Naresh Fernandes in Mumbai sent sound recordings and other helpful source materials to me in 2009. The staffs at the National Archives of India in New Delhi and the U. P. State Archives in Lucknow were supportive of my requests for access to newspapers and other material. The staff at the Media Center of the New York Public Library facilitated access to the Lucknow edition of the *Pioneer* newspaper. The staff responsible for the India Office Records and Private Papers at the British Library in London accommodated my many requests for access to original manuscripts and photographs. All errors are my own.

This book is dedicated to Elizabeth, Ivy, and Stella.

Introduction

On July 8, 1865, the *Englishman* newspaper reviewed a performance by blackface minstrel showman Dave Carson at the Town Hall in Bombay. Carson was from Montana in the United States, and he had arrived in India with the San Francisco Minstrels four years earlier. That month, Bombay was at the center of a financial crisis caused by the price of cotton. The American Civil War (1861–65) decreased cotton exports from the United States and increased their value in India, and speculators in Bombay bet that the price of cotton shares would remain consistent or increase. Known as "share mania," share values increased substantially until April 1865, when the exuberance suddenly ended. On the other side of the world the Confederate armies surrendered to the Union forces to end the war. US cotton exports suddenly had the potential to reach prewar levels as the American industry regained its footing. The price of cotton in India plummeted.

The speculative economy structured to support the exchange of these commodities in Bombay collapsed on July 1, 1865, and cotton shares became almost unsellable. Banks, financial associations, insurance companies, joint-stock companies, law firms, and many other financial institutions failed, and the personal wealth of large numbers of businesspeople in Bombay declined. Dave Carson's blackface minstrel productions were known for their raucous ridicule of local people and recent events, and his performances in early July parodied the irrationality of the crash mere days after its highpoint. He entertained audiences of professional and middle-class patrons, including Europeans, British, and Indians. The *Englishman* review of his performance directly references the financial crisis, and even jokes about it:

> Dave Carson himself was as brilliant and as brimful of local hits as ever. His songs in illustration of the crisis now existing in Bombay, though extravagantly comic in their way, yet possessed a touch of the tragic in them, which, no doubt, many present felt, by sad experience, as in reality, the relation of an "ever true tale." We hear that the demands for tickets to each performance

are so numerous, that the company intend making a longer stay amongst us than they at first anticipated. On the whole, it appears to be a far better "spec" [speculation] to turn "minstrel," than anything else on the cards. The shares in a new San Francisco Minstrel Company, Limited, with Dave Carson for Manager and Secretary, would go up to a rapid premium, without much risk of loss.[1]

Carson confronted audiences with the truth of their unbalanced financial behavior and made them laugh and lament at the same time.[2] Though the Bombay crash was a recent painful memory, Carson's blackface minstrel routines were popular and his shows sold out. One can imagine that audiences in Bombay suffering the effects of the cotton trade collapse because of the US Civil War might be captivated by an American performer like Carson. In the mid-1800s, entertainers such as Carson's San Francisco Minstrels traveled to India on steamship passenger routes and brought with them transnational entertainment that could be reconfigured to be relevant to local populations. Blackface minstrel shows marked the beginning of many decades of exchanges between the popular music cultures of India, the United States, and England.

This book studies American popular music during Britain's rule in India—especially in Calcutta (modern Kolkata), Lucknow, and Bombay (modern Mumbai)—and focuses on blackface minstrelsy, ragtime, jazz, and representations of Hollywood film music in live cabarets and Hindi cinema. The book is episodic. Over the course of a century, it identifies key musical moments in the development of these styles, articulates a theoretical orientation to give meaning to music across a broad historical spectrum, and outlines the entertainment idioms and frameworks that supported their growth. In this process, it identifies musical intersections between the United States, England, and India, and argues that the popularity of American music in India often depended on its popularity in Britain, especially London, and that these three countries together constituted a trilateral entertainment network supported by global commercial and military enterprises.

I use the designation "American" in the title of the book because the music had recognizable stylistic qualities originally attributable to the United States, either in terms of musical characteristics or association with American history or culture. Yet the styles I discuss interacted with other music and changed over time and across space. No music is static, and by using the designation "American music" in this book, I acknowledge that its status as originally American was not always apparent or relevant as it interacted with localized traditions in England, India, and elsewhere. In fact, I offer a number of examples to illustrate that we must be careful when attributing musical characteristics to any one people or place, especially in light of the immense creative change and conscious variation that occurred over the decades I discuss. Musical variation is an underlying theme in most of the book's chapters, so I typically use the genre qualifier "American" to suggest heredity, not musical characteristics or contexts. It is also important to note that American music was not necessarily more commanding or pervasive than other forms of popular music, but for reasons I will discuss throughout the book, it was part of the music landscape of Britain's Raj from at least the mid-1800s.[3] Finally, although the designations "America" or "American" are sometimes used to encompass all of North and South America, in this book I use the terms to refer only to the United States.

Dave Carson was one of the most popular blackface minstrel performers in India, and he followed blackface minstrel formal structures from the United States and England, including programming a master of ceremonies (often called "Mr. Interlocutor"), an olio (miscellany) section of specialty acts or stump speeches, one-act sketches, and group or solo song-and-dance productions.[8] His shows parodied African American life in the United States, but he also used Indian melodies, Hindustani phrases, and stereotyped manners of Bengalis, Parsis, and Europeans in his routines. (Parsis are a religious minority community originally from present-day Iran; Bengalis speak the Bengali language and are from a geographic region that includes Calcutta and the state of West Bengal.) Audiences were enthusiastic about Carson's performances, and other blackface minstrel troupes throughout India reperformed his shows. Chapter 1 argues that blackface minstrelsy went through a complicated process to become part of the Indian entertainment landscape in the 1800s, but were popular in large part because of their references to both American life and local events. The aesthetic merit of Carson's performances and his humorous, racially charged accounts of the Bombay crash shaped part of the narrative about life among Europeans in India in the summer of 1865. He urged audiences to reflect more deeply on commerce and trade in Bombay through humor, and his shows represented the capacity of global entertainment to compel people to ponder everyday business life in Bombay, including the role of the United States.[9] These transnational connections operated in a business environment shaped by commercial exchanges between British, Indian, American, and other international economies in a profitable free-trade system.[10]

Since blackface minstrelsy and the black mammy costume were not considered originally British, they represented a cosmopolitanism that had meaning within a complex matrix of historical and cultural reference points that resonated on a global scale.[11] They embodied specialized knowledge of the wider world and contemporary representations of race, and stimulated the imaginations and fantasies of audiences that desired direct access to American and British entertainment. These two examples illustrate a key argument of the book, namely, that commercialized music from the United States became popular in part because of a common desire to access and express the world beyond local horizons or circumscribed boundaries, but in a manner that reflected the interests of local performers, composers, and audiences. I do not mean to imply that there is a direct musical line between blackface minstrels and jazz, but that the history of American encounters I discuss in this book resonated with people in diverse ways and, for various reasons, music associated with African Americans was sometimes most compelling for audiences.[12]

Music making is a creative process often influenced by commerce. Musicians, audiences, composers, and others must sometimes act on and respond to flows of capital or larger forces of globalization.[13] As this study will discuss, entrepreneurs built multipurpose performance theaters in Bombay and Calcutta to accommodate foreign variety troupes in the 1800s (chapter 1), art deco ballrooms in cinema halls and hotels to accommodate jazz performers in the 1930s (chapters 2 and 4), and clubs for Allied military personnel during World War II (chapter 3). Gramophone companies produced discs of commercialized jazz in the sound studios and factories of Calcutta in the 1930s and 1940s (chapters 2 and 3), and Hindi film music composers included foreign jazzy sounds in their compositions (chapter 5). In many of these circumstances, activities centered around globalized entertainment included acts of consumption or acquisition of assets or money that supported local, regional, and national economies. Music was the product of agency and intentionality, often understood through economic manifestations, and it facilitated access to the outside world through commerce and global streams of capital.[14]

Outline of the Book

Nineteenth Century

The chapters in this book are chronological, with the exception of chapter 4, which is a case study of a single city. Chapter 1 studies the decades between the 1850s and the 1910s when the economic and industrial foundations of the entertainment economy supporting American popular music took shape. During these decades, blackface minstrelsy, ragtime, early jazz, and other musical styles became commercial success stories in Bombay, Calcutta, and elsewhere, demonstrating to entertainment entrepreneurs that music from the United States was accessible and, with the right business plan, profitable. During these years the political and economic frameworks of colonialism continued to bring investment and transportation to interior India. With the arrival of the British military, young audiences eager to hear Western music spread to small cities and towns across the subcontinent, and distribution networks for printed music brought material to amateur performance groups made up of Europeans, British, and, more rarely, Indians. The chapter also traces the story of ragtime, which has a history similar to blackface minstrel shows and jazz in terms of the role of trilateral entertainment exchanges between America, England, and India. In the 1910s, ragtime—typically considered originally American—became popular in England in part because of the revue *Hullo, Ragtime!*, which opened in London on December 23, 1912, and ran for 451 performances at the Hippodrome Theatre. It also had numerous sold-out performances at the Royal Opera House in Bombay (see fig. I.1). From 1913 on, ragtime was part of the performance lineup of theater houses and clubs offering Western entertainment in urban centers across India.

In the nineteenth century, large numbers of British, European, and Indian businesspeople engaged in transnational capitalist markets and commercialized global exchanges in India. People, commerce, and art poured across international borders, and millions of British voluntarily migrated from England for economic opportunities. Transnational ideas and actions were integrated into these movements, and new technologies and innovations in the mid-1800s reconfigured spaces between England, the United States, and India, including passenger steamships and the telegraph. Gary Magee and Andrew Thompson observe that these movements made transnationalism a way of life among the British during the nineteenth century, and migrants often sought to preserve a sense of British identity overseas, which had material and concrete implications in terms of the proliferation of Western music.[15] I will discuss the economic structures that opened India's interior cities to entertainers in chapter 1. In short, a wide variety of commercial networks stitched together British subjects in India to England and facilitated movement in and out of the subcontinent with greater ease. These networks operated across national boundaries and nurtured a shared sense of community and purpose, expanding and reinforcing a perception of worldwide British belonging.[16] Music traveled these literal and imaginative domains of empire with more ease and regularity during the mid-nineteenth century, and music helped British subjects living in India for long periods of time to overcome social separation from England.

Blackface minstrel shows were a commodity in the nineteenth century. People profited from them—whether through printed music and instrument sales, paid performances, or advertising and marketing revenue—and their dissemination reflected the power of money to successfully traverse art, commodities, and entertainment across great distances. In tracing the growth and development of music in the British Empire in the last half of the nineteenth century, Jeffrey Richards notes that belief and pride in the success of the empire was inculcated in part through "well-developed and

Figure I.1. Advertisement for the show *Hullo, Ragtime!* at the Royal Opera House, Bombay. *Times of India*, November 15, 1913. Image reproduced by permission from ProQuest LLC.

commercialized leisure industries."[17] Economics inherent in the development of mass market entertainment, including rising wages, more leisure time for the masses, an efficient and integrated transport system in the railways, capitalist entrepreneurs willing to develop new leisure industries, and cheap mass production of commodities,[18] heavily influenced the character and availability of blackface minstrelsy in India, as elsewhere.

The nineteenth century also brought into view musical milieus that were a product of new time-space compressions of globalization created by England's imperialist ambitions.[19] Blackface minstrel routines in India were stylistically English, at least in part, because they included characteristics unique to blackface minstrelsy in London. Simon Frith notes that the impressive rise in popularity of blackface minstrel shows was in some respects "as much an English as an American phenomenon" because of its stylistic growth in the United Kingdom.[20] British in India were aware of the favorable reputation of minstrel shows in London, and it is likely that they would not have been as popular in India had they not developed distinct styles in England. Yet, the fact that black and blackface minstrel performances were considered originally American, or that they referenced African American life in the United States, communicated a greater global sense to audiences. This trilateral link—England, India, and the United States—represented a geographic expanse of at least half the globe and enabled music to traverse Anglophone commercial networks. With entertainment enterprises that supported traveling blackface minstrel troupes, British audiences in India could ponder representations of African American life in the distant United States and view entertainment that was popular in London, all in performances that tightly embodied these associations.

Indian entertainment of all sorts supported the market for American popular music. Local Parsi theaters often provided venue space, marketing infrastructure, and performance support staff for blackface minstrel shows. Parsis came from present-day Iran to the region of Gujarat centuries ago. They settled in the 1700s in Bombay, where many became prosperous businesspeople and began cultivating the theater and drama in the early and mid-nineteenth century. (Parsi dramas intermixed music, poetry, stagecraft, and narrative in Persian, English, Hindustani, and other languages.) In Bombay, Parsi theater owners opened or managed many of the theaters that attracted foreign performers, including blackface minstrel showpeople on their global tours.[21] Most theater venues were open for use to entertainers regardless of community affiliation or the language of the performance. These theaters attracted both Indian and European audiences, and reached out to all professional classes, not just elites.[22] The Grant Road Theatre and the Gaiety Theatre were among the most popular for blackface minstrel performances. Dave Carson frequently performed at these venues. These and other established theaters enabled interactive networks between European, British, and Indian managers and performers, and they facilitated an efficient line of communication between theater administrators and touring minstrel groups from the United States and elsewhere.

American music in India in the nineteenth century symbolized the potential of stable economic circumstances to support entertainment and leisure activities, both individual and collective, and the capacity for entertainers to profit from these activities.[23] As I will describe in chapter 1, commercial managing agencies fostered economic growth across the subcontinent and were crucial to the practical development of a minstrel circuit beyond large coastal cities. These agencies created networks of laborers, businesspeople, and capital infrastructures that made entertainers feel comfortable about traveling outside urban centers. This managing agency system provided venture money and management expertise, and was an important solution to the problem of inland movement and business development in the nineteenth century.[24] Managing agencies, at their own risk, set up companies such as jute mills and tea gardens, and after gaining successful repute attracted investors' capital into existing and new companies. Based on small private partnerships, this system enabled companies to adapt innovatively and flexibly to the challenges of economic progress.[25] Beginning in the 1830s, the system contributed in part to the creation of a class of British and Indians who confidently conducted business in India, and it was profitable and reliable until the 1890s. Entertainers tapped into social networks associated with these agencies and traveled to interior cities to perform for professional class audiences.

Trading in international shares began in Bombay in the 1830s after the establishment of the Bombay Commercial Bank, the Chartered Mercantile Bank, and the Agra Bank, among others, and US commerce and business enterprise influenced share exchanges in India from the beginning.[26] By the 1860s, the time of the share mania described above, about sixty share brokers were operating in Bombay.[27] Because the United States exported a relatively small quantity of goods to India in the mid- and late 1800s, share trade and commodity exchange with Great Britain were the primary US contributions to the economics of trilateral encounters outside the entertainment industry.[28] By the mid-1870s, the United States was a princi-ple market for the sale of British merchandise, and Great Britain was by far the largest market for US exports.[29] Though the United States and Britain viewed each other with mutual hostility and suspicion in much of the nine-teenth century, business ventures connecting Great Britain to India and the United States encouraged widespread information sharing and confi-dence in business exchanges, which facilitated interpersonal connections and international distribution of goods and capital throughout much of the Anglophone world and beyond.[30]

Turn of the Twentieth Century

After the turn of the century, consumers became more aware of the capacity of media and technology to make the transnational movements of art and music more efficient. This era included technologies capable of mass medi-ating commercialized music, including gramophones, the radio, and film. Gramophones were among the earliest mechanical reproduction technolo-gies and were widely available from at least 1898 in most urban centers and by mail order in India. They disseminated the latest music and brought mechan-ically reproduced sounds to public and private spaces where live music was not possible. Figure I.2 shows a Gramophone Company Ltd. advertisement in 1908 claiming that gramophones "enable residents in Mofussil Stations, where a good band is unprocurable, to enjoy a dance to music played by the finest bands and orchestras."[31] "Mofussil Stations" in this instance are regions outside of heavily populated areas. This advertisement features an image of a ballroom dance with a gramophone player prominently placed in the foreground, and states that the Gramophone Company supplied var-ious kinds of music for ballroom dances. Ball participants are dancing to the music and marveling at its presence, almost as if it were a distinguished participant in the ball, towering over the dancers. The advertisement also emphasizes that the Gramophone Company recorded the best orchestras and bands from Europe, and that listeners could "hear them to perfection in [their] own home."[32] Gramophone discs were sold in all manner of stores and were advertised in newspapers and other periodicals for decades. For European audiences in India, part of the appeal of the gramophone was that it made available entertainment from home. Stephen Hughes notes that the marketing strategies of gramophone companies in India often emphasized that their products were "a way of collapsing the time and space restrictions of a live performance for domestic consumption and control."[33]

DANCING TO THE
GRAMOPHONE

All the most POPULAR DANCE MUSIC by

FAMOUS BANDS and CELEBRATED ORCHESTRAS.

Apply for our SPECIAL LIST of DANCE PROGRAMME RECORDS which has been compiled with a view to enable residents in Mofussil Stations, where a good band is unprocurable, to enjoy a dance to music played by the

FINEST BANDS AND ORCHESTRAS.

We present with each set of DANCE PROGRAMME RECORDS

100 BALL PROGRAMMES.

The GRAMOPHONE is the only talking machine recognised by the GREATEST ARTISTES and enables you to hear them to perfection in your own home.

PRICE of our PERFECT RECORDS, 10inch, Rs. 2·8, 12inch, Rs. 3·12.

Write us for Catalogues and Name and Address of Nearest Dealer.

THE GRAMOPHONE COMPANY, LD.,

Post Box 48, CALCUTTA.

Figure I.2. Gramophone Company Ltd. advertisement. *Times of India*, December 3, 1908. Image reproduced by permission from ProQuest LLC.

The Indian gramophone market relied on a robust climate for commercialized entertainment in the early 1900s, and it supported a massive system of mobility and movement of music and culture within India. These domestic commercial connections enabled and shaped all kinds of cosmopolitan expressions.[34] For example, jazz was available on gramophone discs as early as the 1920s in India. One of the first recordings of a jazz song in India, "House Where the Shutters Are Green," by Lequime's Grand Hotel Orchestra, was pressed in 1926 on HMV (His Master's Voice) in the gramophone recording factories of Calcutta, and was available through mail order throughout India. Calcutta's location as a production and distribution hub for gramophones throughout Asia supported the jazz gramophone economy of India and encouraged local and traveling jazz groups such as Lequime's Grand Hotel Orchestra to find their expression in recording studios.

From the beginning, the Gramophone Company tapped into the potentials and possibilities of the gramophone market for many styles of music across the subcontinent. The long-term prospects of gramophone trade in India depended on developing a product that would appeal to a broad audience base, and Indian music constituted the most expansive market.[35] F. W. Gaisberg recorded Indian artists as early as 1902 with the Gramophone and Typewriter Ltd.[36] His most successful early recordings showcased Gauhar Jaan, a famous *tawa'if* (courtesan) singer. Gauhar Jaan eventually became the first commercially viable gramophone star in India and her popularity expanded the reach of disc sales to a more extensive audience.[37] Gaisberg states that her fame and the approximately six hundred records she recorded were the foundation for the Gramophone Company's presence in South Asia.[38] Indian musicians and artists constituted the primary artistic pool for gramophone recordings and they often focused on semiclassical styles such as *qawwali*.[39] The songs of professional Indian theater traditions also figured prominently in the early releases of the Gramophone Company. According to Michael Kinnear, "it is the recordings of prominent actors, actresses and singers of the theatres, . . . who provided The Gramophone and Typewriter, Ltd., with the recordings which were to achieve the highest sales figures."[40] At the turn of the century, gramophones were sold by a number of companies, including the Gramophone and Typewriter Ltd. (which had at least two offices in Calcutta), the Universal Talking Machine Depot, T. E. Bevan and Company, and the Oriental Phonetic Recording Company, among many others.[41] By the 1930s, this gramophone industry supported jazz musicians and orchestras in India seeking to record jazz standards for domestic consumption. Because of this impressive market, many jazz performers became recognizable recording artists—including Teddy Weatherford, Roy Butler, Ken Mac, Chic Chocolate, Reuben Solomon, and others.

Audiences became even more linked to the entertainment industries of Britain, Europe, and the United States with the advent of the film industry. The commercialization of film took place in India around the same time as in the United States and England, and projection technologies such as the *cinématographe* and chronophone became popular entertainment mediums. The earliest screening of a film in India likely took place on July 7, 1896, when the Lumière Brothers' *cinématographe* was exhibited to enthusiastic audiences at Watson's Hotel in Bombay,[42] seven months after its premiere unveiling in December 1895 in Paris.[43] The *cinématographe* was a camera, projector, and print machine all in one. Many screenings featured instrumental accompaniment on the piano or percussion, or with less sophisticated synchronization using gramophone players, and touring exhibitors often used the same venues that had been used for variety performances.[44] The chronophone used more advanced sound synchronization technology and was introduced after the turn of the century. The America-India Theatre in 1908 used the chronophone to feature sound shorts that, according to advertisements, consisted of "talking, singing, and Musical animated pictures" and featured "Grand Opera, Light Opera, Choruses, Duets, Solos, Recitals, Ballads, etc."[45] Moving pictures were exhibited in variety shows, magic shows, dramatic plays, burlesques, and even ballroom dances, and often featured projection onto 25' by 20' screens.[46] As chapter 2 will discuss, films in the 1910s brought attention to dance and music trends from Europe, England, and the United States—including Apache dancing, the maxixe, ragtime, and many other styles—and cabaret scenes in films created demand for live jazzy cabarets in Bombay and Calcutta.

The 1930s and 1940s

Chapter 2 discusses racial iconographies in performance marketing materials, and advances in sound and media technologies, especially gramophones and film, in the 1920s and 1930s. It focuses on jazz and Hollywood representations of black music. It details exoticism associated with African American musicians in India, outlines the place of jazz and Hollywood film music as a cosmopolitan art, and comments on advertising strategies used in the dissemination of these styles in India. Before the 1930s, exhibitors often screened films in the same venues that featured variety perfor-mances, but in the 1930s decorative new cinema halls formalized films as stand-alone entertainment that reinforced the sophistication of the cin-ema. These halls featured names such as the Eros, the Mayfair Cinema, the Capitol, the Empire, and the Empress, and offered first runs of fea-ture films from the United States and England. Hollywood films created enthusiasm for jazz, and local jazz orchestras frequently performed songs from films. As I will discuss in chapter 2, the Universal Pictures film *Show Boat* was screened in Bombay in August 1936, and was reconfigured into a successful cabaret at the Taj Mahal Palace Hotel titled "Show Boat Dance." The hotel show included songs, dance, and tap dancing from the film, all performed by black jazz musicians living in India at the time.[47] Similar to blackface minstrelsy, jazz in India was popular in its early years in no small part because of its popularity in England. But in contrast to the minstrel circuit, jazz became widespread largely because of new sound and media reproduction technologies.

Chapter 2 also observes that African American musicians represented contact points with cosmopolitan lifestyles, but were consistently sub-ject to a stubborn provincialism.[48] Racial iconographies were integrated into jazz marketing and advertising strategies when African American jazz musicians arrived in India in the 1930s. African American musicians Teddy Weatherford, Roy Butler, Crickett Smith, Rudy Jackson, Creighton Thompson, Bill Coleman, Leon Abbey, and others came from Chicago, New York, and elsewhere and lived in India for months or years at a time. These musicians heavily influenced the development of jazz in India, yet were frequently represented using plantation images and so-called darky iconographies. Figure I.3 is a photo of four African American jazz musi-cians at the Taj Mahal Palace Hotel in Bombay. These four performers, Creighton Thompson, Crickett Smith, Rudy Jackson, and Roy Butler, started a group called the Plantation Quartet, which is shown here. They were often advertised in planation garb as laborers lacking sophistication, or sometimes with overstated red lips, which hints at blackface minstrel images. Other times they were advertised in formal tuxedos singing into a large microphone. Such representations illustrate an attempt to show-case both the cosmopolitan sophistication of urban jazz musicians and the primitivism (or exoticism) associated with jazz music and musicians, which together compelled audiences to peer into an imagined African American lifestyle. For British and foreign audiences, they became manifestations of nostalgia and an opportunity to experience images from home.[49]

Figure I.3. Plantation Quartet, Taj Mahal Palace Hotel, Bombay, 1934. Photographer unknown. Reproduced by permission from the Chicago Public Library, Visual and Performing Arts Division, Roy Butler Collection.

Some program booklets layered an air of sophistication onto blackface minstrel images. Figure I.4 shows the front page of the 1938–39 season program booklet from the Taj Mahal Palace Hotel. It features an image of Teddy Weatherford, a jazz pianist and bandleader who performed in India for much of the 1930s and 1940s, and includes representations of minstrel images such as exaggerated lips, white gloves, and a balloonish head, but Weatherford is also wearing a tuxedo and holding a baton, creating the impression of class and refinement.[50] African American musicians in India were viewed favorably but, as we have seen, in some respects lived under a restrictive racist lens. Teddy Weatherford was from an underprivileged family, but he had talent as a pianist, which enabled him to travel the globe, including to Shanghai and other Asian cities, and to live a cosmopolitan lifestyle that was at times luxurious. Roy Butler, Crickett Smith, and Rudy Jackson had similar class backgrounds. Working in luxury hotels and elite venues in India was partially a strategy to live outside the racism of the

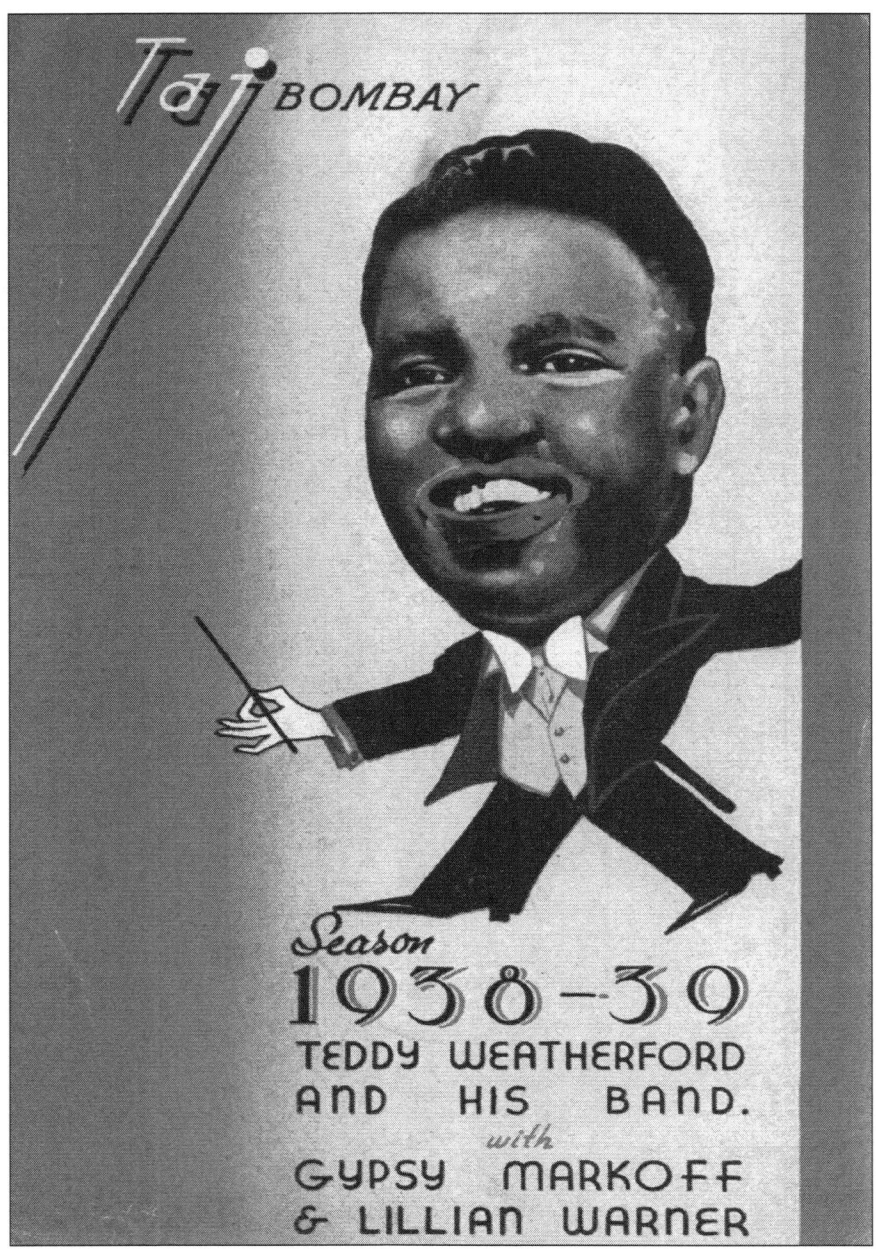

Figure I.4. Teddy Weatherford and His Band with Gypsy Markoff and Lillian Warner season brochure at the Taj Mahal Palace Hotel, 1938–39. Artist unknown. Reproduced by permission from the Chicago Public Library, Visual and Performing Arts Division, Roy Butler Collection.

United States and beyond the racism of India, and these promotional images were a tactic that used race to create opportunity. Sometimes issues surrounding race inform music appreciation, even when the music represents innovative frontiers of creativity. To be sure, American entertainment in India did not necessarily symbolize tolerance or respect for diversity or acceptance of cultural difference.[51]

Chapter 3 investigates the entertainment economy of wartime Calcutta and the Allied military buildup between 1943 and 1945. It studies performances of the United Service Organizations (USO), the nonprofit organization that brought live entertainment to US troops, and the British Entertainments National Service Association (ENSA), which brought entertainment to British armed forces. The chapter comments on the tense relationship between British and American military personnel in the city, and outlines the scope of radio broadcasting and gramophone disc distribution from both foreign and domestic sources. England, the United States, and other Allied countries established supply routes across China, Burma (modern Myanmar), and India, and Calcutta was their headquarters for much of the war. The military built roads and constructed airfields across India and took advantage of existing British military infrastructures and know-how. This buildup influenced Western entertainment throughout India. Jazz musicians saw their audiences expand significantly, and the gramophone industry benefited from a new market, at least temporarily.

Chapter 3 also explores the relationship between commercial and military entertainment markets in Calcutta. With the arrival of tens of thousands of Allied troops in the city, including many from the United States, part of the urban environment was reconfigured to meet the entertainment needs of these young men and women. The Allied military restricted the movements of troops during their leisure time and allowed soldiers to patronize a limited number of entertainment establishments. Select jazz venues focused on the needs of these new military patrons, adapting and restructuring accordingly, including by booking American jazz musicians and supporting ad hoc and amateur dance band performances. A secondary discussion in the chapter addresses the dramatic inequality in the consumption of jazz. George T. Heinemann, a US military officer stationed in Calcutta, lamented that entering Firpo's Restaurant and Bar, a jazz venue frequented by troops, patrons stepped "over corpses to walk into this place, laying on the doorstep."[52] Heinemann is referring to Calcutta during the Bengal famine (1943–44), when at least three million died from starvation and disease. Firpo's Restaurant and Bar and other jazz venues insulated troops from the hardships of Calcutta, and the chapter touches on some of the incongruities associated with jazz consumption in India.

Chapter 4 presents a case study of Lucknow, a small city in the state of Uttar Pradesh. The chapter draws most of its material from ethnographic research I had conducted with elderly individuals in Lucknow who had performed and consumed jazz in the late 1930s and 1940s. It analyzes the local music economy during these decades, and comments on the character of dance clubs, cafés, and cinemas that were built to cater to a growing awareness of jazz. It identifies a change in the character of music consumption among the British population of Lucknow beginning in the 1930s, and comments on the distinguishing traits of jazz in a small interior city. I include this case study to give voice to everyday consumers of jazz and to illustrate jazz's influence on Goan Christians and Anglo-Indians, two communities that constituted a primary audience for jazz in Lucknow. (The Anglo-Indians I discuss in this chapter were born and raised in India and have both European and Indian ancestry.)[53] For example, James "Jumbo" Perry was a guitarist who first played in the late 1930s in Lucknow. I feature his musicianship to articulate factors contributing to the growth and development of a young jazz musician who did not achieve recognition outside of Lucknow. Shelia D'Costa, a member of the Women's Auxiliary Corps (India), organized dances during the war at both free social events and for-profit commercial establishments. I include her voice to illustrate a young woman's enthusiasm for organizing Western entertainment far from the cosmopolitan centers of Bombay and Calcutta. Dorothy McFarland, an avid collector of jazz gramophone discs, was especially keen on songs from Hollywood films. She often spoke to me about purchasing new and used gramophone discs from salesmen who came to her house when she was a young woman during World War II. I introduce McFarland to illustrate the vast proliferation of jazz gramophone discs for sale across India, and to show that commercial encounters with jazz occurred in the intimate environment of the home, even in small cities and towns. These are just a few examples of the individuals I will introduce to show that cosmopolitan encounters influenced the everyday lives of consumers, stimulated their imaginations, and facilitated intimate commercial interactions.

Chapter 5 claims that music from the United States was occasionally integrated into Hindi film music. A number of early Hindi film music composers embraced Hollywood music for source material in their compositions. From the 1940s, C. Ramchandra, the composer duo Shankar-Jaikishan, and Naushad Ali creatively used musical material from Hollywood to contribute to a stylistic continuity developing in Hindi films at the time, commonly referred to as *filmi*, or "film-style." The chapter focuses on songs composed for cabaret scenes in Hindi films between 1943 and 1951. It is well-known that Hollywood music influenced the early years of Hindi film music, but much less is known about the detailed compositional process involved in in these musical interactions, including the role of jazzy caba-rets in Bombay. I analyze several song-and-dance sequences to demonstrate the manner in which these composers sought to fit into the developing *filmi* stylistic approach, and I detail the role of the Bombay cabaret industry in this process. I articulate their exchange of musical ideas over the course of these few years, and I suggest that although their global vision sparked at least some of their initial compositional practice, musical exchanges in Bombay always influenced their nuanced embrace of these global visions.[54] Chapter 5 describes the interaction between global and local music in the soundtracks of early Hindi films and the stylistic variations made manifest in this relationship. Taken together, these five chapters explore ideas about popular music development within larger patterns of music commoditiza-tion and dissemination under colonialism, and articulate a variety of enter-tainment encounters between England, America, and India.

The book as a whole reveals that musicians and businesspeople regularly collaborated, and that musicians in many cases were successful because of effective entrepreneurial activity.[55] Ragtime performers, jazz musicians, blackface minstrel show people, and Hindi film music composers achieved creative autonomy and were active agents in embracing new modes of sound and film reproduction, advertising platforms, and commercial dis-tribution networks. Whether through printed sheet music (Dave Carson), gramophones and radio (Teddy Weatherford), or the availability of Hollywood film songs as creative material (C. Ramchandra), music makers often assimilated to the realities of entertainment commerce, embraced the opportunity to answer the musical needs of masses of audiences, and empowered themselves through media, marketing, and new technologies.

Finally, it is important to mention that the relationship between England and America in the nineteenth and twentieth centuries ebbed and flowed, improving at certain times and falling by the wayside at other times. But through most of this period, the exchange of goods, people, capital, and culture across the Atlantic proliferated. Even during periods of challenge and tension in this relationship, common interests and goals brought the American and English political or military establishments together. In chapter 3, I outline the tensions between American and British troops during World War II. According to Christopher Bayly and Tim Harper, Americans were sometimes offended by what they saw as the prejudices of the British Empire and imperialism in general, and viewed the government of India as "anti-American," incompetent, and corrupt,[56] perhaps unmindful that the United States and its military were segregated along racial lines. Yet the China-Burma-India (CBI) allied operations during World War II, which brought tens of thousands of US and British troops to India, required nuanced military collaboration across South and East Asia. Troops collaboratively built landing strips, roads, and military bases over vast areas and were successful in holding back the Japanese military. In this instance, winning the war involved skillful collaboration, even while surface tensions persisted.

Scope

This book is not intended to be linear or comprehensive. Similar to Andrew Jones's pioneering work on the jazz age in China,[57] I take the approach that to understand the discursive and social formations that produced, received, and deployed music, it is important to study cultural meaning over the course of several decades and expound on the diverse ways in which people engaged music. I follow Jones's strategy of tracing the development of music in the context of a larger colonial entertainment culture, and at times I attempt to bridge the gap between popular music and colonial life.[58] I frequently focus on jazz and articulate occasions and trends in its development, but my concern is with the broader contexts and meanings inherent in musical links between the United States, England, and India, and in this process I study blackface minstrelsy, ragtime, and film music. I also follow Sara Cohen's strategy of focusing on single cities or neighborhoods to understand the production and consumption of commercialized music.[59] I examine new spaces in the global music encounter, from the neighborhood of Hazratganj in the small town of Lucknow that was known more for developing Indian styles of music and dance, to Calcutta during World War II when US military personnel reinvigorated a market for jazz in defined military spaces, and to Bombay in the mid-1800s during a global financial crisis. Each time and place compels us to view globalization not just through an international lens but also through the lens of city spaces, including the movement of music, people, industries, capital, and commerce between neighborhoods.[60] Jazz was not pervasive across all of India, so it is necessary to focus on key cities and neighbor-hoods to formulate larger arguments on the commercial and musical exchanges connecting Calcutta, Lucknow, and Bombay to each other and to the world.

We should also consider that the United States was by some measures an imperial power in its own right and that blackface minstrelsy, ragtime, jazz, and Hollywood films fully subscribed to racist stereotypes and cultural outlooks.[61] Furthermore, my focus on American music should not be seen to negate the leadership of many Indians in producing modern visions and spaces, musical or otherwise. For example, most of the ballrooms, clubs, and cinemas I reference were established and operated by success-ful Indian businesspeople, among whom one of the most noteworthy was Jamsetji Tata, born in Gujarat. Tata established the Taj Mahal Palace Hotel in Bombay in 1903. From the 1920s to the 1950s (and beyond) the ball-room was a primary venue for the performance of jazz and jazzy cabarets,[62] and its creative directors designed thematic shows that influenced a hand-ful of early Hindi film song composers, including C. Ramchandra. The hotel was also on the cutting edge of radio relay technologies and orches-tras broadcast live jazz from the main ballroom. The United States was becoming an economic powerhouse during the period I examine, so it is understandable that its popular culture might proliferate across the globe. American music was part of a long history of imperial movements into South Asia, and it was in some respects a feature of the imperial landscape because both the United States and England determined the guidelines by which audiences could become a part of the social life of this music. Thus, consumption of American music in some ways represented an imperial cosmopolitanism because it was often reimagined and supported in India through colonial institutions, commercial enterprises, and social codes. It was thus part of a process to which only economically or racially privileged communities enjoyed access. In short, the consumption of American music was not necessarily part of a democratic process that supplied entertain-ment to everyone who was interested.[63]

It is important to note that some of the imperial networks and other globalized processes I discuss began decades before the mid-1800s. From the early years of the British presence in India, music facilitated elite lines of communication across international borders. Ian Woodfield argues that late eighteenth-century performances of European music in Calcutta were similar to the manners and inclinations of the concertgoing public in London.[64] He observes that the character of many performing institutions and clubs in India at this time matched "exactly those of most English provincial centres, and musical tastes in the [British] community followed no less closely those of the concert-going public in London."[65] Music recitals were held in private homes at this time,[66] and a steady demand for European instruments, including pianofortes and sheet music, began in the 1780s.[67] Orchestras and bands performed in Calcutta as early as the mid-1780s, and a large-scale performance of George Frideric Handel's *Messiah* in 1797 was an attempt to mirror similar events in London. Small instruments such as violins and flutes were readily available and easy to secure from England, and by the late 1700s these instruments "poured into Calcutta in very large numbers" to support military bands.[68] Instruments and music were available through companies specializing in music or through informal networks of friends and acquaintances who could bring instruments back with them from England.[69] These networks supported European classical and British regimental music, although I did not find that American popular music was a significant part of these musical exchanges.

A brief word should be said about jazz audiences. Indians whose backgrounds connected them directly to the English language or Christianity were often front-runners in the production and consumption of Western music. Individuals in these classifications—Anglo-Indians, Parsis, and other minority groups with similar associations—together with Goan Christians and foreigners constituted the majority of consumers. (Goa was a separate nation on the west coast of the subcontinent and is now a state in India.) According to personal history narratives I collected from elderly Anglo-Indian jazz connoisseurs in Lucknow and Calcutta, the youth of the Anglo-Indian community at the time enthusiastically embraced Hollywood films and listened to jazz on gramophones and the radio. Goans similarly embraced jazz, and instruction in European music in parochial schools in Goa under Portuguese rule was probably a primary motivating factor. For these musicians, Western music was not necessarily foreign, but rather the music of a self-demarcated community in which global and local music had intersected for centuries. In fact, the history of European music curricula in parish schools and seminaries in Goa stretches back to the 1500s. Possibly the earliest recorded instance of ongoing instruction in Western music on the subcontinent occurred in conjunction with the founding of the Jesuit College of Saint Paul in 1542 in Goa, in which converted boys were instructed in music.[70] Giuseppe Sebastiani, an Italian Carmelite priest, later writes describing 1683 Goa: "There is no town or village of the Christians which does not have in its church an organ, harp, and viola, and a good choir of musicians who sing for festivities, and for holy days, Vespers, masses, and litanies, and with much cooperation and devotion."[71] Finally, audiences in this book also included the masses of people exposed to Indian film music. Jazzy elements in the music scores of C. Ramchandra, the composer duo Shankar-Jaikishan, Naushad Ali, and others reached millions of Indian filmgoers of all backgrounds. In all these instances, music was integrated into the interests and aesthetics of a variety of people over many decades. The aesthetic judgments of these composers and audiences represented a depth of complexity that I aim to unravel in this book.

Orientation

The origins of my theoretical arguments come from personal history narratives I collected in North India over the course of fifteen years, but most of this book draws on archival material in a number of public and private collections, especially the Roy G. Butler collection at the Visual and Performing Arts Division of the Chicago Public Library, the Media Center of the New York Public Library, the personal collection of Micky Correa now in possession of his daughter Christine Correa in Brooklyn, New York, and the India Office section of the British Library, which houses diaries and other personal items. I did most of my field research in Lucknow, Nainital, Delhi, Mumbai, and Kolkata. In my study of jazz in chapters 2, 3, and 4, I do not claim to offer a comprehensive survey of musicians, orchestras, or venues throughout India at the time, and I have avoided mentioning certain musicians and orchestras because of a lack of reliable information. Recent studies on the history of jazz in Bombay, including Naresh Fernandes's *Taj Mahal Foxtrot*, address some of the important names and venues I do not explore in detail. A broad study of Western popular music in India is also not within the scope of this book. Scholars have widely addressed popular music in South Asia, and there is certainly much additional work to be done.

Much of this book focuses on music against the backdrop of several important events in the history of India, including the Indian Rebellion of 1857, the Salt Satyagraha and civil disobedience, the Government of India Act (1935), the Khilafat Movement, the Simon Commission, communal riots in North India, and many other political and social proceedings of the Independence Movement. As the move toward independence gained momentum in the 1920s, many minority communities—including Anglo-Indians, Goan Christians, and Parsis—held conflicting positions about the British presence in India. Though some individuals may have expressed overtly political opinions, I do not address political ideologies in this book unless they are relevant to my discussions of music. In doing so, I by no means minimize the importance of significant political events occurring during the decades I discuss.

Finally, at various points during the colonial period, British and Europeans engaged music of all sorts, including Indian music and dance. Ian Woodfield, Charles Capwell, and others have made clear that British and Europeans in India at times embraced Indian entertainment.[72] Woodfield claims that the eighteenth-century "Hindostannie Air," a short piece derived from an Indian original but arranged in a European idiom, represented efforts to engage and appreciate Indian music. Similarly, "nautch" or "notch" dances, performances of Indian dance, entered the vocabulary of British in India in the late eighteenth century,[73] and were popular in public and private settings. In this light, I do not mean to imply that American music somehow affected people more compellingly or resourcefully, but that for reasons that changed over time, people chose music from the United States for a portion of their entertainment. I hope this book is seen as one additional study of the popular music landscape of India, and not as a study on the dominance of Western or American music.

Chapter One

Entertainment Globalization, 1850s to 1910s

This chapter addresses the practical capacity of blackface minstrelsy and ragtime to constitute a significant portion of Western entertainment in India in the mid-nineteenth and early twentieth centuries. In this era of transnational entertainment networks and new mechanical reproduction technologies, these styles of music spread unevenly, yet consistently, across India. This chapter shows that regimental bands and ballroom dances supported the entertainment needs of British and Europeans in India, and asserts that commercial structures and social capital associated with these entertainments facilitated demand for music from the United States. In this process it comments on the spread of printed music, musical instruments, and musicians, and outlines the role of ballroom dances and regimental bands in their proliferation. It then focuses on blackface minstrel shows in the 1800s and ragtime at the turn of the century, detailing their scope and character, including the role of theater venues, gramophone recordings, and foreign entertainment troupes. This chapter concentrates on music whose audiences were primarily British, Europeans, or English-speaking Indians, and suggests that blackface minstrel shows and ragtime were transnational styles that reached India almost from their beginnings.

For audiences in India, knowledge of the African American origins of blackface minstrel shows and ragtime—including cultural, historical, and geographical roots—represented select knowledge of the history of black America. Blackface minstrel performances encompassed many characteristics—comedy, parody, acrobats, and mischief—but also exemplified the recent history of slavery in the United States. Ragtime embodied many attributes—antecedents in "coon" songs, an emphasis on syncopation, and prevalence in American brass bands—and was sometimes considered rooted in the black minstrel or slave music idioms. Accurate or not, these links to African American origins signified black exoticism which was important to value construction and cosmopolitan meaning. Furthermore, as I mention in the introduction to this book, blackface minstrelsy and ragtime were popular in India in many respects because they were popular in England, especially London, and they represented adherence to musical trends in both Great Britain and the United States. Thus, this chapter expands on my earlier discussions of the trilateral musical links between India, England, and the United States.

Commercial Connections, 1800s

Commercial and transportation infrastructures supported the spread of American music in India in the mid- and late 1800s. The opening of the Suez Canal in 1869 and the arrival of the steamship, railroad, and telegraph to India in the mid-1800s presented new opportunities for businesspeople, thus facilitating trading and commercial ventures. These infrastructures increased demand for commodity imports and buttressed exports to China and other countries, particularly in textiles.[1] After the Indian Rebellion in 1857, the British government created a formal administration in place of the East India Company and sought to promote agricultural product exports, encourage foreign investment, and develop infrastructure. These investments in the economy benefited industries, organizations, and other commercial ventures that depended on coordinated business-making across India, including in sparsely populated regions. By the 1860s, India was a significant market for manufactured goods and raw materials, and was a primary contributor to the empire's international profit-making structure.[2]

Managing agencies encouraged investment and channeled capital into industries throughout India. They created a demand for steam tugging, river steamboats, and the railroad, and expanded commercial networks in India that linked city to city and town to town. This managing agency system was somewhat unique to India; its origins are attributed to Carr, Tagore and Company in 1834, and eventually matured into a system that controlled or managed numerous public companies and that took the risk associated with business and entrepreneurial ventures in India, including inland navigation development.[3] The public bought stock in these managing agencies, and smaller mercantile businesses used them to traverse the complexities of conducting business. With the emergence of Carr, Tagore and Company, effective collaborations between European and Indian businesspeople further facilitated interior development, including construction of the railroad in the 1850s and publishing of reliable maps.[4]

A. Claude Brown suggests that during this era cheap and efficient transportation supported foreign entertainment companies seeking performance opportunities in India: "Steamer and railway fares were sufficiently moderate to allow of good-sized [entertainment] companies being brought out [to India], with ample supply of 'props,' at frequently recurring intervals throughout the year."[5] Beginning in 1853, less than 100 miles of railway spanned India. By 1860 that number rose to about 2,000 miles, by 1864 to about 4,000 miles, by 1883 to about 10,500 miles, and by 1897 to 20,391 miles.[6] The exponential increase in the size of the railway service made intra-India travel more efficient and fast,[7] and created what Nitin Sinha calls a "communication grid,"[8] which provided the framework for commodity exchange and business ties among people stationed in interior locations. These ties increased potentials and possibilities in intra-India business ventures. The railroad allowed European exporters to bypass indigenous merchants and middlemen, so by the end of the nineteenth century, a smaller number of prominent merchants established more complete control of the commodity chain, which facilitated more resourceful communication between successful British and European businessmen. Further, a ship transport system connecting San Francisco with Australia, and a system of intercolonial telegraph networks connecting Australia and New Zealand to pacific ports via India in the 1870s enabled transnational travel and communication.[9] These essential connections brought increasing numbers of American entertainers to India, New Zealand, and Australia, and enabled foreign artistes to reach out to entertainment proprietors in India to secure jobs performing for Europeans and British in both urban and rural environs. Dave Carson was one of the first to prove it was possible to make significant profit in this growing economic climate.

Social and Musical Connections, 1800s

British government employees, businessmen seeking to strengthen professional ties, and British troops created a demand for social clubs in both densely populated and remote locations across India. Most British businesspeople to arrive in India in the middle part of the century had backgrounds similar to those of nineteenth-century merchants at the time in England, and club membership was an important part of business life.[10] Social clubs in the mid- and late 1800s in India maintained rigid social codes that facilitated the coordination of business opportunities. Membership criteria were based on a number of factors, but generally involved considerations of class, occupation, and race. Initially considered primarily residential and dining quarters, social clubs grew in the latter part of the century to become comfortable sites for business discussions, sporting events, and entertainment, including ballroom dance and military music programs.[11] Mrinalini Sinha suggests that "European social clubs in India served to incorporate Europeans abroad into an emerging new colonial political and social order . . . and played a vital role in the homogenization of the domestic life of Europeans abroad."[12] This homogenization included conscious efforts to program Western music.

Regimental bands were integrated into these social and commercial connections. They performed marches and other popular songs of the era in social clubs (and other private and public venues), and they populated interior cities and towns with musicians, not an easy task in the mid- and late 1800s. J. Mackenzie Rogan notes that regimental bands were tightly integrated into the social life of smaller towns:

> Services of a band for amusement and relaxation at stations, where the troops are entirely or almost entirely dependent upon themselves, are invaluable. Dances, concerts, theatrical performances, and entertainment of every description are practically dependent upon the band for their success, while cricket, football, polo, and gymkhanas owe much to the assistance of regimental bands. Church services are in many stations dependent upon bands for the musical portion of the service.[13]

During the Victorian era thousands of bands were active in the empire and were important indicators of life back home for the British.[14] They stimulated trade and commerce for local businesses, and provided music for all sorts of entertainment. British troops were stationed in India for years at a time, for at least ten years in the middle of the century and for about six years or more toward the end of the century,[15] so becoming a member of a band represented active participation in musical ties to the homeland over the course of several years.

It is important to note that these regimental bands were not always considered profitable, easy to maintain, or composed of skillful musicians. An anonymous article in the *Bombay Times and Journal of Commerce* in 1848 claims:

After a world of trouble, expense, and exertion, [a band plays] . . . a march or two, and some quadrilles and waltzes; the youngsters, who have no more idea of *taste* in music than they have of the science of optics, are delighted, and invite you to come and hear their band. To gratify the vanity of your friends you accompany them, and your politeness places you on the tenterhooks for an hour or more. Well, two days after this, one of their performers dies of cholera, dysentery, or some other of the numerous evils that flesh in this country is peculiarly heir to—their band is so crippled by the loss that it is quite laughable to listen to it.[16]

In spite of these challenges, military bands accommodated the demand for British music and supported commercial and artistic endeavors. An anonymous article in the *Bombay Times and Journal of Commerce* in 1847 suggests that "a band in a regiment conduces highly to its appearance in a military point of view, as well as its being a great source of amusement in camp or cantonments."[17] Bands contributed to the social life of European and British audiences and, in spite of the presumed shadow of death waiting around the corner, proliferated.

British regimental bands expanded the market for instrumental method books and printed music.[18] These published materials became popular in the mid-1800s when the market for training amateur musicians in regimental bands increased and publishers became more ambitious to meet this need.[19] Boosey and Sons from London contracted authorized agents in Bombay, and their literature was available by storefront and mail order throughout India from at least the 1850s.[20] Their inventory included instructions for forming and maintaining a military band and guides for composers of instrumental music. Much of this material aimed to provide training for amateur musicians at early stages and offered instruction on a wide variety of instruments.

Sheet music was in broad circulation as well, and consumers in small towns in interior India could purchase it through mail order from Bombay, Calcutta, and other large urban centers. Rudolph Sibold sold sheet music postpaid in India, including collections of music performed in parades, a common practice in London at the time.[21] By 1851, Sibold's books available in India included slow marches and works that featured some of his original compositions and arrangements.[22] He also sold quick marches for movement on parade in four-inch booklets that could be attached to instruments while in formation. Some of his quick marches included "negro tunes," which were probably songs from the black or blackface minstrel repertoire.[23] Lists of sheet music arriving on streamships, often from

Singapore, also frequently list "negro songs," which were sold by Sibold and other distributors.[24] Titles such as "Dalhousie" and "Punjab" referenced locales in India, and some of these items were available by subscription, arriving once each month in score or with full band parts. Sibold's collections were advertised as "approved arrangements" for parades and sanctioned by Prince Edward and prominent musical directors in England.[25]

Entertainment designed for British in India was based on assumptions about the nature, role, and meaning of music, issues of legitimacy, the socializing potential of music, and the legacy of English music in general. Music reaffirmed practices and precedents in England, and at the same time reflected ideas and values unique to the British in India, perhaps no more clearly seen than in ballroom dances. Balls facilitated meaningful interpersonal interactions, reinforced social codes, and facilitated productive social exchanges. Both Europeans and Indians organized balls across the subcontinent. Sir Edward Braddon writes in 1872 that

> there are balls given . . . by the Viceroy, the Governor, Lieutenant-Governors, and Commanders in Chief; there are regimental balls; there are balls given at large stations to some great star who has fallen on them; balls given by the civilians to the military; balls given by individuals who have [money] to throw away; subscription balls and reunions. In every station there is a room which is large enough for the purpose.[26]

Regimental bands often performed the music.[27] Because of their popularity, balls boosted demand for orchestras, instruments, and sheet music. They promoted cooperation among participants and put on display shared musical values and expected behaviors.

Balls were taken seriously. They commanded significant resources and attention, and reinforced contemporary ideas about the value of music and dance, often by accentuating ornate decor. Descriptions of balls in Calcutta's Town Hall are numerous throughout the nineteenth century. One anonymous description in 1894 hints at tasteful decoration:

> A large *shamiana* [large tent shelter] canopied the steps which give access to the main entrance, the steps being carpeted and the whole being illuminated by electric lights specially set up for the occasion. The staircases were very tastefully decorated with foliage plants, while the vestibule was arranged as a drawing-room with luxurious furniture. Entering the hall, the scene was one which baffles description. The roof was chastely draped in Louis XV style with light blue and white, the colours of the Order of the Star of India . . . and Indian Empire the latter being of a deeper blue than the former. The stage at the south end had been removed, and in its stead a dais [raised platform]

was erected in the middle of the main hall, from the centre of which a mag-
nificent palm spread its leaves over a veritable cloth of gold. Here and there
along the wings of the hall, pleasant arbours were erected[.] The band was
accommodated in the gallery[.] The supper-room below was profusely decorated with flags and other bunting [decorative cloths], the Viceregal table
being surmounted by strips of red and white, the Lansdowne colours.[28]

This event was carefully planned and the venue was elaborately adorned.

Balls facilitated productive exchanges among participants. They carried
social weight and invitees took interpersonal interactions at dances seriously. Courtesies between partners and dance skills were recognized and
treated with the utmost importance, and balls facilitated dancing and informal conversation in a relaxed setting.[29] Jane Maria Strachey recounted her
experiences at a ballroom dance in Simla in June 1863 in rare detail in her
diary, and many of her entries reference interactions with dance partners.
In the excerpt below she comments on the final dance of the evening,
which the band performed in fast tempo. Making a good effort, she was
able to keep up with the tempo, and and she took seriously a compliment
she received from her dance partner, Captain Grant. She also writes that
she did not leave the dance until daylight the next morning:

> I never heard such a pace as the band played it at; they were tired and wanted
> to tire us. At the first pause, Capt. Grant said, "This is an impossible pace; we
> can only just do it in time and there is not any one else in the room, at any
> rate no other lady, who could." I was rather proud of the compliment, but
> confess to having been thoroughly "done" when it was over. I could not speak
> and could hardly breathe. It was about a quarter of an hour before I could
> go. I think we were the very last ladies. It struck four just after we left and we
> went home in broad daylight.[30]

Eventually, blackface minstrel material flowed into the repertoire of balls
and other social events.

Blackface Minstrels

What was the character of blackface minstrel shows? Who were the performers? On November 17, 1869, American folklorist Charles Godfrey
Leland mentions in a letter to his sister Dave Carson's astonishing success in performing minstrel shows in India. He recounts Carson's work in
India frankly, boasting that Carson "made $100,000 by singing nigger [*sic*]

minstrel songs in broken Hindoo English in Oriental dress." Calling him an "enterprising American,"[31] Leland was captivated with Carson's commercial enterprise, his keen business sense, his capacity to integrate art with business in India, and his success in securing significant income in India from entertainment. How did Carson profit so appreciably, and what commercial enterprises were put in place during this era that supported contemporary popular entertainment?

The cotton crisis in 1865 mentioned in the introduction to this book had an important initial influence on the practical support of the minstrel circuit in urban theaters. According to Robert Lee, this financial crisis "together with technical changes and structural innovations in the export trade, pushed many Indian merchants out of business, . . . they lacked the business connections to Europe to finance their exports and sell their merchandise."[32] Though European businessmen continued to rely on Indian merchants to act as guarantee brokers, many turned to wealthy English-speaking Parsis, who became increasingly successful and more integrated into urban business practices.[33] Parsis built and managed theaters that featured English, Indian, and Parsi dramas, and their close ties with British businessmen meant that supporting blackface minstrel shows was commercially possible and profitable.[34] The first Parsi theater production is usually dated to 1853 at the thousand-seat Grant Theatre in Bombay. After this date, Parsi theater owners booked minstrel shows from the United States at the Grant Theatre and other venues, often hiring troupes for months at a time.[35] Minstrel performances, especially Dave Carson's shows, often brought significant income. Traveling companies such as the Georgia Minstrels, Southern Star Minstrels, Dave Carson's Minstrels (also known as the San Francisco Minstrels), the Victoria Loftus Troupe, and the Australian Froliques performed at the Grant Theatre and other halls. Shows were advertised in local English-language newspapers and well-attended .[36]

Black and blackface minstrel shows were transatlantic entertainment almost from the beginning. Pioneering blackface solo performer Thomas Rice performed early manifestations of blackface in England in 1836,[37] and according to a contemporary account in the *London Satirist,* Rice spread minstrel show mania through "all classes."[38] By 1843, the Virginia minstrels, the first established blackface troupe, visited Britain, and three years later the Ethiopian Serenaders performed for Queen Victoria, which made blackface minstrel shows acceptable to larger numbers of British consumers.[39] Though blackface minstrelsy was performed as early as the

1820s in urban centers in the United States,[40] it became popular in India a few years after becoming acceptable in London in the 1830s.

The primary appeal may have been the humor and unruly routines of minstrel performers onstage, rather than the parody of African American lifestyles with which the audience had little (or no) familiarity. Sarah Meer claims that blackface minstrelsy in England was distinct in costume, music, puns, and terminology, and that London had a number of uniquely British blackface minstrel troupes. She suggests that "minstrelsy was not only as popular in Britain as in the United States, but it developed distinctively British offshoots with the formation of local British troupes and even a recognizably British style of blackface."[41] Many London minstrel performances focused on the Mr. Interlocutor character, typically a responsible man that countered or kept in check blackface end men or sidekicks.[42] Often elegantly dressed in a tuxedo and top hat, Mr. Interlocutor was even-handed, calm, often Caucasian, and he struggled to keep order. Blackface minstrel shows in India similarly focused on disorder at the hands of a calculated white overseer in the domestic environment, and skits often parodied impulsive servants. Miss May Livingston, a performer with Mr. Sheridan's Company in Bombay in 1886, performed successful minstrel routines at the Gaiety Theatre in Bombay. A review of her performance on December 6 emphasizes her capacity to exaggerate the mannerisms of an imprudent servant:

> She was, perhaps, a trifle too boisterous at times, but this was a fault which was amply counterbalanced by the general cleverness she displayed. Her negro songs, delivered in the character of an impudent and mischief-loving black domestic, were rendered with a spirit and breadth of humor which convulsed the house. There was no resisting the restless roll of her eyes, the facility with which she used her mouth and even her tongue to give a ludicrous finish to her song, or the general extravagance of her actions.[43]

European audiences may have enjoyed these routines because many employed domestic servants.

Audiences in India certainly found meaning in references to African American life in the southern United States. Critics often observe that minstrel shows across the globe reinforced the nostalgia and exoticism apparent in the social distance between African Americans and white audiences, a primary reason for their appeal. In fact, minstrel shows in India (and elsewhere) were often called "plantation impersonations," a loose reference to the African American South. According to John Strausbaugh:

One of the oddities of the minstrel show was the way it balanced its cruel, dehumanizing jokes at the expense of Black people with a fond, often tear-jerking nostalgia for the South—a South few of the performers, and fewer of their audience members, knew anything about. The minstrel South was another fantasy onto which White folks could project their desires—a lost preindustrial paradise . . . [a] mythic Eden filled with ripe watermelon and stacks of steaming hoecakes, smiling mammies, kindly massas, wily catfish and ringing banjos.[44]

Minstrels troupes in both England and India promoted this fantasy.

Instruments, sheet music, and other print media were available to black-face minstrel troupes in India from the early 1850s. The bones, the banjo, and burnt cork used to blacken the face—all important components of blackface minstrels routines—were sold as early as 1853 in India, and equipped local and traveling performers with the necessary gear to perform current songs and sketches.[45] Minstrel sheet music was sold from at least the mid-1850s as it became available on merchant ships, including the popular Stephen Foster minstrel tune "Nelly Bly." It was prominently listed in inventory catalogs in 1856.[46] Mr. E. Mackney, a London music hall performer, mass printed sheet music of minstrel songs and sold collections titled "Mackney's Negro Songs" in Bombay in the 1860s. His collections were perhaps the most widely available minstrel tunes in India.[47] Almanacs printed in the United States listed information useful to touring minstrel performers, including the names and fees of potential contractors proficient in designing and overseeing productions in India. American theater manager Harry Miner circulated information for theater and variety organizations seeking to travel to major cities in India in the 1880s. In the *American Dramatic Directory: Route Around the World* written in 1884, Miner recommends contractors and lists labor prices in Calcutta:

> Bill-poster, Wm. Saunders; contracts for season at 25 rupees a week; good man. Job printer, Erasmus Jones, No. 5 and 6 British India street; good work; reasonable rates. Stage hands, etc., average 20 rupees a month; this work is all done by coolies. Furniture and properties—Lazarus Brothers, Chowringhee Road. Ushers, ticket-sellers, door-keepers, etc., receive 1 rupee a night; musicians, 3 rupees a night; doorman or sepoy watchman, 1 rupee a night. Any good company can play to big business for three months here if able to change programme twice a week.[48]

Miner's publication also lists theater venues and their seating capacities.

Like minstrel shows in other countries, performances in India referenced the struggles of slavery, emancipation, and class identification.[49]

Harriet Beecher Stowe's *Uncle Tom's Cabin* (1852) brought significant attention to African American life.[50] British attitudes toward slavery, race, and class were interpreted in many dramatizations of *Uncle Tom's Cabin* in London,[51] and the novel sparked interest in race relations in the United States and inspired material for minstrels. However, blackface minstrel performers in India, including European and American showmen (among others), expanded the scope of thematic material to appeal to larger audiences. Issues of parted lovers, separated families, and loss were common motifs, and Dave Carson included words and phrases in Hindustani and Bengali. By giving local meanings to universal themes, minstrel showmen designed productions that went beyond plantation themes to appeal to a broad spectrum of audiences. In shows called "Bengali minstrels," for example, Dave Carson parodied stereotyped behaviors associated with Bengali businessmen and parodied ethnic, class, and religious stereotypes in Calcutta.

The New York Serenaders were probably the first troupe to bring minstrelsy to the Subcontinent in 1851.[52] They traveled to India after touring Australia.[53] But it was not until 1861 that blackface performer Dave Carson proved that blackface minstrels were in demand and could potentially generate significant income. He toured his professional troupe, the San Francisco Minstrels, throughout India in 1861 after a circuit in Australia. He performed current blackface minstrel material from the United States and London, and remained in India for the next five years. He returned to South Asia on a number of occasions in the 1870s and 1880s, and even performed in smaller towns and cities such as Varanasi, Allahabad, Lucknow, Agra, and Simla, where according to one early twentieth-century account, he "astonished the Hindus and Mohamedans not a little with [his] representations of the sports and pastimes of the Ethiopian race in the United States of America . . . and a host of natives from all parts of Asia, greeted [him] with delight and hard silver."[54]

Carson achieved some proficiency in Hindustani, which he used to his advantage, and he even studied local accents.[55] An article in the *Englishman* newspaper on November 28, 1863, says, "he pass[es] in Hindustani with full honours and put[s] into most effective practice his research in politics."[56] Another article in the same paper on March 10, 1866, asserts, "By far the greatest merit he has displayed has been the courage and skill with which he had determined to amuse Anglo Indians [British] with that around them."[57] Poonam Trivedi and Nand Kumar suggest that Carson's localized material heavily contributed to his success and that he often punctuated songs with words in Hindustani.[58] Carson effectively designed shows that tapped into the everyday life of both Indian and European audiences in India, and often drew from controversial local events such as the market crash in Bombay. In one particularly successful routine in 1865, "Scenes in the Bombay Police Court," Carson used material from a negative experience he had with the Bombay Police. He also understood the popularity of Indian *nautch* (dance) performances for the European elite, and his dancing-girl routines brought their controversial popularity into the open. (*Nautch* dances for Europeans were sometimes associated with prostitution.) Here he Indianized the trend of cross-dressing in minstrel shows and created an act titled "Zuleika, the Pearl of Punjab," in which he dressed as a "Hindoostani Nautch Girl,"[59] which he parodied through exaggerated dance routines.

He successfully portrayed stereotypes and farces of Bengali businessmen, Parsis, and Europeans, as well as Hindus and Muslims. Because his thematic material referenced locally inspired content, including discrimination between British and Indians, many of his shows were widely attended by Bengalis when he was in Calcutta and Parsis when he was in Bombay. Joseph Charles Parkinson writes in his diary in 1870 that Carson had "acquired considerable reputation for his delineations of native character, making the Parsee laugh at his caricature of the Hindoo, while the Hindoo is convulsed at his clever skits of the Parsee."[60] Carson considered Parsis an important target market, understood their economic interest in the urban theater industry, and designed shows to appeal to this community. One of his most popular characters, Davejee Carsonbhoy, was a Parsi character he created in 1865 that, according to an article in the *Times of India* on June 6, displayed the "true Parsee cast of features—sloping forehead—long full nose, on an elongated face—full lips, large mouth, with chin slightly receding—long neck and shoulders falling."[61] Carson also performed this character during his later trips to India. Another Parsi character, "Rati Madam," was an independent woman who wore tight clothing. Routines featuring Rati Madam were popular at the Grant Road Theatre in Bombay. Sir Dinshaw Edulji Wacha, a Parsi resident of Bombay, recalls in 1920, it "was that humorist, Dave Carson, who really made the Grant Road Theatre famous among the play going folk of Bombay and for years altogether attracted thousands to the house . . . and was never more happy than when he donned the garb of the Parsi masher of the period and made love to 'Rati Madam.' The house used to roar with laughter."[62] In his enthusiastic tone, Wacha suggests that Carson's shows drew more attention to the Grant Road Theatre than Indian, Parsi, and other English dramas, at least for a while.

One of Carson's most popular characters was the "Bengalee Baboo" [Bengali Babu], an Anglicized Indian from Bengal who unsuccessfully attempted to imitate European manners and dress.[63] Carson performed this character for years, including during the 1878–79 season at the Royal Theatre in London. Audiences in India and London referred to his routine as the "Bengali-Minstrel" show,[64] and he catered to the audience appetite for mockery of British refinement, or efforts by Bengali businessmen to achieve such refinement. The British used the term *Babu* to reference the social-climbing Bengali businessman. Borrowing from its British definition, Carson mocked the economic acquisitiveness of "Babus" as storeowners, clerks, and low-level traders.[65] During the 1877 season at the Theatre Royal in India, Carson performed a skit titled "The Bengalee Baboo in England," which portrayed the character in London (see fig. 1.1).

As we have seen, Carson's performances comically reinforced ethnic, racial and class differences in India through local stereotypes. Because he was American, his expressions of upsetting stereotypes and prejudices in India were perhaps more easily viewed in a comical light. His shows put uncomfortable stereotypes center stage and confronted audiences with a truthfulness that for a brief moment avoided serious recoil. He compelled audiences to acknowledge their biases and he exaggerated excesses and differences, yet people were still inclined to attend his shows. For Indian audiences, it was perhaps the blackface component of these shows that, as Poonam Trivedi suggests, "made him seem like . . . [an Indian], facilitating and making more palatable his stinging jibes."[66] Carson was able to speak to audiences in a more meaningful way than most other American entertainers who hit the shores of India, at least until jazz and ragtime musicians arrived in 1919. He was considered a professional performer who could draw large crowds and perform well under any circumstances. At his performance at the Town Hall in Calcutta in July 1865 described in the introduction to this book, Carson's troupe performed for a packed house under exceptionally hot and humid conditions:

> The Hall was inconveniently crowded, and the sufferings of those poor unfortunate "gentlemen in black" who, from lack of seats, did duty as "wall-flowers," far removed from the soothing influence of the ever-welcome *punkah* [fan], were pitiable to behold. To all appearance, they seemed to be undergoing, as of old, the Inquisitorial torture of the slow fire, and there is every probability that had there not been a plentiful supply of "iced pegs" procurable within convenient distance, some serious accidents might have taken place.[67]

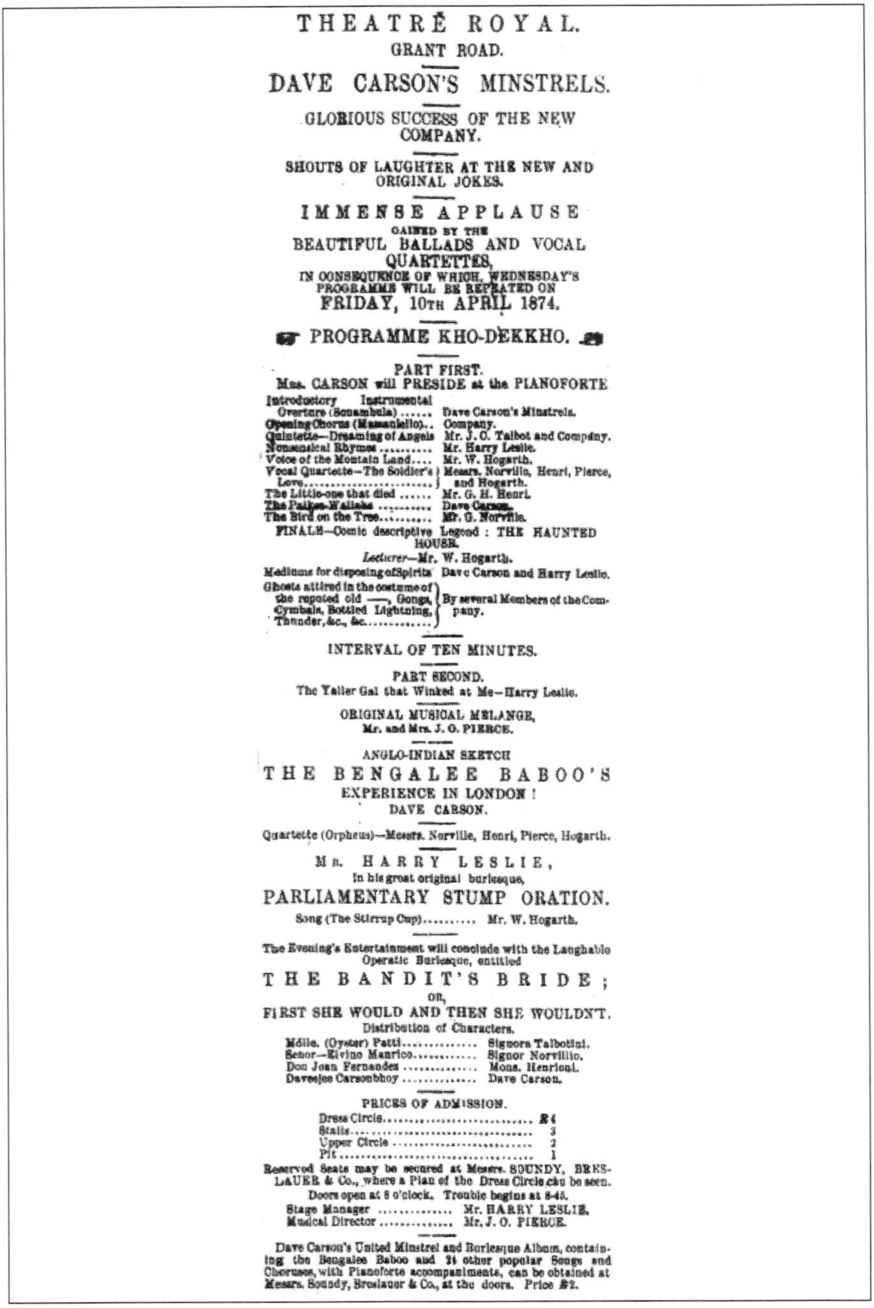

THEATRÊ ROYAL.

GRANT ROAD.

DAVE CARSON'S MINSTRELS.

GLORIOUS SUCCESS OF THE NEW COMPANY.

SHOUTS OF LAUGHTER AT THE NEW AND ORIGINAL JOKES.

IMMENSE APPLAUSE

GAINED BY THE

BEAUTIFUL BALLADS AND VOCAL QUARTETTES,

IN CONSEQUENCE OF WHICH, WEDNESDAY'S PROGRAMME WILL BE REPEATED ON

FRIDAY, 10TH APRIL 1874.

PROGRAMME KHO-DEKKHO.

PART FIRST.

MRS. CARSON will PRESIDE at the PIANOFORTE

Introductory Instrumental Overture (Sonambula)	Dave Carson's Minstrels.
Opening Chorus (Masaniello)..	Company.
Quintette—Dreaming of Angels	Mr. J. C. Talbot and Company.
Nonsensical Rhymes	Mr. Harry Leslie.
Voice of the Montain Land....	Mr. W. Hogarth.
Vocal Quartette—The Soldier's Love........................	Messrs. Norville, Henri, Pierce, and Hogarth.
The Little-one that died	Mr. G. H. Henri.
The Palkee-Wallahs	Dave Carson.
The Bird on the Tree..........	Mr. G. Norville.

FINALE—Comic descriptive Legend: THE HAUNTED HOUSE.

Lecturer—Mr. W. Hogarth.

Mediums for disposing of Spirits	Dave Carson and Harry Leslie.
Ghosts attired in the costume of the reputed old —, Gongs, Cymbals, Bottled Lightning, Thunder, &c., &c..............	By several Members of the Company.

INTERVAL OF TEN MINUTES.

PART SECOND.

The Yaller Gal that Winked at Me—Harry Leslie.

ORIGINAL MUSICAL MELANGE,

Mr. and Mrs. J. O. PIERCE.

ANGLO-INDIAN SKETCH

THE BENGALEE BABOO'S EXPERIENCE IN LONDON!

DAVE CARSON.

Quartette (Orpheus)—Messrs. Norville, Henri, Pierce, Hogarth.

MR. HARRY LESLIE,

in his great original burlesque,

PARLIAMENTARY STUMP ORATION.

Song (The Stirrup Cup).......... Mr. W. Hogarth.

The Evening's Entertainment will conclude with the Laughable Operatic Burlesque, entitled

THE BANDIT'S BRIDE;

OR,

FIRST SHE WOULD AND THEN SHE WOULDN'T.

Distribution of Characters.

Mdlle. (Oyster) Patti..............	Signora Talbotini.
Senor—Elvino Manrico............	Signor Norvillio.
Don Joan Fernandez	Mons. Henrioni.
Daveejee Carsonbhoy	Dave Carson.

PRICES OF ADMISSION.

Dress Circle..............................	₨ 4
Stalls..............................	3
Upper Circle	2
Pit..............................	1

Reserved Seats may be secured at Messrs. SOUNDY, BRESLAUER & Co., where a Plan of the Dress Circle can be seen.

Doors open at 8 o'clock. Trouble begins at 8-45.

Stage Manager	Mr. HARRY LESLIE.
Musical Director	Mr. J. O. PIERCE.

Dave Carson's United Minstrel and Burlesque Album, containing the Bengalee Baboo and 24 other popular Songs and Choruses, with Pianoforte accompaniments, can be obtained at Messrs. Soundy, Breslauer & Co., at the doors. Price ₨2.

Figure 1.1. Advertisement for Dave Carson's group at Theatre Royal. *Times of India*, April 10, 1874. Image reproduced by permission from ProQuest LLC.

Professionalism was important to Carson's reputation, and a number of reviews comment on his capacity to offer orderly, streamlined entertainment in the face of a challenging climate and undesirable work conditions.

Amateur showmen performed the Bengalee Baboo character at European ballroom dances and social clubs across India.[68] Carson sold sheet music of the Bengalee Baboo routine at his performances,[69] disseminating his material to regimental bands and amateur variety troupes. In the 1870s and 1880s, his repertoire drew more heavily from the songs and skits of blackface minstrel groups in England; he learned songs as he traveled more frequently in and out of India, and thereby exposed audiences and performers in India to the newest material. Carson's sheet music and traveling shows inspired others to organize minstrel routines, and he significantly influenced the showmanship of local amateur troupes.

By the 1870s, members of regimental bands were forming amateur blackface minstrel troupes, often to increase capital flowing into band coffers. These groups were popular and sometimes contributed to the sustainability of struggling bands, especially those stationed far from large urban centers. The Gloucestershire Regiment Crow Minstrels performed in Ahmedabad in 1888, and according to a review in the *Times of India* they performed "chorus, songs, and jokes peculiarly characteristic of the nigger [*sic*] community."[70] The term *Crow* is likely a reference to "Jim Crow," which by 1888 had burgeoned into a complex of meanings, but in this instance probably referred to blackface performers.[71] The names of groups were telling, and showed a clear interest in highlighting the blackface components of performances. In Karachi (now in Pakistan), a group of twelve British and Indian military and administrative personnel organized a minstrel troupe called the Kurrachee (Karachi) Kaffirs. "Kaffirs" was an offensive term for black Africans. They often performed in Frere Hall, an upmarket Venetian Gothic building.[72] In another instance, the 6th Brigade Royal Artillery organized an ensemble called the Coloured Opera Troupe (sometimes called the Coloured Royal Opera Troupe) in the 1870s. A review in the *Times of India* on November 20, 1874, claimed that the ensemble featured "negro songs and choruses, chiefly in a comic vein."[73] They frequently performed at formal ballroom dances. They were enthusiastically received among ball participants and, according to the same review, were known for their technical ability.

Performers embraced a wide spectrum of minstrel character types and designed shows with multiple costume changes. Cross-dressing was often a source of humor. At one performance on May 26, 1880, at the Gaiety

Theatre in Bombay, Dave Carson joined forces with Miss Clara Stanley's variety company to perform minstrel sketches and other variety entertainment, which necessitated choreographed costume changes:

> Two very clever members of the company gave a unique and humourous negro minstrel sketch, which was one of the best items on the programme. The two gentlemen appeared on the stage as an old lady and gentleman, and after going through a vocal duet, disappeared behind the wings, almost immediately reappearing attired in ordinary negro minstrel costume with their faces blackened in the orthodox manner. The transformation was very rapidly effected, and elicited considerable applause.[74]

Men often dressed in a black mammy costume to perform comic farces that satirized attempts to keep the household in order.

Blackface minstrel routines were a feature of many ballroom dances. They were often described in reviews as "witty," "farcical," or "comical" in contrast to the ballroom dance music that dominated the evening. Some reviews of balls suggest that audiences received blackface minstrels with more enthusiasm than classical music and formal dance. A ball at Lowjee Castle in Bombay on March 14, 1874, featured elaborately ornamented halls and an orchestra performing ballroom music, but the minstrel entertainment was met with the most enthusiasm: "The curtain rose on one of the finest drawing-room Negro entertainments that was ever given by the amateurs of the Coloured Royal Opera Troupe of the Royal Artillery. We will say nothing further about the performance than that it was all that could be expected . . . the most amusing of which were the 'Bengalee Babo.'"[75] In this instance, the Coloured Royal Opera Troupe of the 6th Brigade Royal Artillery borrowed from Dave Carson's character Bengalee Baboo.

Not all minstrel performances received positive reviews. The local group Koi Hai Minstrels performed at balls and formal dances in Calcutta in the 1880s. In one review of their performance at a ballroom dance in the *Times of India* on July 21, 1884, the reviewer claims, "Christy Minstrels when good are the very best performance for a Calcutta public,"[76] but suggests that ambiguity in the structure of minstrel performances, in contrast to the tight structure of theater plays, was difficult to accept. The following excerpt indicates that Koi Hai Minstrel productions involved large numbers of performers and musicians, which contributed to a confused stage:

> The house was crowded and the applause was hearty and continued all through, but a good many came away somewhat disappointed with the

performance. To the uninitiated outsider the fault seemed to be that there was no beginning or end to it, and ... the performers came in, without rhyme or reason, as far as one could see, with black faces and hands. A Christy Minstrel performance always draws, and in this case there were lots of talent, good voices, and large amateur orchestra, and a company consisting of quite twenty Christios [blackface performers], but with all this there can be no doubt the performance was not what it might have been.[77]

Yet at the same time, this review suggests that blackface routines were popular and that blackface minstrel events were usually well attended.[78]

The formal structure of minstrel shows loosely followed the typical structure in England and the United States, including an opening chorus or solo piece, then the interlocutor with a monologue or in dialogue with other performers, followed by a series of variety acts. However, many amateur groups departed significantly from this structure. A review of a performance organized by the stationmaster of the railway station in Bhusaval, Maharashtra, on December 1, 1890, gives us a detailed sense of the organization of late nineteenth-century amateur variety shows that included a blackface component:

The entertainment was opened by a solo on the pianoforte. . . . This was followed by the rise of the curtain, and the singing by the company of the opening chorus "Down the River." The chorus was well and expressively rendered, and elicited a burst of applause. After the usual introductory conversation between the Interlocutors, Bones and Sambo, a rather long programme was gone through. . . . The songs were well rendered throughout, and the parts of Bones and Sambo were well and spiritually acted. The first part of the programme was brought to a close by the singing . . . of the "Old Brigade." After an interval of five minutes the second part of the programme was commenced. The first item was a banjo solo . . . after this came a character song entitled "I'm not the Old Man I used to Was," [followed by] a medley called "General Jumbo's Army" . . . concluded with a very amusing farce entitled "Black Lunatics."[79]

Bones and Sambo were popular minstrel characters. Though these shows were loosely organized around minstrel themes, they were likely not as structured as the routines of Carson or other foreign traveling troupes. This show included solo and ensemble material, both instrumental and vocal. It is likely they used songs locally available on sheet music or song collections. "Down the River," for example, was listed in contemporary collections of minstrel music, including the widely disseminated volume *Bryant's Songs from Dixieland* (1861), and the lyrics referenced boating down the Ohio River:

... Oh! The master is proud of the old Broad-horn,
For it brings him plenty of tin;
Oh! The crew they are darkies [*sic*], the cargo is corn,
And the money comes tumbling in.
There's plenty on board for the darkies to eat,
And there's something to drink and smoke;
There's the banjo, the bones, and the tambourine,
There's the song and the comical joke.
Oh! The river is up, and the channel is deep,
And the wind blows steady and strong;
Let the splash of your oars the measure keep,
As we row the old boat along
> *Chorus*
> Down the river, down the river,
> Down the Ohio;
> Down the river, down the river,
> Down the Ohio[80]

The review claims this performance was "in the shape of Christy Minstrel Entertainment,"[81] so the lyrics to "Down the River" probably reflected an effort to unify the evening theme through exoticized references to rural life in the United States. At times minstrel shows, such as this production, were possibly more akin to variety shows with tunes that loosely fit into the "negro" song genre of the time or that used minstrel instruments such as the banjo, bones, and tambourine.

Ragtime at the Turn of the Century

John Philip Sousa's performances at the World's Columbian Exposition in Chicago in 1893 helped launch the spread of popular band music in the United States. Sousa sought to create respectability and legitimacy for bands, and his sheet music sales and phonograph recordings proliferated in the American mainstream.[82] He was a pioneer in recording songs on phonographs, and his band made some of the first ragtime records.[83] He regularly performed ragtime live, and traveled to Paris in 1900 to enthusiastic reception.[84] A key characteristic of ragtime was its syncopated (or "ragged") rhythms layered on a steady, marchlike bass, which facilitated its integration into band repertoire. Harry Stecopoulos attributes much of the success of ragtime to brass band arrangements, including the pioneering Sousa song "Hu-la Hu-la Cakewalk" in 1901.[85] In 1903, an anonymous article in the *Times of India* detailed the work of Sousa and traced the popularity of ragtime across Europe: "Paris has been wildly enthusiastic over the rag-time music which goes with the American cakewalk, and all over the Continent [Europe] musicians have been tearing American rag-time to shreds. Mr. Sousa discovered while in England 'that the only thing which would keep King Edward awake at a concert was rag-time.'"[86] This account suggests that ragtime was a transnational phenomenon, and its author reveals the interest in global proliferation and its capacity to excite all classes. By the time Irving Berlin produced the quintessential ragtime piece, "Alexander's Ragtime Band," in 1911, ragtime had been commercialized for consumption by the masses in the United States and spread overseas through the recordings and performances of Sousa, the US Marine Corps Band,[87] and many other bands and orchestras.[88]

Since military bands were still pervasive in the early 1900s in India, it is understandable that ragtime would become part of the band repertoire and variety show industry. Known today mostly as piano music, ragtime also encompassed ensemble music and songs. The band of the B. B. and C. I. Railway Volunteers regularly performed a "Ragtime March" beginning in December 1904 in Bombay and included it in their repertoire through 1905.[89] Also in 1904, the Black and White Minstrels, composed of thirty local amateur and semiprofessional performers, performed the cakewalk at the Gaiety Theatre in Bombay accompanied by the 121st Pioneers military orchestra. The review of one performance details the popularity of the cakewalk in the show: "The finale consisted of a cake-walk. This was one of the best items on the programme and was performed with great skill, the gentleman taking part accomplishing difficult steps in a very expert manner. There was a general demand for a repetition of the dance, but the curtain was down and 'God Save the King' was played without the desired repetition."[90] The cakewalk was less syncopated than ragtime, and was often used in band arrangements.[91] It was sometimes considered an early manifestation of ragtime.[92] This production also included "coon" songs and a "Banjo band," and the format loosely followed minstrel shows:

> The programme was carried through with great spirit and the audience caught the enthusiasm of the performers and were ready to encore everything. The voices were nicely balanced, and under Mr. Mallandaine's direction the choruses went with a cheerful swing. Captain Johnston fulfilled the indispensable roll of Massa Johnson, interlocutor Mr. Walker was Massa Bones, Mr. Sheringham, Massa Sambo; Captain Hobbs, Massa Tambo and Mr. Binning, Massa Squash. The programme commenced with a song by Massa Squash, with chorus, and this was followed by the charming song

"Pansy Faces" which was sung by Mr. Knight and warmly applauded. "The Darkies Dream" by the banjo band was another signal for an outburst of applause and the banjos had to repeat their contribution. Mr. Faulkner gave an effective rendering of "My Pretty Red Rose" and Mrs. McCarthy obtained an undeniable encore for her singing of the coon song "Why don't you love me Honey?" Massas Bones and Sambo intervened with a cleverly performed dance and Miss. Dyer whistled very prettily "The Coon's Birthday."[93]

"Coon songs" were a staple of Tin Pan Alley[94] and are often considered to be an antecedent to ragtime[95] and the cakewalk. The song "The Darkies Dream," composed by G. L. Lansing sometime in the late 1880s or early 1890s, was available as sheet music,[96] and was typically categorized in contemporary advertisements under either banjo or piano music.[97] Bands recorded it as a march.[98] It exhibits ragtime traits such as quick syncopations and dotted rhythms.[99] An original 1905 Edison Gold Moulded Record recording in the United States by the Edison Military Band begins the performance of the piece with an unaccompanied dialogue that starts, "Get up there you lazy Nigger [sic], get a move on, you all the time sleeping."[100] Racist stereotypes continued after the turn of the century, including in this instance a suggestion of laziness articulated in the title. Performances that included ragtime and its antecedents in India also embraced these discriminatory references in one form or another. The Bombay performance represents one of the first instances in India when a large number of early (or antecedent) ragtime songs were performed in a single event, and illustrates the common practice of mixing elements of standard variety shows with blackface minstrel material. The first variety show in India that used the term "ragtime" in a context outside of regimental "Ragtime Marches" probably occurred in 1908. The Fairmonts, a dance team touring with the Empire Vaudeville Company, performed at the Gaiety Theatre in Bombay that year.[101] Acts in their shows also featured the cakewalk.

Among new entertainment venues built in India at the turn of the century that booked ragtime were the Empire Theatre in 1908 and Royal Opera House in 1912. Maurice Bandman, a theater manager and entertainment entrepreneur, partially financed the construction of the Royal Opera House and produced many of the ragtime and cakewalk performances there. He managed much of the entertainment in its opening months, including vaudeville and film productions, and he brought the most up-to-date music, dance, and variety troupes directly from London and the transatlantic circuit. Also financed by J. F. Karaka, a Parsi businessman, the Royal Opera House represented a new aspect of entertainment possibilities in the urban context and symbolized an age of increasing commodification of entertainment supported by lifestyle changes of the growing middle class.[102] The Empire Theatre was built in a Renaissance style, but by one newspaper account was "wholly modern" and boasted "modern devices which make the theatre the most up-to-date in the East."[103] The interior was decorated in Louis XIV style, and featured a complex ventilation system with fans and electric lights. With the opening of the Empire and Royal Opera House, previous venues such as the Gaiety may have lost some of their reputation as modern venues.

Ragtime's loose association with "banjo music," "coon" songs, and the cakewalk were important to its proliferation across the globe. James Weldon Johnson, an American author and activist, claimed in 1916 that "American Negro music in its triumphant march has swept the world,"[104] and suggested that the African American roots of ragtime constituted much of its enthusiastic transnational reception. Six years later, Johnson asserted that ragtime "is the one artistic production by which America is known the world over. It has been all conquering. Everywhere it is hailed as 'American music.'"[105] Marketing imagery often borrowed from minstrel iconographies, and audiences were attracted to ragtime in some respects because it was originally American and represented a successful crossover between white and black music. It also made audiences feel modern.[106]

In many cases, American ragtime performers in India achieved the most recognition, and ragtime shows that featured Americans were often the most heavily advertised. For example, the US entertainment trio "The Chasers" performed ragtime at the Excelsior in Bombay in late 1921 and were marketed in advertisements as the "American ragtime and jazz company" and the "Great American Rag Jazz Trio."[107] This group featured xylophonist Tod Sanborn, pianist Harry Levine, and dancer George Crotty. One advertisement claimed they were "real Broadway experts" who performed jazz and ragtime "as it should be played" (fig. 1.2).[108]

As with blackface minstrels, much of the entertainment designed for British, Europeans, and other foreigners in India in the 1900s and 1910s also gained notoriety and variation in London, and this was certainly the case for ragtime, especially in 1913. As stage critic Lionel Carson argued in 1914, "1913 dawned with the ragtime craze in full blast [in England], and though sunset has come [in 1914] with the desire diminished and the attraction less pronounced, there can be little doubt that the curious syncopated music which hailed from America has left its mark in England."[109]

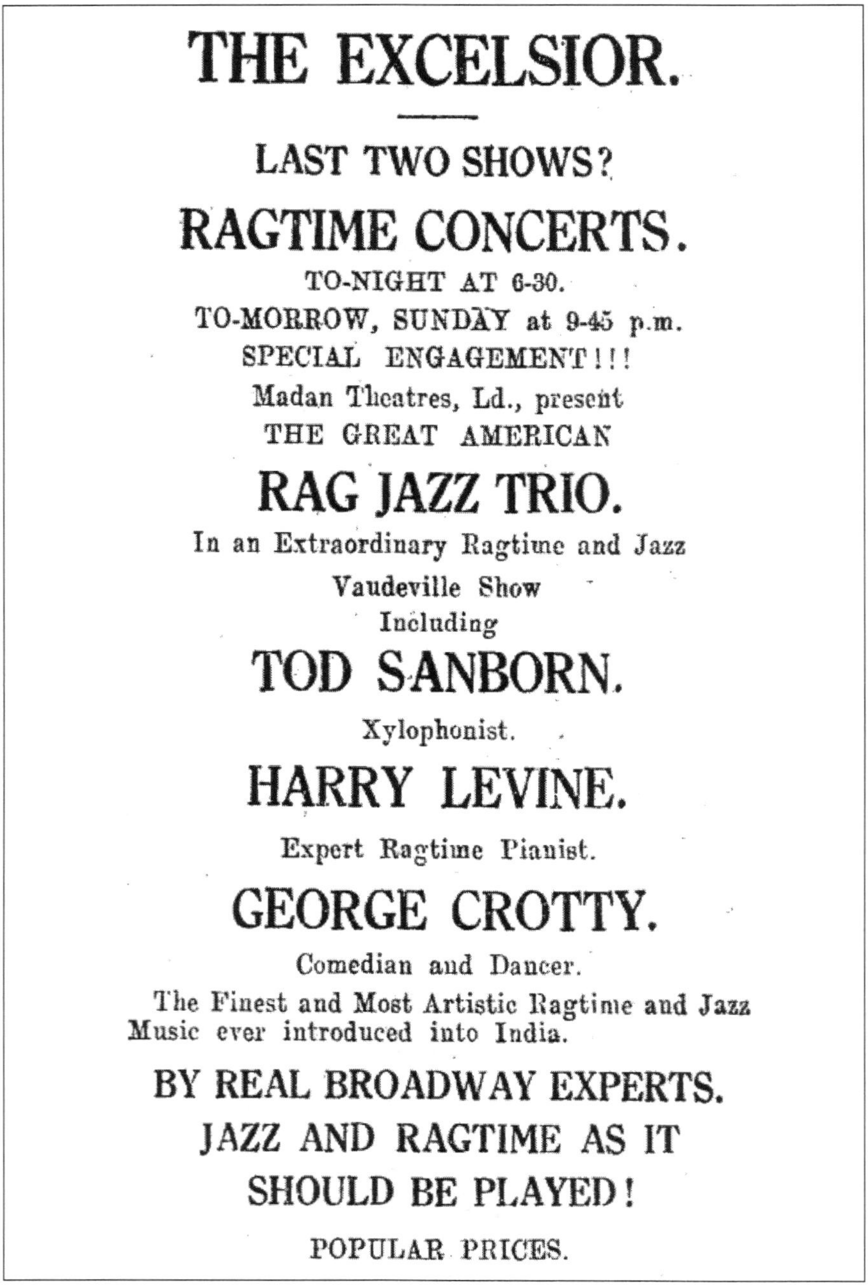

Figure 1.2. Advertisement for the Rag Jazz Trio at the Excelsior. *Times of India*, November 26, 1921. Image reproduced by permission from ProQuest LLC.

By 1913, ragtime was performed and danced across all classes of society in the United States and England.[110]

Commentary on ragtime increased in 1913 in India, and included musings on its African American origins and popularity in London. According to the *Times of India* on January 21, 1913, in London,

> the prominent feature of every single programme is "rag-time." What is ragtime? An American lady told me the other day that it means the time when the negroes break off work and go and amuse themselves, and that it dates really from the old slave days in the southern States of America . . . at any rate "rag-time" is music and dancing founded on old negro tunes and dances, but very much altered in its passage through the hands and feet of New York musicians and dance . . . even waltzing is dying out in the ballroom under the overpowering influence of rag-time.[111]

The fact that it achieved "passage through the hands and feet of New York" gave it additional legitimacy, and the article goes on to claim that "there is one thing certain about this rag-time music—that it sticks in the head more pertinaciously than any music that was ever written before. It won't leave you alone. It has a queer syncopation beat which is all-conquering, and its tunes are somehow individual and marked in character for all their triviality and vulgarity. And it is capital stuff to dance to."[112] These references to the southern United States are similar to portrayals of blackface minstrelsy years earlier. Ragtime was treasured for its association with London, New York City, and the African American South.

Interest in ragtime in India likely peaked in 1913, probably because of the popularity of the London revue *Hullo, Ragtime!* at the Hippodrome Theatre that year.[113] It frequently featured Irving Berlin's music,[114] including "Alexander's Ragtime Band," and was replete with familiar ragtime songs.[115] From its early years, the popularity of ragtime in England and Europe inspired American musicians to travel across the Atlantic for jobs in shows,[116] and many *Hullo, Ragtime!* productions in London were partially composed of American performers.[117]

Hullo, Ragtime! also ran in Bombay at the Royal Opera House in 1913 (see fig. I.1). Performed by the Bandman Londoners, it was under the direction of Maurice Bandman and was billed as the "London Rage." Advertisements directly referenced its popularity at the Hippodrome in London, and performances at the Royal Opera House in Bombay were often sold-out.[118] The *Times of India* reviews of *Hullo, Ragtime!* emphasized the show's attention to new material, and one review claimed that it represented "polyglot form, with English as a foundation [on] which will be erected a super-structure of various foreign tongues."[119] Advertisements invited readers to attend the shows and "be in fashion."[120] The Gramophone Company Ltd. ran advertisements for recordings of the music in Calcutta and Bombay, and they exploited the buzz for ragtime by advertising all of Irving Berlin's music.[121] His Master's Voice (HMV) claimed in advertisements that year that HMV was the "Champagne of Ragtime" and that they sold ragtime music "straight from the States"[122] (fig. 1.3). Billed as quintessentially American and stylistically English, music from *Hullo, Ragtime!* and ragtime in general was sold on gramophone records and performed in theaters, social clubs, and cabarets.

After the peak of ragtime in 1913, revue artists continued to feature it in theaters in urban centers throughout India. Perhaps the most popular performer was Miss Addie Leigh, who organized several shows in 1915 at the Excelsior in Bombay. A review of her performances in May that year reveals, "Miss Addie Leigh appears singly as an operatic vocalist and singer of ragtime as well as in the double turn, and the audiences during the weekend have not been slow to appreciate her singing, which is much above the average that is heard at the musical hall in India . . . Those who like ballad get ballad, and those who like ragtime get ragtime."[123] In this instance, Leigh's popularity is supported by her capacity to sing in an "operatic" style. Both Leigh and the Empire Vaudeville Company traveled to New Zealand and Australia before or after their tour in India. These performances often showcased Bioscope or other film technologies. Leigh's shows included color (Kinemacolor) films screened in the background.

Toward the end of the decade, the Banvard Musical Company from the United States produced a number of shows with ragtime, and performed in a variety of theaters, social clubs, and hotel ballrooms—including the Excelsior Theatre and the Town Hall in Bombay. They arrived in December 1919 and their shows included what reviews called "catchy jazz,"[124] suggesting that they may have performed ragtime or other styles of music in a swing rhythm or with improvisation. Their American background was heavily promoted, and advertisements described their style as "All American."[125] A review of their performance in the *Times of India* on December 12, 1919, claims they offered,

> a little daring rhythm of movement and dainty dancing. . . . The fare which is served up may be classed as musical comedy in the land of the dollar. . . . It is a mixture of ragtime and revue in which there is nothing very musical but rather the reverse, yet providing plenty of fun and frolic. The company

Figure 1.3. Advertisement for His Master's Voice Records. *Times of India*, July 22, 1913. Image reproduced by permission from ProQuest LLC.

comes from America. Those who last night saw its first production . . . need no detective faculties to discover that fact. The American accent was "right there." Sometimes you could cut it like a knife. . . . This adds to the enjoyment rather than detracts from it.[126]

This review suggests that the "fun and frolic"—and not necessarily its musical intricacies—constituted its primary draw, and even their American accents were catchy. The company also included a chorus of girls, which one review boasted was an "American picked 'Beauty Chorus' [that] is said to be the best group of singing and dancing classes ever seen in the Far East."[127] Much of their success can be attributed to Miss Pearl Jardinere, who oversaw the chorus in late 1919 and early 1920.[128] Jardinere performed on Broadway,[129] which brought additional esteem to the show. Banvard's performances at the Excelsior integrated both ragtime and chorus girls into successful productions.[130]

Cabaret and stage show scenes in foreign films in the late 1910s compelled Banvard, Maurice Bandman, and others to showcase chorus girls in their ragtime shows. The Bandman Opera Company's Bombay stage revue *The Bing Boys Are Here* in 1917 featured a chorus of girls, and was described in one review as "a lot of noisy rag-time, a little dancing, a whole arm full of pretty girls and a whole shop full of gorgeous dresses, all generously seasoned with jests."[131] The film *Primrose Path* was screened at the Olympia Cinema in Bombay in 1916, and the advertisement in the *Times of India* states, "Lovers of the screen will find an extraordinary combination of a unique plot, most unusual situations and a cabaret scene that is remarkable even in these days of lavish production."[132] Another film, *Midnight at Maxim's*, screened at the Empire Cinema in 1917 in Bombay, was advertised as a "spectacular cabaret show" that featured the Maxim Cabaret Girls performing "the best and the latest numbers which are the rage of the civilized world."[133] Sometimes films featured cabaret themes in narrative plots. Screened in March 1916 at Bombay's Excelsior Theatre, the Pathécolor film *Rose Amongst the Briars* had a plot that centered on the trials and tribulations of a cabaret girl. One review writes that the story "shows the trials of a simple girl, who, left on her own resources, goes in for cabaret dancing."[134] These and other silent films were typically screened within a year or so of their initial release in the United States. Audiences wanted to experience what they saw on screen, and a number of live performance venues began to adjust to this demand.[135] However, chorus girls were not uniformly seen in a positive light. Dennis Kincaid suggests in his 1938 memoir that the management of Firpo's Restaurant and Bar in Calcutta attempted to book a cabaret soon after it opened in the late 1910s but "for ten years the police imposed a ban, to the relief of most of the influential [British] who heard with concern of the state of undress permitted to performers in London cabarets and considered that the effect on the Indian public of the spectacle of European girls as professional dancers in a public restaurant would be unfortunate."[136] In this example, entertainment demands were peripheral to maintaining status and standing.

Changing Entertainments

By the 1920s, new hotels and dance halls increasingly booked cabaret formats that included dancing and live music (including jazz), and small, intimate tables where patrons could eat dinner and drink alcohol. The term *cabaret* encompasses many definitions, but was first used during this decade and in this context to describe evening entertainment with music, dance, alcohol, and dinner. Restaurants such as Firpo's Restaurant and Bar in Calcutta, and hotels such as the Taj Mahal Palace Hotel and Green's Hotel in Bombay hired resident orchestras and organized evening and afternoon cabarets. These hotel orchestras set the stage for successful private investment in dinner dances, and many venues that previously featured ballroom dances or staged variety shows began to accommodate cabarets, a trend that continued for decades.[137] Some cabarets included burlesques and follies that were comical or farcical, and others showcased variety groups or jazz.

The 1910s mark the end of certain Victorian-era limitations and controls on acceptability. With the advent of cabarets, audiences in India increasingly wanted to live in a consumer world supported by global commerce and international connections. New cultural energy loosened ideas about audience participation in dance, and lines between performers and audiences lessened as both began to share the same floor and dance to the same music. The increasing acceptability of alcohol loosened inhibitions. As I will mention in the next chapter, Maurice Bandman probably brought the first jazz music to a large audience in India at the Excelsior Theatre in 1919, yet these initial performances were presented on a stage with audiences seated in a theater format. Over the course of the 1920s, jazz became more accepted by all classes and was integrated into commercial cabarets. Its dissemination through media such as gramophones and sheet music expedited its availability. Even though the capital of Britain's Raj shifted to New Delhi beginning in 1911, much of the commercialized music and dance remained centered in port cities such as Bombay and Calcutta. The next chapter will articulate these shifts in entertainment in more detail.

Chapter Two

Technologies, Exoticism, and Entrepreneurs, 1920s and 1930s

Jazz traversed India and influenced audiences and music makers of all backgrounds, and successful musicians navigated this diversity conscious of its business potentials, engaging commercial realities and estimating audience demand as necessary. The African American vocal group Plantation Quartet used Hollywood representations of black American music to promote identification with global culture. Performing in Calcutta, Bombay, and elsewhere, this group used Hollywood film songs and so-called darky promotional images to contextualize their performances in blackface minstrel and antebellum plantation histories. The most successful musicians in the 1920s and 1930s often exhibited keen business skills and marketing savvy. Ken Mac first heard jazz in 1921 at the Cavalry School in Saugor (modern Sagar) while on holiday, and he later became a key jazz figure in India.[1] The school is located in interior India, far from the larger urban centers more typically associated with the development of jazz and other transnational commercial enterprises. After this performance, Mac learned to play the drum set by listening to imported gramophone recordings from the United States, and his music studies at the Lawrence Royal Military School in Sanawar provided resources for his early successes in jazz performance. Saxophonist Micky Correa started his work in the jazz music business in Lahore and moved to Bombay in 1938 to perform at elite venues and network with African American musicians. His band's success in Lahore required learning effective advertising strategies to target the European consumer base. This chapter will address the work of Correa, Mac, the Plantation Quartet, and other jazz musicians, and articulate how sound technologies, film, entrepreneurial activity, and exoticism associated with African American musicians supported popular music in the 1920s and 1930s.

Plantation Quartet

On November 10, 1934, the Plantation Quartet (sometimes called the Deep South Boys or the Taj Quartet) performed at the Taj Mahal Palace Hotel in Bombay. The group was composed of African American jazz musicians Creighton Thompson, Crickett Smith, Rudy Jackson, and Roy Butler. The quartet sang Hollywood representations of black music and dressed in costumes that depicted plantation life in the southern United States.[2] Advertised as a "Plantation Gala," the theme of the evening was "A Night Down South." In describing the event, an anonymous article in the *Times of India* romanticized the creativity of slaves working on plantations and linked African Americans to cotton fields and the banjo:

> To transport the guests into the scenery and atmosphere of the south of the United States is the object of the Taj management at the Plantation Gala[.] From one's earliest recollections, American negros have been connected with cotton fields and plantations—recollections aroused by books like "Uncle Tom's Cabin," and kept alive through many generations by ditties such as "Swanee River," "Poor Old Joe," etc. Stories of these old days, when the plantation hand's chief pleasure was music, both instrumental and vocal, still hold a fascination for young and old, and one instinctively connects the banjo and singing of "spirituals" with the coloured people of the Southern States, whose quaint phraseology and manner of speaking have long disappeared before the advent of education.[3]

The quartet headlined at the Taj Mahal Palace Hotel for many years and performed in a number of venues in Bombay, Calcutta, Sri Lanka, and elsewhere.

The Plantation Quartet's performances represent a number of important elements that illustrate continuity with and contrast to the entertainment economy I discuss in chapter 1. First, a production team designed the cabaret at the hotel, and it was not a staged theater performance. The goal of the proprietors of the hotel was to profit from food, drink, and entrance fees. The evening included dinner, dancing, and alcohol consumption, which presumably brought more profit than fixed-seat theater productions. Second, according to the review, music from cotton fields and plantations became timeless through literature classics such as *Uncle Tom's Cabin* (1852). Even eighty-two years after its initial publication, *Uncle Tom's Cabin* still served as a reference point for black music. As I mention in the introduction, *Uncle Tom's Cabin* was available in India in the early 1850s and became part of the popular imagination in the ensuing decades.[4] In this case, attention to the novel brought attention to black music. Third, the "chief pleasure" of slaves in cotton fields was music, and a primary instrument of this association was the banjo. References to slave life, plantations, and the antebellum South were pervasive in descriptions of American music of the 1930s and 1940s. According to the article, the Plantation Quartet preserved a dying plantation culture through songs such as "Swanee River." American songwriter Stephen Foster wrote this song, originally titled "Old Folks at Home," in 1851 for Christy's Minstrels, a blackface minstrel troupe from Buffalo, New York.[5] The main theme, nostalgia for the plantation, is best exemplified in the line, "Still longing for the old plantation, and for the old folks at home." Though the culture of the antebellum South was lost by the time of the Plantation Quartet performance in 1934, it could be temporarily revived through staged entertainment, which added intrigue and exoticism to performances.

The article in the *Times of India* claims that Luis Pedroso, a Cuban tap dancer, played the character Rastus, "the boy who can't sing but can shuffle his feet."[6] Rastus is a comical character first seen in American mass culture in early silent films such as *Rastus in Zululand* (1910) and *Rastus' Riotous Ride* (1914). In these films, he was typically a happy-go-lucky African American man who lacked the wherewithal to stay out of trouble. The Rastus character, also pervasive in American popular culture outside of film, was most commonly seen as the jolly, confident man who was the face of Cream of Wheat.[7] The Plantation Quartet also included parodies of the black mammy. In their 1934 photo taken at the Taj Mahal Palace Hotel in Bombay (see fig. I.3 in the introduction), we see one member cross-dressed in a black mammy outfit. By the 1930s, stories and images of the domestic slave as a dependable servant, most often represented by the mammy, had entered American popular culture. One of the most familiar images was Aunt Jemima, the cheerful, full-faced character that sold pancake mix. According to Micki McElya, Aunt Jemima was first seen in American popular culture as early as the 1890s at the World's Columbian Exposition in Chicago in 1893, and the origins of the mammy narrative were probably first seen as early as the 1830s, when the planter class recited stories "to animate their assertions of slavery as benevolent and slave owning as honorable."[8] (This narrative continued in Hollywood films in the twentieth century.) Karen Cox claims that Rastus and the black mammy represented some of the earliest advertising images that came from the southern United States,[9] and they embodied antebellum respite from the modern industrial world. Their nostalgic representations were important to the advertising strategies of the Plantation Quartet, and the use of terms and phrases such as "old days," "disappeared," and "earliest recollection" in the *Times of India* article also reflects these sentiments.

The steam-powered paddle-wheeled riverboat and bales of cotton in the background of the photo of the Plantation Quartet further construct imaginary imagery from the rural South. Similar nostalgic and romanticized representations of plantations were seen in Hollywood films of the late 1920s and 1930s, perhaps most successfully in *Gone with the Wind* (1939). The Great Depression in the United States and nostalgia for the timeless, simple way of life in the antebellum South attracted audiences to these representations, both in film and on stage. Melvyn Stokes proposes that Hollywood often sentimentalized plantations, even slavery itself, through portrayals of plantations with benevolent white owners who were cultivated, courteous, and whose slaves served willingly.[10] Bruce Chadwick clams that cooperative black slaves were "typically shown as helpful mammies, obliging butlers, smiling carriage-drivers, joyful cotton-pickers and tap-dancing entertainers,"[11] all images seen in the performances and marketing photos of the Plantation Quartet. Similarly, according to Warren French, "Hollywood in the 1930s . . . presented an idyllic South overflowing with wealth and populated by refined ladies and gentlemen surrounded by faithful servants."[12] Other advertisements for Plantation Quartet performances reinforced southern antebellum idealism through photos similar to the depiction shown in figure I.3.

Juxtaposed within the photo of the quartet is a symbol of new international mobility. The ship in the background has a streamlined design, linear aesthetic, and repeating horizontal evenly spaced circles reminiscent of cruise liners, which are art deco motifs. By representing art deco through plantation nostalgia, this staged photograph illustrates much of the meaning and appeal of performances of its type in India, grounded in stereotypes and imaginary anachronisms of African American life in the United States, yet contextualized within a modernist sensibility unobtrusively accentuated in art deco. Through musical and iconographic stylistic devices, advertisements for the quartet reinforced the idea that the performers were from somewhere else, and that the music pointed toward a place or setting that was unlike India.

The appeal of the Plantation Quartet rested not only in its focus on plantation imagery, but also in its stylistic connections to Hollywood's expansive, nebulous definition of black music. The Planation Quartet followed Hollywood's lead when choosing repertoire. Representations of black music in Hollywood films were first seen in the late 1920s when sound films made it possible to feature singing on screen. According to Jack Kirby, early films such as *Hearts in Dixie* (1929) and *Hallelujah* (1929) were "ringing with banjos and brimming with high-kicking, happy darky stereotypes." The film *Hallelujah* incorporated a fad at the time that Kirby calls the "exotic negro"—mysterious, musically gifted, and lacking a moral compass.[13] Ed Guerrero writes that, between 1930 and 1945, "there was hardly a plantation film made that did not contain some sort of sentimentalized musical interlude performed by the devoted slaves on the plantation or the black servants of the postbellum years."[14] These representations were seen in musical comedies such as *Dixiana* (1930) and *Mississippi* (1935).

The members of the Plantation Quartet in many respects defined themselves through songs and images created by these and other productions. The quartet's music repertoire often included material from current foreign films, especially productions with plantation or riverboat themes. In August 1936, almost two years after the quartet's first performances, Regal and Capitol Cinemas in Bombay screened the Universal Pictures film *Show Boat* (1936). Though this film does not focus on a plantation, it evokes elements of Kirby's "exotic negro," most exemplified in actor Paul Robeson's character Joe, a musically gifted laborer negotiating a difficult life filled with racism. The Taj Mahal Palace Hotel, seeking to profit from the popularity of the film, designed a cabaret titled "Show Boat Dance" (fig. 2.1) that premiered a week before the film's release, and was presented in collaboration with Universal Pictures.[15] Crickett Smith's Symphonians performed jazz, the Plantation Quartet sang, and Cuban drummer Luis Pedroso sang and tap-danced: "The Taj Quartet is going to sing some of the melodies from the film. Creighton Thompson's basso profondo should be well suited by 'Old Man River'; and no doubt 'Can't help loving that man'—one of the finest 'blues' ever written—will be sung. The Band's drummer, whose tap dancing is now famous, will do his stuff to 'Make Believe.'"[16] These songs are from the film. The Plantation Quartet and the tap routines of Luis Pedroso created a successful thematic evening event. (Not coincidentally, tap dancer Bill "Bojangles" Robinson's films such as *Harlem Is Heaven* (1932) were screened in Bombay that same year.)

This integration of themes and music from the film *Show Boat* into a local cabaret in Bombay illustrates Hollywood's influence on domestic entertainment. By the 1930s, Hollywood films had shaped ethnicity and race into consumable products. They injected fluid racial stereotypes with glamour and consumerism, and the global marketability of Hollywood

Figure 2.1. Advertisement for the "Show Boat Dance." *Times of India*, August 28, 1936. Image reproduced by permission from ProQuest LLC.

films such as *Show Boat* essentialized and idealized racial differences with real-world referents. In *Show Boat*, African American laborers sang with ease, but they were also disenfranchised, and race was at the heart of both elements. Sarah Berry calls this broader trend in Hollywood "exoticism-as-masquerade,"[17] in which the complexities of African American life are oversimplified and masked in films, but the challenges of racism still form their core.

The song sequence "Ol' Man River" in the film features the character Joe singing in a deep, voluminous style at a slow tempo. Laborers dressed in work clothes populate the scene—sometimes carrying bales of cotton on their backs, other times rolling the bales across a dock in unison as machines would. Joe sings in a plaid shirt on dock, and his demeanor evokes melancholy and strength. Camera shots feature strong yet fatigued laborers struggling to get through the day, at times downhearted, and at other times engaged in transgressions such as drunkenness. The song "Ol' Man River" symbolically conflates the struggles of life in the United States with the relentless, uncaring flow of the Mississippi River. It begins with the following lyrics: "There's an old man called the Mississippi / That's the old man that I'd like to be / What does he care if the world's got troubles / What does he care if the land ain't free." Arthur Knight maintains that narratives in films such as *Show Boat* often defined the character and scope of black music and musicianship in films.[18] Through Joe's songs and the larger narrative structure, audiences could lament discrimination in the United States and construct a relationship between revealing lyrics and black music as a definable style. In the case of "Ol' Man River," Joe sings to convey a simpler time, to express discrimination, and to represent Hollywood's singing African American archetype. The cabaret "A Night Down South" at the Taj Mahal Palace Hotel marketed these nostalgias and stereotypes, summed up best in the *Times of India* review article mentioned above, which claims that cabaret audiences "instinctively" connect certain styles of music and instruments to African Americans.

In the British entertainment industry as well, primitivism informed ideas about the commercialized representations of black music portrayed by Paul Robeson and in *Show Boat*. Primitivism here means a belief in the capacity of black music to express an idealized historical time, especially as it expresses the mystery of music or humanity in general, and confidence in black musicians' capacity for a simpler, more human musicianship. The Drury Lane Theatre in London produced a theater version of *Show Boat* in 1928, and in the cast was Paul Robeson, the same actor from the film. Robeson also gave concerts in London during the run of *Show Boat*, including performances with the Drury Lane Orchestra conducted by Hermann Finck, which were met with positive reviews.[19] In the *Daily Express* (London) on July 5, 1928, James Douglas wrote, "His songs are the Bible as we heard it at our mother's knee. They are the mother-songs of mankind, the hidden songs that all men and women hear whispering in their buried memory. It is not only the dreaming negro soul that yearns in these cumulative refrains. It is the sad soul of humanity reaching out in to the mystery of life and death." This review is yet another example revealing that, at its core, black music was considered mysterious and hidden, yet "buried" somewhere in all of us.

To be sure, the repertoire of "A Night Down South" featured pieces that did not necessarily represent race or the American South. The song "Make Believe," sung by Luis Pedroso in the cabaret, is a love dialogue between the leads portrayed by Allan Jones and Irene Dunne in the film. Allan Jones attempts to express his love for Dunne in this duet: "Only make believe I love you / Only make believe that you love me." Sung in the film in a loose operetta style, this piece likely appealed to audiences at the Taj Mahal Palace Hotel who sought Hollywood representations of romance.

The performances of the Plantation Quartet were part of broader trends that circulated global media and commercialized performances. Vocal music described as "plantation" songs had been performed in the past in India, including once on a tour by the Westminster Glee Singers in 1924, part of a circuit designed to "revive interest in the national music of [Great Britain]."[20] A contemporary newspaper review suggests that their music was "British Minstrelsy" repertoire, which included "English National Airs, Irish Folk-Songs, Scottish Melodies and Welsh Airs," but they also performed "American Plantation Ditties."[21] The Westminster Glee Singers performed unaccompanied, and were recognized and respected in London. The "Louisana [*sic*] Quartette," a group from the United States, performed at the Excelsior in Bombay for about a week in 1921. One review emphasized that they specialized in "negro melodies and quaint old plantation harmonies."[22] But by the time the Plantation Quartet formed in 1934, Hollywood films and resident African American jazz musicians created plantation imaginaries that were modern, global, and nostalgic. It is important to emphasize once again that the Plantation Quartet typically performed music from Hollywood films, which was usually considered outside the scope of traditional black spirituals.

Other Exoticisms

Exotic iconographies were not limited to black or southern histories. The Plantation Quartet performed an "Apache Gala" in February 1935 at the Taj Mahal Palace Hotel. This gala included Native American themes and accessories, and advertisements encouraged patrons to "come in Apache costume."[23] A review of the performance in the *Times of India* states that the theme also focused on the Apache dance, a style that emerged in the 1910s in Europe and the United States. It was an aggressive couples dance that included semiviolent tosses, turns, hair pulling, and dragging. Originally from Paris, it received its name because of its primitive connotations with Native Americans and ritualized extremes of sexual domination and submission between the male and female dancers.

Maurice Mouvet and his French dance partner Madeleine d'Arville are typically considered to have brought the dance to the United States at Louis Martin's Café de Paris in New York in 1910. Mouvet wrote that it was "an intensely brutal dance, but it is not vulgar with deliberate vulgarity. It is the dance of realism, of primitive passion; as a picture of life in the raw it has beauty and artistic strength."[24] He claimed the dance was unrestrained, and that "Indians, and in fact, every savage tribe, . . . dance wildly, madly, before they go to war."[25] By Mouvet's own account, his performance in 1910 launched the cabaret format in New York City: "This was the opening of cabaret in New York. . . . While I was dancing at Martin's there was also a Spanish solo dancer and one or two singers. The long intervals in between gave the guests a chance to chat, and this was the nearest approach to the ideal cabaret that New York has ever had."[26] Theater reviewer Yetta Geffin claimed in 1915 that Mouvet's first performance was "unlike anything that New York had ever witnessed before."[27] The Apache dance in the United States created a sensation in cabarets and dance halls, and was even used in vaudeville as a stunt dance.[28]

The dance's transatlantic movement between the United States, England, and France probably enhanced its appeal. It became popular in France with the film *Bebe Apache* in 1910, in which the two lead characters perform an Apache dance in a seedy cabaret.[29] In India, a number of American films were screened that featured the dance in a cabaret setting, including *The Stronger Vow* (1919), *l'Apache* (1919), and *Shattered Dreams* (1922). Audiences viewed American silent film stars such as Dorothy Dalton and Geraldine Farrar perform (or witness) the dance. It was also performed in variety shows at the Excelsior and elsewhere in Bombay during these years.[30]

By the time the "Apache Gala" was organized in 1935, the Apache dance had a history of stage performance in the theaters of India. But with the arrival of African American musicians and for-profit dance halls, its performance became associated with cabarets, and venues were decorated in themes that transformed the entire performance area. Reviews of the 1935 dance describe the main ballroom at the Taj Mahal Palace Hotel as adorned "to create the impression of a 'dive' in Montmartre . . . with specially prepared and painted scenery and effects . . . [to create] a cellar."[31] This décor references the intimate underground cabarets in Paris that popularized the Apache dance in the 1910s. The Taj Mahal Palace Hotel provided Apache costumes and accessories such as pistols and daggers to complete the atmosphere. Patrons were taught a ballroom version of the dance, the Plantation Quartet performed songs related to the theme, and Creighton Thompson and his orchestra performed with a "beauty chorus of Apache girls."[32] Once again we see African American musicians capitalizing on exotic adulation and demonstrating expansive musical skills, all the while mindful of their warm reception. David Krasner argues that "because of the rising interest in 'primitivism (the so-called link between black people and the subconscious nature), black artists and performers had to walk the tightrope bridging the mainstream and the 'exotic.'"[33] American musicians in India often willingly jumped off this tightrope and adjusted their musical style and repertoire to accommodate popular genres and performance practices.

In all the above examples, musicians were inventive in the ways they set about creating a livelihood in this foreign labor market. They embraced certain types of enterprising behavior to establish and maintain a comfortable position in local jazz and variety show economies, and they secured cooperative networks with those working in the film industry to strategically take advantage of the cinema as a source of work possibilities. They also worked in partnership with hotel proprietors to collaborate with supportive networks of musicians, arrangers and producers. Innovative practices in the "Show Boat Dance" or the "Apache Dance" had an economic impact. These productions drew audiences to live venues such as the Taj Mahal Palace Hotel and required that musicians, producers, and others achieve a skill set and creative capacity to accomplish successful performances, which also included, in part, drawing attention to the African or African American backgrounds of a handful of the musicians. A pervasive network of jazz connoisseurs did not exist in India to nearly the same extent as in the United States or England, so we should consider that African American musicians in India in the 1930s were sometimes less valued for their technical ability in music performance and more for their capacity to contribute to production value. This may be one reason that representations of race and social status in marketing and advertising materials were partly expressed in terms of social position and racial status.[34] Their racial background created opportunities for profit in a manner that otherwise may not have been possible among Indian musicians.

Early Jazz

The literature on jazz in India is still emerging. Naresh Fernandes has articulated some of its development in India, focusing on the Taj Mahal Palace Hotel in Bombay,[35] but little additional research as been done on the more expansive presence of jazz in India. Therefore, the next two sections of this chapter will give a descriptive account of some aspects of the early development of jazz, including the practicalities involved in its growth and expansion. The account is not intended to be comprehensive, but seeks to briefly highlight the character of jazz performed by both foreign and domestic entertainers.

Audiences in India were captivated by jazz after World War I. As it spread across the globe, conversations about its definition and genesis were found in newspapers and print media throughout India. Some of the earliest references to jazz in India emphasize its African American origins, often inaccurately. In 1919, Ross Sobel, a British bandmaster living in India, suggested that jazz and its dances were not necessarily new:

> It has been danced all over America for the last twenty years and is simply a variation of the old ragtime played by the old nigger [sic] band consisting of trombones, clarionettes, pianos, and trap drums. The word "jazz" is just a variation of "jazzbo," an American nigger [sic] greeting. . . . The real Jazz music is composed of the beautiful nigger [sic] melodies from the Southern States but it is being sadly murdered by the American musicians, who cannot impart to it that native charm which is the principal reason for its world-wide popularity.[36]

Evoking the designation "native" suggests a primitivism similar to that seen in Plantation Quartet marketing strategies, and Sobel argues that black musicians from the southern United States are the original performers, a primary reason for its expansive reach. He seems to conflate jazz music with jazz dance, which at the time could encompass social dancing to jazz or non-jazz music including ragtime and other similar styles.[37] It is understandable that in 1919 he might struggle with classifying jazz and distinguishing between music and movement in its African American origins.

Jazz was integrated into global entertainment markets from its beginning, and India was no exception. Maynard Owen Williams wrote in 1921 that jazz had already embodied commercial and transnational underpinnings in Calcutta: "Calcutta, of all India's cities, has suffered most from commercializing tendencies. Besides the store where Benares brocades are sold, American shoes shine lustrously under electric lights, and close to the curio shop where Tibetan temple treasures are exposed for sale a costly cabaret offers 'jazz' to jaded pleasure seekers."[38] Williams hints that in Calcutta pleasure was commodified and jazz commercialized, which he views as a somewhat negative factor. Williams is possibly referring to Firpo's Restaurant and Bar, which was among the first private establishments to regularly book jazz and cabarets in Calcutta.

Jazz was performed in North India at least two years before Williams's article was published.[39] Maurice Bandman probably booked the first shows including jazz aimed at large audiences, at least in Bombay. In April 1919, Bandman, an entertainer and theater manager from the United States, hired the Jazz Band of the HMS *New Zealand* (which was docked in Bombay that month) to perform at the Excelsior Theatre in Bombay.[40] They performed "The Bing Boys on Broadway," the London theater song "Chu Chin Chow," and the early ragtime piece "Yankiana Rag."[41] Though reviews of their performances do not list jazz pieces, one review on April 12 claims they introduced "jazz effects into a full orchestra" including a "jazz drummer."[42] Another review claims that "jazz music has been especially arranged for."[43] As was the case around the globe, jazz at this time was vaguely defined, and these early performances may have featured variations of ragtime or American stage show music that included a jazz-style drum set or drumming techniques associated with jazz.

The finale of a multinight performance series organized by Maurice Bandman at the Excelsior Theatre two months later in June may have included jazz or jazz dance. An advertisement for this final performance stated, "A feature in connection with the last night will be the introduction of the latest London craze the Jazz dance, by Miss Alice May and Mr. Clayton Robbins. These performers made a study of Jazz during the last few months they were in London."[44] May and Robbins were theater performers, and the designation "jazz dance" may refer to the W. Benton Overstreet song "The Jazz Dance" (1917), whose lyrics name dances of African American origin such as the Shimmy-She, the Buzz, the Texas Tommy, and the Eagle Rock.[45] Whatever its meaning, Bandman often advertised that his performances exhibited the most up-to-date material from the United States, and at least some of his repertoire may have included music at the vague intersections of jazz and ragtime.

Perhaps the earliest foreign jazz musician to tour India was Zimmy the Jazz Drummer. He first performed at the Excelsior in late 1919 at the invitation of Bandman,[46] and was popular for months, performing in a number of venues. He played with singer-composer-dancer Madeline Rossiter in a variety show format, and advertisements and reviews indicate that their repertoire included early jazz or ragtime tunes. They likely met while performing with the Royal Strollers, a variety group that performed in New Zealand and Australia, where Zimmy was once described as a "trick drummer and manipulator of many instruments."[47] Zimmy and Rossiter performed together in India throughout the 1920s to mostly positive reviews, and by many accounts they were popular and successful. Zimmy was described as the "Live Jazz Man,"[48] and his regular presence in Bombay, along with other local musicians and traveling orchestras, suggests that by late 1919 or early 1920 audiences had at least limited access to the earliest manifestations of live jazz. Audiences purchased printed music of jazz as early as 1919, which generated further interest. Marcks and Company Ltd. in Bombay and Pune, one of the largest sheet music distributors in and around Bombay, sold pieces described as "the latest jazz music" in stores and by mail order.[49]

Reviews of variety shows during this period suggest that Maurice Bandman found it difficult to find proficient performers, so he often secured talent from passenger ships and took over the management of traveling troupes to enhance their marketability. Dave Carson's successful minstrel runs in India inspired Bandman to travel to the subcontinent with his company for a brief tour in 1900.[50] He returned in 1905 and became a middleman for a number of touring companies for years, having established connections to theaters, skilled labor, and marketing resources. Bandman was flexible in his performance lineup, mixing and matching entertainers as he saw fit. He was one of the most successful proprietors of his kind in North India, and his command of the English-language variety theater probably supported the first ongoing performances of jazz in India, at least in Bombay, and he often included Zimmy the Jazz Drummer.

Other groups performed jazz in late 1919 after Zimmy arrived, including the Banvard All-American Musical Comedy Company. They organized variety shows under the direction of Bandman. Most reviews of their performances do not mention jazz and claim that the music was a mix of ragtime and revue music,[51] but a review on December 2, 1919, states that "the comedies abound in merriment, witty dialogue, catchy 'jazz' song hits and a variegated variety of dance." The word *jazz* is in quotation marks, which suggests that reviewers in India, as elsewhere, were still struggling with its defining characteristics. As jazz became associated with the United States, advertising its American origins became an important marketing strategy, as illustrated in Banvard's frequent use of the designation "All-American" in their title and marketing materials.[52]

In the early 1920s, jazz groups performed in a variety of contexts. Though the earliest jazz performances took place in theater venues, the spread of jazz in India is also associated with cabarets and social clubs. Some cabaret organizers booked both jazz and classical performers at the same event, and the approach to decor was sometimes similar to the fairyland themes seen at formal ballroom dances, as discussed in the preceding chapter. Jazz performances seemed to fit well with the fantasy trends seen in formal ball decor. In Bombay in 1923, when the League of Mercy booked the Renown Jazz Band, a traveling group, at the Ladies' Gymkhana, the venue was decorated with a "fairyland of coloured lights and lanterns peeping in and out of the many trees and bushes, which were effectively decorated with bunting, streamers and flags." A review describes the performance as "unflagging; and dancing enthusiasts could not complain of a lack of encores. Such a cheery band of players . . . [drove] away the 'blues' of the most depressed at any time."[53] On June 9, 1923, the Poona Hotel organized a "Carnival and Fancy Dress Ball" that included illuminations, fancy decorations, and confetti fireworks.[54] The Broadway Boy's Jazz Band from Bombay performed jazzy tunes and an operatic ballet dancer, Miss Patricia Gorman, performed a Waltz form the ballet *Coppelia* (1870) composed by Leo Delibes.

Jazz quickly gained steam in the early 1920s.[55] A newspaper article in the *Times of India* describing available entertainment in Bombay in 1920 even suggests that music for European audiences consisted almost entirely of jazz and popular music: "The musical fare provided for the Indian public is jazz and selections from musical comedy and tinkling music hall tunes."[56] Music critics debated about the quality of jazz. One newspaper article in 1919, "Judge on the 'Jazz,'" claimed that jazz was "reminiscent of, although . . . far less fascinating than, the barbaric tunes we have heard arising from the old Wazzah Bazar in Cairo, the Malay Quarter in Cape Town, and from the haunts of the nautch girl in India."[57] In spite of the occasional critical stance, audiences responded to jazz with fervor in 1919, causing some critics to suggest sarcastically that audiences considered it sacrosanct. An anonymous syndicated article that year in the *Times of India* claims that "judging from the seriousness of the face of some of [jazz's] celebrants it may be religious."[58]

African Americans and Exoticism

As in most other places, jazz in India had profit value. People made money on it, sometimes in performance venues or on the radio, and sometimes through sales of gramophone discs, sheet music, or films. It was featured in social clubs, dance halls, hotel ballrooms, railway social institutes, and numerous other private and public venues, many of which were for-profit. Jazz became more prevalent in the 1930s in part because of orchestras composed of African Americans touring India. The first major traveling groups to arrive in India in the mid-1930s, such as Joseph Ghisleri's Symphonians, Leon Abbey, and Herb Flemming's International Rhythm Aces (fig. 2.2) were partially or totally made up of African American musicians. Herb Flemming traveled to India in December 1933 to play at the Grand Hotel in Calcutta. He stayed in residence until the end of the winter season in April 1934. His group included African Americans Roy Butler on saxophone and Crickett Smith on trumpet, as well as Cuban drummer and tap dancer Louis Pedroso, all of whom chose to remain in India. These three musicians later joined a French orchestra, Joseph Ghisleri's Symphonians, in Bombay in 1934, a traveling band that boasted African American Rudy Jackson on saxophone. Writing about these musicians, Ralph Gulliver maintains, "In contrast to the bleak opportunities for musicians in depression-ridden America, these men were treated royally. . . . Pay, working conditions and accommodations were all superb."[59]

In Bombay, the arrival of Joseph Ghisleri and His Symphonians in 1933 created a jazz scene that included international jazz performers. The proprietors of the Taj Mahal Palace Hotel booked Ghisleri from France at great expense. M. Gunsett, a manager of the hotel at the time, traveled to Europe to secure Ghisleri's contract. Ghisleri's orchestra was administered from Paris, and his musicians signed contracts written by Ghisleri in French with salaries listed in francs.[60] As a more comprehensive circuit of musicians and venues was established between 1934 and 1935, hotel proprietors in India managed and paid orchestras locally.

When Ghisleri left India, African American musicians Roy Butler, Creighton Thompson, Rudy Jackson, and Crickett Smith converged on Bombay to start Crickett's Symphonians. This group was the first orchestra organized in India by African Americans. Pianist Teddy Weatherford joined the group, which was later renamed Teddy Weatherford and His Band. In 1936, jazz violinist Leon Abbey traveled to the Taj Mahal Palace Hotel, bringing with him a number of notable American musicians, including

Figure 2.2. Herb Flemming's International Rhythm Aces, 1933. Photographer unknown. Reproduced by permission from the Chicago Public Library, Visual and Performing Arts Division, Roy Butler Collection.

trumpeter Bill Coleman.[61] Abby influenced the blossoming jazz scene in Bombay with his cutting-edge style. On December 19, 1936, he wrote in the *Chicago Defender* that "old numbers and old ways were called for by conservatives." At the opening night performance at the hotel, Abbey boasts, "Every table, and then some, had been reserved, and the Cool Ballroom was merrier and madder" than it had been for some time.[62] Fernandes hints that Abby's tour in Bombay shook up the hotel entertainment economy and created additional demand for innovative styles from the United States.[63] American musicians witnessed a broad range of performance opportunities in local entertainment economies, especially in elite hotels. The convergence of well-known, professional traveling orchestras and the arrival of African American musicians between 1933 and 1936 in Bombay and Calcutta together increased excitement about jazz.

African American jazz musicians performed regularly in South Asia until 1945 and achieved financial stability and job security. Money was a primary reason that many musicians chose to stay. Saxophonist Roy Butler, based in India from 1933 to 1944, once wrote to his family in the United States that living in South Asia was "simply a millionaire's vacation with pay and passage."[64] Teddy Weatherford and Roy Butler, who always maintained celebrity status as representatives of the early development of jazz in the United States, lived comfortably in India. By choosing to remain in South Asia, American musicians proved to audiences and local musicians that financial security was possible in jazz performance. In spite of the benefits, most American performers chose to leave India in the early and mid-1940s because they felt that cutting-edge musicianship was not pervasive or feasible, among other reasons. Infrequent interactions with jazz musicians in the United States and Europe prevented the development of recognizably new or distinct styles of jazz, and by the 1940s many jazz musicians found no sizable audience for music that was not associated with Hollywood films. African American musicians living and performing in India probably excited audiences more than new musical directions in jazz.[65]

Jazz promoters and advertising strategists used blackface minstrel or darky iconographies and nostalgic representations of the American South to define African American jazz musicians in India, especially in the mid- and late 1930s. These sorts of representations of jazz and black jazz musicians exemplify Ted Gioia's "primitivist myth" concept,[66] the idea that jazz is unformulated, anachronistic, and originally from elsewhere, and that it signifies romantic longing for a different time or something unexperienced, a seductive mystery.[67] These representations suggest that exoticism created aesthetic appeal, a process that, according to Ralph Locke, involves "evoking in or through music . . . a place, people, or social milieu that is not entirely imaginary and that differs profoundly from the 'home' country or culture in attitudes, customs, and morals."[68] Jazz's African American roots, its association with black performers in India, and its global mediation through Hollywood cinema contributed to its popularity.[69]

Pianist Teddy Weatherford fronted many of the orchestras made up of African American musicians in India at the time, and he was often represented in promotional material that used variations of blackface minstrel images. Weatherford was a skilled jazz pianist from the Chicago jazz scene.[70] He took his Chicago style to India in 1936, traveled between Calcutta, Bombay, and Colombo, and made frequent trips to other Asian and European cities.[71] Hotel proprietors in India heavily marketed Weatherford's image. A tall, heavy-set musician, he was also frequently represented as an awkward sophisticate because of his size and characteristically slow gait. The front page of the 1938–39 season booklet from the Taj Mahal Palace Hotel (discussed in the introduction) is a good example (fig. I.4). His white gloves, exaggerated red lips, and large head have antecedents in minstrel iconographies. Promoters used these images throughout Weatherford's stay in India.

Program booklets often featured African American musicians in plantation garb. Figure 2.3, which shows the front page of a brochure from the Galle Face Hotel in Sri Lanka, borrows directly from minstrel or plantation iconographies, and includes exaggerated inky blackface performers with bright red lips, and a banjo player sitting front and center on a barrel. The musicians did not perform minstrel music, but jazz and classical dance pieces. Such representations were common even though the musicians performed in some of the top venues and hotels in South Asia. Program booklets frequently featured exaggerated or stereotyped vernaculars, with some describing the lineup of bands with the sentence: "Dis are de order they cumes on" instead of "This is the order they will play."[72] Similar exaggerations were seen in showmanship on the stage or bandstand. Saxophonist Roy Butler related that Crickett Smith walked with an overstated limp during performances of the Plantation Quartet and "relied heavily on comedy to get by . . . he was funny looking to begin with, short, black and with pop eyes."[73] According to Walter White, in the United States, performers embraced these sorts of stereotypes to increase their recognizability.[74] But in India, African American musicians secured upmarket accommodations and were paid well,[75] so it is likely that hotel proprietors and other promoters felt that these representations offered additional marketability.[76]

Why were these iconographies used to promote black musicians in India? Part of the answer is that references to primitivism and blackface in jazz figured prominently across the globe in the early years of the genre. Historian and critic J. A. Rogers, in his pivotal 1925 article "Jazz at Home," described jazz as a "thing of the jungles—modern man-made jungles."[77] Similar descriptions of jazz primitivism were common, and black provincialism was pervasive in American popular media, perhaps most revealingly on the mainstream radio show *Amos and Andy* broadcast on NBC. By 1931, the program about two African American men from Birmingham, Alabama, had reached an estimated audience of forty million.[78] *Amos and Andy* shaped audience perceptions of southern blacks in the United States, and the skits and stereotyped vernacular of the show were in some respects an extension of nineteenth-century blackface minstrel shows that emphasized ignorance and laziness. Douglas Craig suggests that Amos and Andy

Figure 2.3. Program brochure of a performance of Teddy Weatherford and His Band at the Galle Face Hotel in Sri Lanka, July 29, 1939. Artist unknown. Reproduced by permission from the Chicago Public Library, Visual and Performing Arts Division, Roy Butler Collection.

were sympathetically portrayed, but both displayed these archetypes: "The show's humor arose from their mispronunciation of words, . . . [and] both characters spoke in an exaggerated minstrel dialect."[79] In addition, the iconic Al Jolson sound film *The Jazz Singer* (1927), popular in both the United States and England,[80] features Jolson singing American songs in blackface, and Simon Frith suggests that British jazz musicians in the 1930s occasionally dressed in blackface.[81] Creating an audience for jazz in India was not easy, so promoting iconographies and representations familiar to British and American entertainment industries was a practical marketing strategy.

Furthermore, hot jazz was not regularly broadcast on the BBC in England until the mid- to late 1930s,[82] in part because some in England considered jazz a threat to national identity.[83] According to Genevieve Abravanel, there was a fear that hot jazz could "modernize England out of itself" and render its pastimes and traditions homogeneous with America.[84] Hotel and club proprietors in Calcutta and Bombay probably viewed the lack of hot jazz in England as a marketing and advertising opportunity. The density of jazz narratives at the time and the significant generalizations seen in conversations on the source of jazz and its racial identity encouraged widely diverse and heavily politicized judgments about jazz in England.[85] In India, by contrast, jazz's hazard to British identity was more distant, and the popularity of jazz probably questioned the standards of social life of the Raj more than it did national identity in the homeland. In fact, some British audiences in India in the mid-1930s might have considered live hot jazz in Bombay and Calcutta more vibrant and enduring than in England at the time. From a purely economic standpoint, it made sense for promoters in India to call attention to African American musicians in Bombay and Calcutta through racial iconographies.

British attitudes about jazz in India were contradictory.[86] Vast differences in class, age, profession, rank, and income among the British influenced patterns of consumption as well as other lifestyle choices,[87] but Dennis Kincaid, a civil servant in India until 1937, claims that the gramophone industry increased attention to jazz among all classes, and he jokes that "the new gramophone with the records recently purchased in Bombay . . . set [the older generation] all swaying a little in their rocking chairs."[88] Yet even those who accepted jazz were not necessarily comfortable with it. In one description of a dance at Bombay's Taj Mahal Palace Hotel, Kincaid expresses relief that he could do a ballroom foxtrot to jazz: "The negro band that played in 'the Taj' in the cold weather and made a specialty of 'swing' music, to which luckily it was, however, quite easy to dance the same old fox-trot one always had danced."[89]

Radio and Gramophones

Sound technologies, including radio, stamped a sense of cosmopolitanism onto the primitivisms and exoticisms associated with jazz. The radio represented technological modernity and connected jazz connoisseurs with each other across India through real-time broadcasts.[90] Enthusiasm associated with radio broadcasting at the time was pervasive. On January 23, 1934, the *Times of India* claimed that radio had become integral to European life in India, and had brought the outside world into the home. The article asserts:

> You in India switch over a little lever, turn a knob and hear voices or music from places which would take you weeks, perhaps months, to travel to. There's still romance in this workaday world—romance which every man can enjoy, thanks to progressive manufacturers. As you sit in ease in your chair,

you may enjoy a concert from Moscow, Grand Opera from Berlin, a commentary on a bull-fight in Spain, tangos from South America, hot jazz from Miami, news from Australia, a talk from New Zealand—in short your receiver will bring to you the whole world's radio entertainments.[91]

The radio was advocated through discourses of modernity and the hard work of manufacturers who built radios of all sorts.[92] It projected authority and innovation into jazz,[93] extended this experience to locally circumscribed listeners in rural areas, and connected audiences to coastal city performances.[94]

Jazz orchestras relayed live shows on shortwave broadcasts from Delhi, Bombay, and Calcutta.[95] Firpo's Bar and Restaurant in Calcutta relayed live dance-band performances on the Calcutta broadcast signal from at least 1930.[96] Ken Mac broadcast his band live on Friday nights out of Delhi in late 1937 and 1938.[97] Crickett Smith and His Boys broadcast occasionally in 1937 on the Bombay frequency in the evening.[98] On Tuesday evenings for several months in 1938, Teddy Weatherford broadcast his performances from the Taj Mahal Palace Hotel and Green's Hotel in Bombay.[99] These broadcasts sometimes lasted more than three hours. One advertisement for Weatherford's performances at the Taj Mahal Palace Hotel that year boasted that live broadcasts attracted enthusiastic patrons: "Anybody in Bombay can now 'go on the air' every Tuesday night. Teddy Weatherford and his band broadcast from 10 to 11 p.m. and the diners furnish the 'atmosphere' for the broadcast, their applause and even their chatter, when the band does not drown it, being relayed. From the listeners' point of view the patrons appear to thoroughly enjoy it."[100] Audiences could participate in the broadcast itself, providing chatter, applause, and "atmosphere." Another review of a relayed performance at the Taj Mahal Palace Hotel in July 1938 claims that live broadcasting contributed to the excitement of the performance: "Teddy Weatherford is, as usual, devising new methods of making rhythmic music more popular than ever. His broadcast last Tuesday was brilliant, and diners were thrilled at being 'behind the scenes' for this occasion."[101] These shows reinforced the popularity of Weatherford and other jazz musicians in Calcutta, Bombay, and Delhi.[102]

Lionel Fielden, director of broadcasting for the government of India between 1935 and 1940, felt that the radio represented an iconoclastic edge that operated along the margins of the British administration of New Delhi.[103] Joselyn Zivin suggests that Fielden and his team "entertained very different notions of progress; they had ideas about how to elevate and unify mass tastes, how to liberate listeners from parochialism, and how to engineer a more immediately inclusive kind of popular politics based on the world of information learned from the radio."[104] In this sense, the radio in India represented progress, antiparochialism, and democratic access to news and information on a global scale, perhaps unlike any other source. At least some in the colonial administration sought to preserve this inclusivity.

The gramophone was another technology important to the proliferation of jazz. The jazz gramophone recording industry in India started in the mid-1920s as more bands toured the country. Lequime's Grand Hotel Orchestra recorded two tracks in 1926 for HMV Calcutta that represent possibly the earliest recordings of jazz in India: "Soho Blues" and "The House Where the Shutters Are Green."[105] Canadian Jimmy Lequime was one of the earliest bandleaders to travel to India; he was hired away from Shanghai, China, to perform at the Grand Hotel in Calcutta for a brief period in 1926. Jazz recordings were also imported. At the end of the 1920s, the total number of annual gramophone imports from England, the United States, Germany, and France numbered in the hundreds of thousands—610,704 from England alone in 1929.[106]

By the 1930s, the gramophone industry was continuing to evolve and expand. Hollywood film dissemination networks in India distributed imported gramophone recordings of the latest jazz,[107] and frequent advertisements for these discs appeared in English-language papers such as the *Statesman*, the *Times of India*, and the *Pioneer*. HMV, Columbia, and other gramophone companies printed advertisements for jazz daily or weekly in many newspapers and listed the latest available titles from Europe, the United States, and Calcutta. Local jazz orchestras recorded hundreds of songs, including the original song "Taj Mahal" by Crickett Smith and His Symphonians in 1936 on the Rex label, which was performed at the Taj Mahal Palace Hotel for years.[108] The latest foreign and domestic jazz recordings were available on gramophones, as were the most recent tangos, maxixes, sambas, and vaudeville or Tin Pan Alley songs. The location of Calcutta as a hub for pressing and distributing gramophone records bolstered the widespread availability of the recordings, and talking-machine commodities became a primary source of income for many storeowners in Bombay and Calcutta who specialized in machinery and high-end items. This foundational gramophone economy and supporting structure for sound recording later enabled jazz artists to record hundreds of jazz standards for sale in local markets (as will be discussed in chapter 3).

Two Case Studies: Ken Mac and Micky Correa

This section presents two case studies of musicians who became prolific performers during the early years of jazz. I choose these two musicians to emphasize that not all musicians were from the United States or Europe, to show that many jazz musicians depended on British institutions for their growth and development, and to suggest that navigating with nuance the pragmatisms of everyday life was necessary to facilitate access to the wider musical world. In the process I suggest that the cosmopolitan encounter with jazz occurred through engagement with local institutions and commerce, and that opportunism and self-promotion were essential ingredients for many professional musicians. One of the first domestic groups to perform in India, the Bohemians, was led by drummer Ken Mac. Mac attended the Lawrence Royal Military School in Sanawar in the late 1910s, where his training in music shaped and supported his interest in jazz. An unpublished 1947 biography written by his longtime trumpet player Stooge claims that one evening in 1921 Mac attended a music performance by a small group of officer-trainees at the Cavalry School Fencing Hall in Saugor, a small town located in the former Central Provinces. At the event he became fascinated with a drum set composed of both a snare drum and bass drum, all "operated by one man." This single-person contraption captivated the drummer, and he learned that the "big drum . . . was operated by a foot pedal while the side drum was clamped to the left top rim of the bass drum."[109] This setup was typical of drum configurations used by early jazz groups in the United States, and Mac was fascinated.

Mac was trained at the military school on the marching snare drum, a percussion instrument typically strapped to the upper body to facilitate performance while on parade. His training on marching drums likely enabled his initial technical ability to play percussion. Early jazz musicians in New Orleans similarly assembled military-style drums into stationary drum kits, and the young Ken Mac picked up on this trend with enthusiasm. Stooge claims that Mac's inspiration to learn the jazz drums came from his having witnessed this single performance at the fencing hall:

> Till then his own experience of music was confined to the side drum acquired as a student in the band of the Lawrence Royal Military Academy, Sanawar, and this new idea so fascinated him. . . . There were other noisy gadgets—cymbals, motor horns, whistles, etc., and a pistol with which shots were banged off occasionally. Was this possibly the "jazz" in America people here were talking about?!! And while he was thus reflecting, the seed to a colorful and successful career was sown.[110]

Mac's kit was similar to jazz drum sets in the United States.

The Lawrence Royal Military School maintained a choir, offered private applied instrumental instruction, and had a brass band and a "percussion band."[111] The school developed an exemplary music department whose teaching program was awarded special recognition by the Prince of Wales in 1922, and it organized a large number of programs and performances each year.[112] It is not likely that the Lawrence Royal Military School or the Cavalry School in Saugor formally taught jazz, but drawing from the above descriptions we can assume that at least some students were interested in jazz during these years. The military school's music curriculum created the capacity to learn new styles of music, and educational institutions such as the Cavalry School provided ready-made audiences of young enthusiasts. Schools with music curricula existed in several hill stations as well as in larger cities such as Calcutta, Delhi, and Bombay. These schools typically based the standards of music education on school programs in England.

Early jazz musicians struggled to find instruments. Mac used military drums to construct his first set, but he needed additional tom-toms and a bass drum pedal to complete the kit. He journeyed to local markets to find the necessary materials. According to Stooge, he sauntered "deep into the native quarter, where, after much explaining, gesticulating and arguing, he managed to convey what he wanted, and finally emerged with a couple of Indian drums."[113] After some correspondence with an engineer friend, "a clumsy looking pedal was forged and, together with the other fittings, his first set of Jazz drums was assembled."[114] Key to Mac's success was the bass drum pedal, which frees the hands and facilitates a simple ostinato on the bass drum. Thus, the items necessary to construct a complete jazz drum set were found in a small town in India.

Mac performed in India for decades. The Bohemians' instrumentation in 1922 included a banjo, cornet, piano, and drums, and their first major job was at the GIP (Great Indian Peninsula) Railway Institute in the Byculla Station, Bombay.[115] They drew a capacity crowd and the show was a success.[116] They later performed for a much larger audience at the New Year's Eve Ball at the Royal Bombay Yacht Club in December 1922. His career as a performer in elite venues began after this show, and he subsequently played in many of Bombay's choice establishments such as the Willington Sports Club, the Bombay Gymkhana, Green's Hotel, and the Taj Mahal Palace Hotel. According to Stooge, "There was not a place of any importance that did not engage [his] services."[117] The Bohemians traveled to London in 1926, where Mac was exposed to new ideas, and upon returning he added a violinist and saxophone player, increasing the orchestra to six members. In the following years they signed contracts at many elite venues throughout North India. The Lawrence Royal Military School provided the initial musical resources to create one of the most successful longtime jazz performers in India.

William Weber suggests that music historians sometimes tend to give musicians too little credit for their agency in reshaping the musical lives of themselves and others.[118] Jazz musicians in India (and elsewhere) were not necessarily subordinate to others in the music business, nor were they simply fashionable talents unmindful of the forces acting on their economic success. They were active agents who took advantage of opportunities around them. In many cases it was not sufficient just to be a good performer—to be successful, most had to find patrons and attract a public, self-promote, and organize productions that appealed to audiences. Saxophonist Micky Correa's early years performing jazz are a good case study. Correa performed in the for-profit cabaret industry in Bombay after learning the ropes with the Optimists Band (sometimes called Correas Band or Correa's Optimists Band), an orchestra established by his brother Alex Correa in 1928 in Lahore. They were based in Karachi from 1928 to 1938. When they first began performing, they relied on British patronage in social clubs and private functions. They learned European classical dance tunes and popular national songs, and Micky Correa was arguably recognized as the musical backbone of the group. Since the Correa brothers (and likely others in the orchestra) conversed in English and were educated in Catholic English-medium institutions that taught Western music, it is likely that they had a marketing edge, and knew the needs of the audience through a knowledge of Western music. Furthermore, they had capacity to establish interpersonal networks and communicate with their British market base, which included people in key government positions.

Micky was born in Mombasa in 1913 and his family moved to Goa around 1918 and then to Karachi around 1924, where he attended Saint Patrick's Catholic High school and learned the violin in the school orchestra. When his elder brother Alex started Correa's Optimist Band, Micky, still a teenager, played the violin and banjo, later switching to the saxophone.[119] They changed the name of the band to the Optimists Swing Orchestra, and performed regularly in venues such as the Government House, the Karachi Gymkhana, the Sind Club, the Boat Club, and the North West Railway European Institute, as well as at private functions including weddings. The orchestra members included Chris Webb on banjo, J. A. Millar on piano,

P. Carrol on baritone saxophone, E. D. Silva on violin, S. D'Souza on saxophone, J. A. Correa on drums, and John D'Souza on double bass.

During this period Karachi was experiencing a climate of enthusiastic optimism. Dennis Kincaid lived in Karachi at the time and claimed that "everyone looked forward to the day when [it] would eclipse Bombay" in commerce and infrastructure development.[120] He boasted that after World War I "everyone in Karachi seemed to have money,"[121] and that social clubs such as Clifton, Sind Club, the Golf Club, and the County Club were overflowing with patrons. Because of its prosperity, Karachi was a profitable city in which to maintain a successful dance orchestra. Understandably, the Correa brothers invoked the word *optimist* in the name of their orchestra as an effective branding and marketing strategy, and they claimed to perform the most up-to-date music. One advertisement maintained that they performed the latest "popular music, received directly by airmail from the leading publishers" in Europe and the United States.[122] In a 2008 personal interview I conducted with Micky Correa, he said that they performed "current standards."[123]

Early promotional materials indicate that they also targeted the market for ballroom music in social clubs, and their advertising pamphlets claimed that they played both "classical and dance music."[124] British patronage was a significant source of income, especially early on, and their promotional literature frequently emphasized that the band played waltzes, foxtrots, rumbas, and other styles of formal ballroom dance music. Much of their promotional material included "God Save the King" prominently displayed. One advertising pamphlet they distributed in 1937 reprinted a letter dated November 17, 1936, from the Government House in Karachi, complete with an official seal. Written and signed by the principle secretary of the governor of Sind, it states that Correa's Optimists Band supplied the music at a Government House dance, and that "they were entirely satisfactory and I willingly recommend them."[125] At the top is written "Under Distinguished Patronage," suggesting that influential administrative figures officially (or unofficially) endorsed the band. To solicit jobs from the British professional class in Lahore, the Optimists Swing Band successfully referenced the structures of colonial rule in marketing material, and they publicly claimed official endorsements. They identified expansive European clientele, and adjusted repertoire and advertising strategies accordingly.

The marketing approach of the Optimists Swing Band changed in late 1937. Much of their promotional material began to emphasize the term *swing*. They used phrases such as "Swing, Brother, Swing," "Swing Action," "Swing High! Swing Low!" and "Marvel Swinging" in brochures and programs (fig. 2.4).[126] Alex Correa was the band's manager, and his attention to marketing and branding suggests that he was a keen businessman, able to identify and adjust to diverse audience demand. They even designed pricing tiers, one advertisement claiming they shaped performances to "suit your pocket."[127] Advertisements for the orchestra often promoted Micky Correa as a "Radio Star" after his successful radio broadcast performance in Bombay in 1937. These marketing and advertising strategies contrast the more traditional promotional approach of the late 1920s and early 1930s that tended to evoke loyalty to older or more established British clientele. The Optimists Swing Band successfully identified audience expectations and was highly adept in recognizing product appeal and reconfiguring marketing strategies. Alex and Micky Correa understood that the music could be promoted as would any other commodity with an effective brand and price structure.

Micky Correa moved to Bombay in 1938 after his successful live radio performance. A newspaper review writes that his repertoire for the broadcast included "Dancing with Tears in My Eyes," a big band waltz, and "Sax-O-Phun," an energetic jazz piece emphasizing a solo saxophone.[128] The review described his performance of "Sax-O-Phun" as the highlight of the program, and suggests that Correa sought to exhibit confidence in saxophone virtuosity.[129] This radio broadcast was a major moment in Correa's life, and he spoke to me about it with particular enthusiasm. After moving to Bombay, he joined Beppo and His Rhythm Orchestra and performed in the ballrooms of the Eros and Majestic Cinemas, which held daily dances and cocktail hours. Opening in the fall of that year, the Eros ballroom boasted afternoon teas, luncheons, dinners, musical concerts, tea dances, and dinner dances. The *Times of India* describes it as a particularly exciting venue:

> Modern décor, with no taint of futurism, and a DANCE FLOOR on cushioned springs. You'll dance as you've never before—on Bombay's final for floor shows. Highballs at the COCKTAIL BARS—one reserved for "les girls"—and an OPEN AIR BALCONY (240 ft. long) where you'll be glad to cool off to sea winds. There's room for 500 guests and, apart from the madding crowd, a splendid private room.[130]

In addition to Beppo and His Rhythm Orchestra, some of the top Bombay jazz orchestras and crooners of the era performed at the Eros, including

Figure 2.4. "Swing High! Swing Low!" advertising pamphlet for Correa's Band. Personal collection of Micky Correa. Reproduced by permission from Christine Correa.

Ken Mac, Lorna Shortland, and the Eros Symphonians. By moving to Bombay, Micky Correa was able to regularly perform in one of the most exclusive venues in India.

While at the Eros and Majestic, Correa encouraged Beppo to include more current dance band tunes. He had brought boxes of sheet music with him from Karachi because the war greatly reduced its availability in Bombay.[131] Members of Beppo and His Rhythm Orchestra were mostly German. They performed through 1938, and disbanded when some members of the orchestra were unexpectedly interned because of their German citizenship.[132] Correa later joined orchestras made up of African Americans, including Teddy Weatherford and His Band, Crickett Smith and His Symphonians, and, after a short stint leading his own group, Roy Butler and His Indian Orchestra in 1941. A July 17, 1954, article in the *Evening News* indicates that Micky Correa "got a big 'break' while playing in 1939 with Teddy Weatherford's Band at the Taj [Mahal Palace Hotel]," and that he was "deputized" by African American band member Rudy Jackson.[133] Correa's experiences performing in African American groups probably improved his reputation and facilitated significant networking potential with key jazz promoters in Bombay, including the proprietors of the Taj Mahal Palace Hotel.

In contrast to his work in Karachi, Correa was part of a new and exciting dance band and cabaret industry in Bombay. The proprietors at his places of employment designed the advertising and marketing strategies and booked the acts, and they did not typically promote his performances using phrases such as "God Save the King" or "By Distinguished Patronage." Performing with African American groups in large hotels, Correa no longer relied on British clientele for sole support and patronage, and he worked with musicians who appealed to diverse audiences in elite hotels. When performing in hotel dance bands, he and others typically lived onsite, did not pay rent, and were given servants. He did not have to self-market or self-advertise his group, and he was paid reasonably well.

Correa started his own band in 1941, played at the Taj Mahal Palace Hotel and Green's Hotel, and was ultimately able to effectively integrate his band's repertoire and approach into cabarets that featured multiple groups working collaboratively. The Taj Mahal Palace Hotel, Green's Hotel, Eros Cinema, and Majestic Cinema—and many other venues—were sites of capitalist accomplishment that promoted repertoire catering to audience demand for jazzy cabarets.[134] Such active engagement was to last for years. Micky Correa became a central figure in jazz and cabarets, and performed for decades in arguably the most elite venues in India. He recognized new networks and flows of capital, and adjusted accordingly, seeking out businessmen, entrepreneurs, and private-sector entertainment proprietors. Leading hotels in India increasingly operated in private entertainment economies, and jazz was empowering and optimistic in this climate of entertainment capital and diverse consumer bases.

Correa became an incubator for swing musicians in Bombay in the 1940s. His orchestras inspired a number of jazz musicians who later led some of the city's most popular groups. Many musicians found early encouragement on his bandstand, including Johnny Baptist, Norman Mobsby, George Pacheco and the Gomes brothers on saxophone, Peter Monsorate, Pete D'Mello and Chic Chocolate on trumpet, and Manuel Nunes, Dorothy Clarke, and Lucilla Pacheco on piano.[135] Correa's star status gave recognition to his band members and helped to jump-start careers. Many of these musicians also worked in the early Hindi film song industry. Correa died in Bombay in 2011 at age ninety-seven.

Correa was an entrepreneur in the most positive sense. He (and his orchestras) manipulated advertising to set up new benchmarks and values in the performance of jazz, which in the 1920s and 1930s in Lahore meant emphasizing that Goan musicians could indeed meet the high standards of foreign jazz musicians and secure the stamp of approval from British politicians and public administrators. According to William Weber, musicians often have to undertake a variety of enterprises to become successful and self-promote, including teaching private lessons, advertising, and establishing interpersonal connections.[136] Musicians must frequently advance themselves through manipulation of the market and entrepreneurial activities that nurture personal, professional, and economic relationships. Jazz musicians in India sought opportunity where it existed. When I interviewed Correa in 2008, he indicated that he could obtain up-to-date printed jazz music in Bombay only through extensive interpersonal networks that stretched to Lahore and Calcutta. "I had to find my own [sheet music]," he said, "Lahore, Calcutta, anywhere I could find."[137] Correa sought independent achievement and respect through a network of productive social connections among musicians and businesspeople that ultimately brought opportunity and success.

Conclusion

The beginning of this chapter describes the way that Hollywood representations of African American music promoted and triggered exoticism and primitivism in musical imaginaries, and how artifacts of modernity—such as the radio, moving pictures, and the gramophone—gave the music its complete cosmopolitan flavor, thus allowing audiences to directly inhabit the globalization of American music. But as the last part of the chapter discusses, it is also helpful to consider the pragmatics of engaging globalized cultural productions. Though Micky Correa spent most of his life outside Goa, he strongly identified with his Goan background, and similar to other Goan musicians I interviewed, he suggests that his Goan musicianship was shaped by Western music instruction as it had existed in Goa over the centuries. Singing and instrumental music were encouraged in the colleges and churches of Goa as a means of evangelization, and were an important part of the education of students in Catholic institutions, a trend that continued for hundreds of years. From at least the 1600s, evidence suggests that Goans were considered to have achieved a high level of musicianship. In 1683 Giuseppe Sebastiani wrote: "I enjoyed many times listening to very beautiful music for feast days, especially that of Saint Ignatius Loyola, which was celebrated with seven choirs and the sweetest *sinfonie* [instrumental piece]. . . . I cannot believe how musically proficient are the [Goans and Konkanis], and with what ease they perform."[138] Victor Anand Coelho suggests that documents from the College of Saint Paul in Goa at the time "show regular payments to musicians for harp and viola strings, as well as for the playing and teaching of the organ during the years 1680–1710 . . . [and also] payments for a choir of twelve, and for certain occasions, twenty-two singers."[139] As a Goan musician, Correa considered himself an extension of the long, proud tradition of Goan musicianship, and he recognized and respected the commercial potentials of Western music that began in Goa over two centuries prior.

Jazz occurred in a rapidly globalizing world and was embedded in daily routines and the practicalities of everyday life,[140] no more clearly illustrated than in Ken Mac's first contact with live jazz in the Fencing Hall of the academy. Mac was a young student with an enthusiasm for music. His encounters with the jazz drum set represented not only the global potentials of jazz but also conveniences and pressures in the everyday life of a young person in school, the capacities of tradesmen in the "native quarter" to build a drum set for him, and school instruction on the parade drum. Cosmopolitanism encounters with jazz were embedded in mundane thoughts, stirring inspirations, and practical musical skills, resources Mac later used to shape the early jazz economy of India.

This chapter has focused largely on Bombay, but jazz proliferated in many urban centers throughout the country, and it gained traction for a number of reasons in diverse circumstances. The next chapter outlines the role of the US military in supporting jazz in Calcutta during World War II.

Chapter Three

Calcutta in the War

Thousands of Allied troops arrived in India between 1941 and 1945, and the United States occupied military stations throughout the country to support a massive force. These war efforts, part of the China-Burma-India theater of operations, created a military economy in India that increased the market for Western entertainment. By late 1943 in Calcutta, optimism about victory had become prevalent, and large numbers of Allied soldiers stationed in the city were enjoying live music, Hollywood moving pictures, gramophone recordings of jazz, and English-language radio broadcasts. This chapter focuses on the influence of the Allied military's entertainment economy on jazz production, dissemination, and consumption between 1943 and 1945. It frames the war in a transnational setting by suggesting that the American and British militaries were catalysts for entertainment globalization, and captures a historical moment during a time of penetrating and somewhat unconventional human movement into the city. It discusses military radio broadcasting, local jazz gramophone disc markets, the scope of military entertainment, and the contextualizing forces that brought meaning to jazz.

For local music industries and infrastructures to be economically successful, there must be large numbers of customers, adequate resources to economize on production costs, and significant density of human capital.[1] Wartime Calcutta had gramophone recording studios and production plants, music stores to sell instruments, radio broadcasting infrastructures, local and foreign musicians, and tens of thousands of troops with money to spend on diversions, all of which supported a dynamic market for Western entertainment during the war. The military administration supported live and mechanically reproduced music for troops in both military venues and commercial enterprises, thus reformulating entertainment economies and reframing the market for jazz. A secondary argument of this chapter is that the active process of embracing globalized popular music sometimes involves ignoring or remaining uncommitted to local concerns. Partially borrowing from Pat J. Gehrke's idea of "uncommitted localism,"[2] I suggest that we sometimes withdraw from local concerns in our quest for cosmopolitan encounters, which in this chapter includes Western entertainment in elite clubs, and I claim that during the Bengal famine of 1943–44, patrons of Firpo's Restaurant and Bar, arguably among the leading jazz establishments in Calcutta, gave meaning and context to entertainment vis-à-vis social ills associated with the famine. In this instance, an uneasy feeling of privilege constituted jazz cosmopolitanism, shaped by images of hunger and malnourishment seen around Firpo's Restaurant and Bar and elsewhere in Calcutta. This brief section of the chapter aims to raise awareness of the need for more musicological studies on the role of popular music in reinforcing segregation and social exclusion in India and elsewhere.

Allied Military

The Allied military in India marked another point in the history of domination of the subcontinent that symbolically branded it as possessed territory. As an urban center on the coast, Calcutta was influenced by the economics of the war and was prone to external market and geopolitical forces. The military populated Calcutta and other cities in India with thousands of troops, especially between 1943 and 1945. The number of British soldiers in India was about 43,000 in 1939, but had risen to about 240,000 by 1945.[3] The number of US soldiers in India in 1943 was about 120,000,[4] and around 250,000 served over the course of the war.[5] As a primary zone of communication for the CBI theater of operations, military personnel were stationed in Delhi, Calcutta, Lucknow, Karachi, and Bombay, as well as in many smaller cities and towns such as Agra, Asansol, Dibrugarh, Dinajpur, Gaya, Guskhara, Jhansi, Mohanbari, Nimta, and Ramgarh.[6] As early as 1942, the US military established command headquarters and temporary military bases and aerodromes throughout North India to facilitate and defend supply routes over Burma and China. During this year, India began to play an important role in the defense strategy of the Allied powers.[7] The Eastern Air Command, established in 1943, was the largest operational command in World War II that controlled both British and US air units and their support structures. Headquartered in Calcutta, part of this organization moved inland to escape Japanese bombing campaigns. The

Eastern Air Command established an intra-India transport system, which spread US military troops and workforces throughout India.[8] An increasingly important military necessity, this command brought extensive military resources to India, including troops, aircraft, and the resources necessary to build roads and landing strips. World War II was a period of unimaginable challenges for troops. The war was tough and deadly, but entertainment continued. The Japanese military bombed Calcutta and Allied pilots engaged in dangerous missions, but many military personnel stationed in North India experienced periods with no direct enemy engagement.

American military personnel in India were from widely divergent social classes and places—rural and urban, rich and poor, educated and uneducated. Troops in Calcutta lived in close proximity to each other, and many soldiers were eager to hear jazz simply because India facilitated their first direct experience with live performances. Calcutta became a place of opportunity for musicians and audiences, and the war was important to the entertainment and social life of the city, feeding it with amateur, semiprofessional, and professional talent, in addition to thousands of consumers. Calcutta was on the receiving end of one of the most penetrating military trajectories in a global war in South Asia, and its population witnessed powerful new transnational networks of people, cultures, and information. Most jazz musicians in Calcutta embraced these new circumstances and calibrated their musicianship and the music business to this military presence.

Mechanically Reproduced Entertainment

Back in Great Britain, the US military leadership established the American Forces Network (AFN) in 1943 to increase the quantity of American jazz broadcast to US troops stationed in the country.[9] At least 279,171 American troops were in the United Kingdom in May 1943 and more than 1.67 million by May 1944.[10] Though the BBC began to broadcast more music by American musicians and orchestras as troops arrived in the country,[11] its administrators maintained strict guidelines on the permissible amount of non-British programming. The AFN in England was a response to these programming restrictions, and the positive reaction to the AFN among US troops in the United Kingdom led the US military in Calcutta to launch the radio station VU2ZU, which regularly broadcast the jazz of both foreign and domestic groups, live and recorded, to Allied military personnel.[12]

British authorities in India strictly controlled radio broadcasting during the war, largely to supervise its potential to support the Indian independence movement. Colonial government bureaucrats and broadcast administrators centralized and consolidated radio administrative entities and maintained almost complete control over the scope and character of programming, drawing from a range of ideological practices and resources to design and implement a national broadcast policy,[13] both before and during the war. VU2ZU operated beyond much of this regulatory climate. I found no evidence that the station rigorously followed colonial government broadcasting guidelines for programming content, though to the best of my knowledge the station did not overtly challenge these standards.

VU2ZU in Calcutta maintained two small, well-equipped studios with soundproofed walls, heavily carpeted floors, and the latest broadcasting technologies. Programming consisted of both transcribed programs from the United States and live shows that showcased amateur skits and performances by local troops. The station opened its first few broadcast evenings with the announcement, "This is station VU2ZU opening tonight's program with a session of *GI-Jive*," which reinforced its emphasis on jazz programming for military personnel.[14] *GI-Jive* was a fifteen-minute program produced in the United States and presented by Martha Wilkerson, often referred to as GI Jill,[15] and was broadcast on AFN stations across the globe. VU2ZU also broadcast transcribed programs featuring American entertainers such as Red Skelton, Jack Benny, Bob Hope, Burns and Allen, and many others.[16] Radio was an important source of entertainment, and shows featuring personnel stationed in India were especially popular. Recordings of the station's original program, *Yanks in the Orient*, were shipped to the United States weekly for nationwide release on the Blue Network.[17] The Blue Network was the direct predecessor to the American Broadcasting Companies (ABC),[18] which reached listeners across the country. An anonymous 1944 article in the US Armed Forces newspaper, the *Command Post*, states with pride that "although the CBI Theater is the most remote of America's war zones, it is the only one represented in the US by a weekly radio program. This show, 'Yanks in the Orient,' is produced by an Army transcription unit known as the CBI Radio Team and is flown regularly to Uncle Sugar [Uncle Sam] in the form of recordings for weekly nationwide release over the Blue Network."[19] Programs in the field were recorded with new wire-recorders,[20] and *Yanks in the Orient* often focused on the sounds of troops going about their daily work, including wire recordings of air and ground combat.[21] Other shows on VU2ZU featured novelty performers, military and amateur dance bands, and interviews with troops stationed in India.[22] Perhaps one of the most popular radio orchestras to perform on VU2ZU was the Army Special Services twelve-piece traveling dance band called the Jive Bombers, stationed at an undisclosed airbase in North India.[23] They regularly broadcast hot jazz performances for a few months in 1945.[24] Another group, the Top Hat Trio, performed novelty show tunes on bases throughout North India and also frequently performed live on VU2ZU. In addition to VU2ZU, All India Radio (AIR) stations occasionally broadcast recorded programs from the United States between 1943 and 1945, which were advertised in the *CBI Roundup*, the military newspaper.[25]

The military used the power of radio to spread propaganda and to create a sense of military presence throughout India. American voices on the airwaves gave the impression of territorial control and connectedness for listeners across thousands of miles. In addition, enemy propaganda broadcasts were a problem for the US military in India, especially on Radio Tokyo, a propaganda station in Japan. A US government survey of US military personnel in the CBI theater found that 24–32 percent of the troops listened to Radio Tokyo "a little" or "a lot." The US military in some instances sanctioned listening to these broadcasts, assuming that unconvincing propaganda might provide comic relief for soldiers. Military authorities contemplated jamming enemy broadcasts, but instead decided to compete for listeners' attention by improving programming for troops.[26] Ted Sherdeman helped to build radio stations for the Armed Forces Radio Network and later explained in 1946 that the motivation for creating the Armed Forces Radio Service during the war was that "if a man could listen to a program by Dinah Shore he would much prefer that to hearing Orphan Ann, your friendly enemy."[27] Dinah Shore was an American singer and actress, and Orphan Ann was the broadcast name of Iva Toguri D'Aauino, a host for Radio Tokyo.

The US military in India trained at least one female radio announcer, Virginia C. Claudon Allen, to counter Radio Tokyo. She was sometimes referred to as the GI Jill of India. Allen later described her work on VU2ZX in Karachi and VU2ZW in Agra, and stated that she was on air for as long as fifty-five minutes each afternoon.[28] Her music and messages were upbeat and meant to maintain troop morale. She worked in this capacity for three months and boasted that her programs were well received throughout South Asia, including in Calcutta: "I learned the intricacies of becoming a G.I. Jill in answer to the Tokyo Rose. My radio messages were always upbeat; and the music was wonderful. Being 'on air' 55 minutes nightly was part of my weekly duty. We had great respect from the service men who seemed to appreciate everything we tried to do for them."[29] Tokyo Rose was the name Allied troops gave to female Radio Tokyo announcers. Allen catered her programming to US military audiences in India and found willing listeners.[30]

In addition to radio broadcasts, recorded discs spread American entertainment to troops in India. V-Discs of jazz were shipped to South Asia and broadcast on VU2ZU and other stations. The US Special Services distributed V-Discs across the globe, and recordings featured a broad repertoire, including music of some of the most popular dance bands at the time. Pressed on large durable plastic discs, V-Discs were shipped in waterproof boxes, each containing between fifteen and thirty records.[31] Recordings were royalty-free, intended for military use, and not for commercial profit. Between 1943 and the summer of 1945, millions of copies of records were manufactured and distributed around the world, with many reaching India for broadcast. In general, popular music dominated V-Discs, and included variety shows produced by the armed forces, movie soundtracks, commentary to increase troop morale, and electronic transcriptions of US radio shows.[32] Among the top-shelf entertainers from the United States who participated in the V-Disc program were Bing Crosby, Frank Sinatra, Glenn Miller, Benny Goodman, Harry James, Tommy Dorsey, and many others.[33]

Recorded music from Hollywood films was in high demand. With V-Discs unobtainable in local commercial markets because of copyright restrictions, and the availability of imported gramophone discs sharply decreasing because of the war,[34] local performers recorded Hollywood film songs to coincide with a film's debut in Calcutta. Jazz orchestras in the city, both foreign and homegrown, recorded hundreds of these tunes in Calcutta's recording studios and may have been prized as much as the original imported discs. Many local orchestras achieved recognition and notoriety through these record sales, which promoted the perception that respectable jazz groups were working in Calcutta and elsewhere.

For the first time since arriving in India, African American musicians performed for large numbers of their fellow Americans, and they (and others) learned the most marketable material for troops and regularly recorded music from Hollywood films.[35] Teddy Weatherford was especially popular in Calcutta during the war, and after moving there in 1941 he worked with Columbia and HMV. Most of his recordings were from recent Hollywood productions, and, between 1942 and 1944, Roy Butler often recorded with him. The Grand Hotel, one of the top venues for jazz in the city at the time, hired him in 1941. Weatherford played nightly while in residence at the hotel, and he performed as a guest pianist in military venues, including at the British-run Garrison Theatre. Weatherford died of cholera in 1945 while at the hotel. In Weatherford's obituary on May 26, 1945, in the *Chicago Defender*, Deton J. Brooks wrote:

> Among the first victims of the cholera scourge now sweeping this overcrowded city was the "Count Basie" of the Far East, Teddy Weatherford, American Negro pianist and band leader whose reputation extended throughout the entire orient. . . . Since the outbreak of the Pacific war, resulting in thousands of American troops being stationed [in Calcutta], Weatherford had become a byword among GIs. Nightly both white and colored soldiers accompanied by the Anglo-Indian version of the bobby socks girls crowded the dance floor at the Wintergardens [at the Grand Hotel], for Teddy's band produced the best jitterbug music out there.[36]

Weatherford lived in India during the war with his Anglo-Indian wife Pansy Hill, and found that his 1920s Chicago style was in demand among the troops stationed in the city. Jim Holloway wrote in 1946 in *Down Beat* magazine that "he was playing in 1945 much as he did in 1925," and that his piano playing technique was "of the old school, lacking in the inventiveness and intricacies of present day Wilsons and Tatums, a trifle corny perhaps to modern ears, yet solid. He could play real blues."[37] His "old-school" style was the very quality that increased his popularity. He was always in demand as an experienced practitioner, and troops appreciated his role as a 1920s innovator. Weatherford is still considered a historical figure of talent among present-day jazz connoisseurs in India.

Recording songs from Hollywood moving pictures to coincide with a film's release was an effective marketing strategy to increase disc sales. Weatherford's first recordings in Calcutta in September 1941 were medleys produced with Columbia under the name "Teddy Weatherford at the Piano" and included the pieces "Boa Noite" and "I Yi Yi Yi Yi" from the film *That Night in Rio* (1941) with Carmen Miranda, "Moon over Burma" from the film of the same name (1940) with Dorothy Lamour, and "Minnie from Trinidad" from the film *Ziegfeld Girl* (1941) with Judy Garland and James Stewart.[38] In November 1941, Weatherford recorded four tracks under the name "Paquita and Zarate with Teddy Weatherford and his Boys," including "South American Way" from the film *Down Argentine Way* (1940) with Carmen Miranda.[39] These recordings were release around the same time the film was screened in Calcutta. Over the next months, Weatherford recorded several rumbas with this group, including two tracks, "Tropical Magic" and "A Weekend in Havana," from Carmen Miranda's film *A Weekend in Havana* (1941).[40] The market for these local recordings was significant. Advertising space in newspapers reveals that local groups were in demand possibly as much as major names from the United States or Europe were, and music from Hollywood films constituted a large number of advertised titles. Hollywood films were easily available to troops. Around nine moving picture houses screened European and American films during the war, and most featured recent releases.[41] According to the *Calcutta Key*, an official US military pamphlet given to US troops stationed in Calcutta, "The movies you see at the European theaters will be mostly American-made films, surprisingly recent, unless you have just arrived from the States."[42]

Weatherford's recordings with Columbia Records and HMV were advertised in English-language newspapers alongside advertisements of foreign celebrities such as Woody Herman, Vera Lynn, Bing Crosby, and Carmen Miranda, and together were printed in elaborate, full-page layouts. For example, on January 7, 1942, the Calcutta *Statesman* carried an ad that lists Teddy Weatherford and His Band recording two songs from the contemporary film *Great American Broadcast* (1941) starring Alice Faye (fig. 3.1). The same advertisement listed recordings of Woody Herman and His Orchestra and Carmen Miranda.[43] Weatherford's ad placement reinforces the idea that performers working in Calcutta were highly regarded and possibly as marketable as big names from the United States. Lack of imported gramophone discs meant that many jazz consumers purchased Weatherford's recordings instead of the originals from the United States, which spread the word about his work in India among those who might not otherwise be interested in local figures.

Jazz orchestras played these songs live. In 1941, for example, the duo Paquita and Zarate performed music from *Down Argentine Way* with Teddy Weatherford at the Grand Hotel in Calcutta. As mentioned above, the film was repeatedly screened at the Regal Cinema at the same time, and Paquita, Zarate, and Teddy Weatherford released tracks from the film on Columbia in November of that year. In this instance, films, gramophones, and live performances represented a tripartite marketing approach to popularizing music and performers. The Grand Hotel was particularly adept at featuring content inspired by Hollywood films, often with Weatherford at the piano, and performances featured female cabaret dancers and choreography inspired by Hollywood dance sequences.

OF HIT TUNES FROM THE FILMS

"KISS THE BOYS GOODBYE"

"THE GREAT AMERICAN BROADCAST"

"DOWN ARGENTINE WAY"

"THE RELUCTANT DRAGON"

"MOON OVER MIAMI"

MARY MARTIN
Kiss the Boys Goodbye (from film "Kiss the Boys Goodbye") | DB 30058
Do it again

RAY NOBLE & HIS ORCHESTRA
Kiss the Boys Goodbye (from film "Kiss the Boys Goodbye") | 36256
Is that good (from film "Moon Over Miami")

MERRY MACS
Kiss the Boys Goodbye (from film "Kiss the Boys Goodbye") | FB 40095
Honk Honk

TEDDY WEATHERFORD & HIS BAND
I've got a bone to pick with you
I take to you (both from film "Great American Broadcast") | FB 40070

JOHNNY LONG & HIS ORCHESTRA
Where you are (from film "Great American Broadcast")

WOODY HERMAN & HIS ORCHESTRA | DB 30059
Loveliness & Love (from film "Moon Over Miami")

RICHARD HIMBER & HIS ORCHESTRA
The Reluctant Dragon (from film "The Reluctant Dragon") | FB 40006
For want of a star

CARMEN MIRANDA
South American Way (from film "Down Argentine Way") | O 3178 Brunswick
Touras em Madrid

Distributors for Western India :

RHYTHM HOUSE,
Fort, BOMBAY. 'Phone 26328.

COLUMBIA GRAMOPHONE CO., LTD.—CALCUTTA.

Authorised Dealers :

James & Co., Fort.
International Trading Corp., Lamington Road.
Maison Musique, Colaba.
Metro Music, Kalbadevi.

James Mfg. Co., Kalbadevi.
Music Nest, Bandra.
Reid & Co., Secunderabad.
Empire Music House, Poona.

Figure 3.1. Gramophone disc advertisement from the *Statesman*, January 7, 1942. Image reproduced by permission from ProQuest LLC.

It is important to note that Goan and Indian communities broadened the audience for jazz during the war in Calcutta and elsewhere, and skilled jazz musicians from a diversity of backgrounds found a positive reception. These musicians included Burmese musicians Reuben Solomon and Cedric West, as well as notables Rudy Cotton, Tony Gonsalves, Pat Blake, Frank Fernand, and George Banks, all of whom performed regularly through-out India.[44] Reuben Solomon was among the most recognized performers to work at the Grand Hotel in Calcutta. His group, Reuben Solomon and His Jive Boys, recorded twenty-six tracks between 1942 and 1944. Many of Weatherford's band members joined Solomon's group when Weatherford died.[45] These and other musicians defined the direction of jazz and influenced generations of jazz musicians. An anonymous article in a March 1982 special feature of *Debonair* (India) suggests that "these years, some-time before the war upto [*sic*] the late forties, were perhaps the most creative years. . . . Indian musicians under the tutelage of the black jazzmen who played there, were slowly finding their styles."[46] Claiming that Indian musicians worked "under the tutelage" of African American musicians is probably inaccurate, as these and other musicians were respectable per-formers in their own right.

Famine and Live Music

It is instructive to briefly pause and contextualize jazz within the Bengal famine, which was at its peak in 1943 and 1944. I feel compelled to men-tion the famine because it was quite literally at the doorstep of American troops patronizing live-music venues, as we will see later. An astonishingly large number of memoirs reference dead or dying beggars at the entrance to Firpo's Restaurant and Bar, a key Calcutta venue for Western entertain-ment. This section also suggests that listening to jazz in Calcutta was in some respects a provincial act. I use the term *provincial* here not in the judgmental sense, which might assume narrow-mindedness or lack of sophistication. Rather, I view provincialism in this section as a musical ori-entation focused on jazz with little or no attention to music beyond mili-tary life.[47] I found no evidence, for example, that troops attended Indian music performances outside of the circuit of military-sanctioned clubs, at least not to any large degree.[48] Restricting troop movement to certain locations in Calcutta also contributed to this provinciality. American nurse LaVonne Telshaw Camp in her memoir about life as a military nurse in

India during the war explains that in Calcutta, troops "always engaged in things that were American as we consciously separated ourselves from things that were foreign." She regularly attended dances at officers' clubs and other locations such as hospitals, and observed that "evenings spent in the clubs were fun because we usually met people who had crossed our paths at other times and in other places."[49] The US military, by its very policies and procedures, largely sought to limit troop interaction with others. In discussing troop movement in Calcutta during the war, Yasmin Kahn asserts that "many parts of cities such as Calcutta . . . were declared off-limits to soldiers[,] and military police patrolled these areas to ensure compliance,"[50] in large part to prevent undesirable activities, including prostitution. Troops lived, worked, and engaged in entertainment within defined boundaries clearly demarcated by the military.

Limiting movement to military-sanctioned spaces in Calcutta isolated troops from the hardships of the Bengal famine. The reasons for the famine are numerous and contested, but it was one of the worst catastrophes in modern Indian history, in which three million or more died. Large numbers of starving people came to Calcutta from outlying areas in Bengal, where food was in impossibly short supply. The *Calcutta Key*, the US military pamphlet given to troops in Calcutta, references these starving migrants in a section titled "The Homeless Man":

> At some time or other while you are here you will witness the sight of a crowd of men, women, and children who seem to move together like a herd of sheep. They huddle together, or they rush across the street in a mob, or they gather in a group shouting and jabbering—they are new arrivals in the city. Driven here by the famine, by flood, drought, or other causes, they come from Bengal itself, from Bihar, Orissa, or Assam.[51]

Using the designation "herd of sheep" implies that certain fragments of the population lived in a different world altogether, unable to function in Calcutta society. Clive Branson, a British soldier in Calcutta at the time, gave some of the most telling accounts of the famine. In his diary in 1944, he comments on famine victims in the outlying areas of Calcutta: "In speaking of them, one is not speaking of the slum dwellers whose standard of living is 'higher.' Millions upon millions of poorest peasantry—ill-fed, uneducated, down-trodden—patiently accepting their hideous lives only because they cannot see anyway out. This immense abuse of all human decency by our British Imperialists."[52] In another instance he describes a train ride through Bengal toward Calcutta:

The endless view of plains, crops, and small stations, turned almost suddenly into one long trail of starving people. Men, women, children, babies, looked up into the passing carriage in their last hope for food. These people were not just hungry—this was *famine*. When we stopped, children swarmed round the carriage windows, repeating, hopelessly, "Bukshish, sahib [Money, sir]"—with the monotony of a damaged gramophone. Others sat on the ground, just waiting. I saw women—almost fleshless skeletons, their clothes grey with dust from wandering, with expressionless faces, not *walking*, but foot steadying foot, as though not knowing where they went.[53]

Branson attributes the causes of the famine to a lack of effective governance, among other reasons, and he believed that India was ruled with little regard for the poor and disadvantaged.[54]

Unfortunately, these striking images were in some respects part of the experience of live jazz in Calcutta. One would presume that pervasive poverty has had an important influence on group formation and popular music meaning in India. Some of the most interesting musicological studies on the effects of famine on music address the Irish famine (1845–52), which Gearóid Ó hAllmhuráin calls "a catalyst in Irish traditional music making."[55] Music became a more privatized affair after the famine in Ireland, and interpersonal interactions between genders during performance events became increasingly supervised,[56] partially changing compositional practice and musical meaning.[57] For troops in Calcutta, temporary displacement from the United States and reaffirmation of a sense of location within Calcutta's military boundaries probably informed musical meaning more than anything else. The war created a keen awareness of location and geography, and for many in the Allied military, music reinforced the distinctness of life in the armed forces. Troops were not threatened with starvation, which validated the integrity of American and British institutions in India, including their role in facilitating global entertainment, creating a sanctuary from hunger, and promoting group coordination and solidarity. Certainly, troops in Calcutta exhibited nuanced behavior in their consumption of all live music, not just jazz, but the motivation for listening to jazz included a belief in its cathartic nature (often associated with black primitivism), its American origins, and, more practically, its capacity to facilitate drink, dance, and other informal interpersonal interactions between like-minded individuals. As Alan Merriam teaches us, music making can be an opportunity to feel something meaningful and reinforce a sense of group identity among people acting together.[58] In the case of Calcutta, jazz (and other entertainment from the United States) was considered to be part of the social fabric of the military, and other music or economic situations outside of the war machine and its economic manifestations were less valid, and therefore less known. In short, troops may have felt that Indian music was someone else's entertainment and the famine was someone else's immorality, at least in part.

This is not to say that no one felt empathy. Clive Branson and others were certainly sympathetic. But the famine existed outside the security of military life and was perceived to be distant, perhaps similar to the awareness one might have of the famine if living in the United States or England. Yet it was everywhere in Calcutta, and in some respects reminded entertainment seekers of the capacity of military life to operate beyond localized hardships .[59] I want to emphasize that my intent here is not to criticize the response to the famine or to condemn the military's presence in India, but to suggest that the function of the total social system of the military justified putting significant resources into entertainment during a time of war and famine, and people followed suit.

As a response to the military buildup, entertainment entrepreneurs designed cabarets that invited patrons to identify with the collective American (or Western) experience, binding them to many entertainment components—music, dance, cuisine, decor, drink, dress—that together had purpose and, by one account, tempted patrons to guiltily "gorge" themselves with food even as people starved at their doorsteps.[60] One of the most popular for-profit establishments to feature jazz in Calcutta was Firpo's Restaurant and Bar, opened in 1918. This venue profited from food, alcohol sales, admission fees, and entertainment, and was prosperous in the private market. It began booking jazz performances soon after it opened. By World War II, it had a long history of featuring the most popular jazz orchestras in the city. Dozens and dozens of dance orchestras performed there through the years, including Ken Mac, Teddy Weatherford, Jimmy Leguime's Band, Frangopoulo and His Band, Francisco Cassanova and His Orchestra, Charles Campbell and His Orchestra, and many other local and traveling groups. According to Mark Addison, who was stationed in Calcutta with the US Army, Firpo's was a key venue in which to hear jazz pianist Teddy Weatherford.[61] The 1943 American Red Cross guidebook for Calcutta during the war claims that Firpo's organized a dance every night "for all troops and all ranks."[62] Donovan Webster states that US pilots who flew missions to China from Calcutta dined on its "dollar steaks and martinis and beer," and suggests that its music and food menu made patrons feel like "high-rollers."[63] Firpo's attracted a diverse audience. Dennis Kincaid, an official with the Indian Civil Service (ICS), boasts that by the late 1930s even senior British bureaucrats were patronizing Firpo's and they "succumbed to the lure of this continental looking place and entertained their friends to dinner there instead of in their own huge Georgian houses."[64] It had a consistently crowded dance floor during the war years,[65] and large sums of money flowed through its doors.[66] The management sometimes organized evening balls under a single theme, but most nights showcased jazz or variety music to supplement fine dining, drinking, and smoking.[67]

Firpo's embodied many of the entrepreneurial strategies that facilitated new consumption patterns during the war. It was a for-profit establishment started by an Italian restaurateur and confectioner and featured rare amenities such as ice cream sodas, steaks, and even the famous "Firpo's Balloon Cocktail," which was highlighted in the 1946 printing of the *Gentleman's Companion*, a publication distributed worldwide. Firpo's was open to any paying customer, inducing Captain Blackford, an army officer during the war, to joke that Firpo's exemplified the fact that a "middle-class gentleman in England, became upper-class once he set foot on Indian shores." He also asserted that it was a place where "anybody who was anybody, in this cosmopolitan metropolis where status mattered, met other class-conscious people."[68] It was considered an international establishment in terms of music, decor, and diversity of patron, but also an example of segregation in entertainment consumption.

During the famine, a number of contemporary accounts criticized Firpo's and other venues in Calcutta for remaining open while starving victims died.[69] George T. Heinemann, a US military officer stationed in Calcutta, lamented that at Firpo's Restaurant and Bar, "you could get a real, live ice cream soda, and I can still remember stepping over corpses to get into this place, laying on the doorstep, during the famine."[70] Heinemann hints that attending live jazz performances in Firpo's was a chance to temporarily disengage from difficult realities, and he pondered the morality of entertainment involving large flows of money for music, dance, and food. John Frederick Muehl with the American Field Service in Calcutta during the war also contextualizes Firpo's within the famine:

> I approached the entrance to Firpo's Restaurant, it was then that the famine first struck home to me. Lying in the doorway, two nude bodies were glistening in the sweat of an agony just past. They were spread-eagled there in the semicircle of light, one face upward, mouth and eyes open. I tried to avoid them as I mounted the steps, but a young captain behind me was

more considerate. Excusing himself from the girl he escorted, he rolled them out into the darkness of the street, continuing his conversation without interruption.

It was not just the anxiety of a hungry man that made tonight's dinner seem like a banquet to me; Firpo's has a reputation for the best food in Calcutta. There were soups and cocktails, salted nuts and fruit, rolls and relishes, savory, desserts, and an almost unlimited choice of entrees. For a moment I was revolted by the thoughts of what I had seen outside and I stared rather blankly at the food placed before me. But I succumbed very quickly to the sight and the smell and I must confess that in the end I gorged myself.[71]

Obviously affected by the sight of famine victims, Muehl nonetheless "gorged" himself, succumbing to Firpo's temptations.

Firpo's was exclusive, yet most troops had easy access. Patrons ate steaks, drank alcohol, enjoyed desserts, listened to Teddy Weatherford (and other prominent performers), and visually marked the space by their uniformed presence. This venue accepted the privileged and rejected or ignored others living in a different economy under appalling conditions. The *Calcutta Key* refers to people subject to the famine as the "homeless, helpless, [and] hopeless . . . [who] die in the epidemics, or . . . just disappear." These unfortunate descriptions reflect the capacity of visitors to the city to remain insulated from broader socioeconomic conditions and, perhaps more disconcertingly, to view a large segment of the population as an unknown people who eventually fade away. These conditions of poverty constructed loose, yet potent, contextualizations that reinforced the uniqueness of Firpo's, including, by Heinemann's account, the process of "stepping over corpses" to enter.[72] Furthermore, the interior of Firpo's was designed in a Louis Quinze style, a decorative movement associated with the eighteenth-century rule of Louis XV of France. Fantasy and exotic landscapes were featured prominently in Louis XV design motifs, including Orientalia, curious animals, and elaborate floral decorations. Modeling the restaurant in such a refined and antiquated manner, while at the same time booking jazz, was a marketing strategy designed to maintain a degree of sophistication so the music would have an expansive market base. The management of Firpo's knew how to balance diverse aesthetics in order to target a large breadth of consumers.[73] These powerful imageries imply that the contrast between jazz venues and the outside world was a distinction between privilege and disparity, cultural globalization and localized suffering.

Entertainment for the Military

Before beginning a discussion of the character of entertainment for the military, it is important to mention that the US military practiced segregation within its ranks. Large numbers of African American soldiers were stationed in the CBI theater of operations, and black troops often sat in segregated sections during entertainment events. An open letter from unnamed African American soldiers in India sent to the editors of several US newspapers describes discrimination and mistreatment:

> We are writing you enlisting your aid concerning segregation of Negro troops in India and we would like you to take an appeal to NAACP. First off on the ship . . . we weren't allowed to drink from the cool water fountains. Then the first thing we encountered in India is segregation. American, British, Indian, Chinese and Negro troops, all attend the same show and the Negroes are piled in a huddle in the rear.[74]

This complaint outlines the persistent practice of segregation in the military entertainment industry, and suggests tension between white and black troops. American entertainment in India was not available to everyone equally, even among US troops.

The *Calcutta Key* perhaps best documented the scale of the demand for entertainment created by the Allied military. This brochure included comprehensive information on the structure of the Indian government, the climate, health issues, the caste system, sightseeing, city transportation, some key phrases in Hindi, and it repeatedly emphasized that India was an ally of the United States. It lists Christian and Jewish religious services, offers advice on shopping and bargaining, and prominently lists two music stores, T. E. Bernard and Company Ltd. and C. C. Saha Ltd., as key places to buy instruments and gramophone recordings. It also lists four radio and radio repair shops: C. C. Saha, Chicago Telephone and Radio Company Ltd, Radio Supplies Stores Ltd., and N. B. Sen. The entertainment section of the pamphlet is the largest and most detailed. It boasts that "there are no finer places in this city to start, spend and finish the day than in the clubs." For enlisted men, the ARC Burra Club, ARC Cosmos Club, Continental Services Club, and the YMCA organized afternoon and evening dances. For officers, it suggests the Bengal Club, the Calcutta Club, the Calcutta Swimming Club, the Swiss Club, the British-American Club, the 300 Club, the Saturday Club, and the United Services Club. All venues included entertainment such as music, dance, tennis, billiards, cards, grills for cooking, polo, and badminton. The *Calcutta Key* emphasizes that the Winter Garden and Princes Room in the Grand Hotel offered, "real jive." It suggests Firpo's Restaurant and the Great Eastern Hotel (one of the most exclusive hotels in the city) for jazz.[75]

The US government made available live and recorded music for American troops worldwide. Just two months after the attack on Pearl Harbor, Eleanor Roosevelt published an open letter to the country in *Musical America*, exhorting Americans to continue music making for morale purposes.[76] Musicians aided the national war effort by performing for charity events and war bond functions, and participation in United Service Organizations (USO) events and tours became somewhat of a badge of honor for musicians.[77] The USO was a civilian agency, but its activities supported entertainment for the American military. Launched in February 1941, it sponsored productions on military posts and stations throughout the world, and by the end of the war, thousands of entertainment troupes had performed with the organization, sometimes without payment and under harsh conditions. Many USO performers stopped over in India before or after tours through China and Burma. Music conductor and arranger Andre Kostelanetz performed in India in December 1941. In a personal letter from 1945, he claimed that troops in India "were some of the most appreciative listeners. . . . The expression on the faces of the fliers, who this very day faced the maximum of dangers, is a study and inspiration. Rapt, smiling and highly attentive."[78] A primary purpose of USO productions in India was to improve troop morale, and the organization maintained an active presence in South Asia.

The US State Department in World War II considered music a powerful tool. Raymond Kendall, the music coordinator for the USO, wrote in 1943, "singing is primarily a weapon, a medium through which men march straighter, give better commands, fight harder, work longer, and move coordinately."[79] The military draft brought a wide variety of young men to the war from diverse educational and musical backgrounds. To identify the most appropriate styles of music to program, the Research Branch of the Army surveyed 4,296 white enlisted men and found that swing and jazz were the preferred style, followed by classical, with hillbilly-western music preferred the least.[80] It is no surprise that jazz and swing formed the cornerstone of musical entertainment for troops. Annegret Fauser maintains that music making "in the military . . . [was] shaped by a complex set of parameters such as contemporary notions of 'good music,' traditional beliefs about desirable activities for soldiers (e.g. group singing) prejudices about so-called highbrow music, . . . and the individual tastes and preferences of enlisted men. That jazz and swing formed the centerpiece of musical entertainment in the armed forces was never in doubt."[81] Fauser further suggests that "music was also perceived as a racial marker and troops viewed African American troops to be crucial to good jazz entertainment."[82] Jazz and African American musicians together informed ideas about good music for troops.

What was the character of entertainment for the military in Calcutta? Entertainment organizations such as the British ENSA and the USO supported all kinds of performers throughout India. The USO brought entertainment directly from the United States, which included Broadway entertainers, Hollywood stars, professional singers, and amateur groups.[83] Organizing USO shows was challenging. One of the most notable Hollywood figures to perform with the USO was Ann Sheridan, a well-known actress. As she wrote in a *Time* magazine editorial titled "Short Circuit" on October 23, 1944, her trip to India was cut short because of an unfortunate lack of services: "At better than a thousand miles a day, playing even two bad shows, eating C- and K-rations more often than hot groceries, much of it standing up, and then when it's little girls'-room time, go down to the men's toilet and wait till it's cleared so that the girl troupers may use it."[84] She considered her trip exciting yet difficult, and her criticisms reflect the immense complexity of bringing entertainment to India. USO productions included other big names from the United States. A production titled "Rhythm and Blues" premiered in Calcutta under the direction of Alberta Hunter, a noted American blues singer. According to one anonymous review, "Miss Hunter, who ranks with the most distinguished Negro artists of stage, screen and radio sings many of the old 'blues' songs which hit a nostalgic note wherever they are heard."[85] They were a radio hit and performed on the Allied radio station VU2ZU.

The British ENSA also organized nightly jazz performances, theater shows, and acts based on Broadway shows in Calcutta and across the subcontinent. They administered the Garrison Theatre in Calcutta, which housed the ENSA Orchestra and a theater repertory company composed of military personnel. It was open to all Allied troops and uniformed auxiliary services. English singer-songwriter Vera Lynn toured India with the ENSA and performed there in 1944, as did Teddy Weatherford and the US Army Swing Quartet. Celia Nicolls crooned with the ENSA Orchestra at the Garrison Theatre and claims that the level of musicianship was high:

In fact it was to be one of the happiest periods in my life. In Calcutta the department for entertainment for the servicemen was really quite good. We had various groups of musicians, including a string section which could be added on to the dance band I was with, and we would call it the ENSA Dance Orchestra. We did some radio work on All India Radio, and I was thrilled to go into the recording studios and hear the Indian musicians playing there too.[86]

Nicolls suggests that Calcutta boasted a wide variety of top-shelf entertainment, and the ENSA Dance Orchestra performed both live and on the radio. They traveled throughout India, reaching troops stationed in remote locales.

A special unit called the Entertainment Production Unit (EPU) supplemented the activities of the USO.[87] In 1944, they organized a traveling troupe in Calcutta made up of 120 men who performed in hospitals and other ad hoc performance spaces across CBI-controlled areas. They produced shows with titles such as *This Is It, Babes in Boyland,* and *Call Me Mister,* which were written by staff and borrowed content from existing Broadway productions. This troupe identified 159 circuit venues, most of which were outdoors, put on 1,349 shows for almost a million men, and produced 53 radio broadcasts.[88] They were always on tour, with one unit preparing a show while another finished a tour. Audience size varied from 25 to 4,000, and their first production, *Over and Back,* traveled 11,000 miles by truck, rail, and air between India and Burma.[89]

Virginia Claudon Allen performed in the musical "Call Me Mister" with the EPU. She describes that a primary appeal was its chorus of girls:

Singer, Tony Martin, oversaw the show briefly; and we were told it was playing in New York where it was a hit. So, temporarily acquiring a number of willing dancers, we kicked our legs in unison, sang the songs and accompanied by the local military band, were overwhelmingly received by the G.I.'s in Calcutta's large open air theater called "Monsoon Square Garden." This success was undoubtedly equally most attributable to our enthusiasm and the short skirted costumes on a bevy of pretty girls.[90]

EPU shows featured well-known entertainers, in this instance American singer-actor Tony Martin, and held auditions to support quality productions.

In addition to the EPU, USO, and ENSA, the military leadership in Calcutta organized jazz orchestras and theater productions. Among the most popular was the Royal Air Force (RAF) Ambassadors Dance Orchestra with the RAF Singers. They performed in Calcutta regularly until the end of the war. Another group, the Monswooners, composed of US military personnel, performed primarily at Hasting's Air Base in Calcutta. The base supported upward of 1,800 US troops and maintained its own club where the Monswooners performed contemporary jazz in the evenings, on weekends, and on special occasions for thousands of US and Allied soldiers.[91] The RAF Ambassadors Dance Orchestra and the Monswooners also performed in auditoriums, hospitals, social clubs, clubs in military bases, and hotel ballrooms.[92]

Local music stores became gathering places for foreign and domestic musicians to purchase imported instruments and find musicians for bands. Occasional "Wanted Ads" in the Calcutta *Statesman* listed a need for proficient musicians and instruments,[93] both of which were in demand and in short supply. A number of music shops sold instruments to US troops to satisfy demand. Francis Braganza, a Calcutta music shop owner and jazz musician during the war, arrived in Calcutta as a young adult in 1938 and opened his store with his family in 1939. I interviewed him in 2001, and he told me that Americans brought large numbers of instruments with them as they arrived in Calcutta: "I was the main store at the time, but there were many [music] companies. Americans imported [or brought with them] all their saxophones, violins, guitars, a lot of things imported. The American military came with their own instruments, lots of instruments, and bands and all that." But Braganza also suggested that Americans used to stop by his store to purchase instruments and other goods, and he consciously sought their business through networks of acquaintances: "The American military used to come in their jeep, and go here and there, all sorts of things, because [they were] friends, you know." He claimed that Teddy Weatherford was one of the most popular performers in Calcutta and he was proud that Weatherford's band included Indian musicians: "Teddy Weatherford was an American Negro Performer. He had a 12-piece band."[94] The arrival of war troops invigorated the local market for jazz commodities.

Amateur bands often featured lighthearted performances that audiences embraced without serious criticism or rejection. The 136th Fighter Squadron (also known as "The Woodpeckers") maintained a dance band while in Calcutta in 1942 that occasionally played at the 300 Club. Gordon Conway, a member of the squadron, reminisces that "whilst not on readiness Calcutta's bright lights offered many temptations in the form of bars and nightclubs. . . . Fun was had at The 300 Club where in the evenings the misguided Jazz band allowed The Woodpecker Jazz fiends to play during their break!"[95] Conway suggests that they were allowed to perform between sets of more serious groups. The availability of instruments, printed music, and scores of consumers supported the dissemination of all kinds of jazz and facilitated performance opportunities for both novice and experienced musicians.

The relationship between US and British military personnel was sometimes tense.[96] Americans occasionally trivialized British rule and sarcastically referred to the acronym of the South East Asia Command (SEAC) in 1944 as "Save England's Asian Colonies."[97] According to Bayly and Harper, tensions between British and Americans were "severe," and the British "resented the intrusion of the Americans into their patch, especially when they had better railway carriages, better beer, better films, more and prettier women."[98] Altercations between British and American soldiers changed perceptions of British authority and influence. As William Fisher wrote in *Life* magazine in 1943, "One thing that distinguishes the Yank in India is the amount of money he has to spend. He gets at least 200 rupees a month, which would be a veritable fortune to a British Tommy. This leads to some hard feeling, especially where girls are involved."[99] African American pianist Teddy Weatherford often witnessed fights between US troops and British soldiers at the Grand Hotel in Calcutta, where he performed during the last years of the war. According to Reuben Solomon, a saxophonist who performed with Weatherford at the time:

> Americans had more money to spend on the girls, so all the girls would be with the American soldiers and none with the British tommies. As soon as a set of Americans would come in the British would watch them, then suddenly, for no apparent reason, there would be a free-for-all, bottles, chairs, the lot. We would be ducking and Teddy would stand and shout, "Okay boys, fighting music!" And we would go into something very two-beat— tarah, tarah, crash, bang—as long as we could. Suddenly you would hear the MP's whistles and everyone would converge on the dance floor. A few bodies would be taken out.[100]

The sight of foreigners challenging British authority affected those who witnessed or heard about these conflicts, which I will discuss in more detail in the next chapter.[101]

Americans sometimes caused other tensions. The September 1944 issue of the *Anglo-Indian Review* accused US military personnel of creating a menace because "a large number of illegitimate children have been born to Anglo-Indian girls in Delhi . . . [and] the putative paternity of these children is almost invariably American."[102] Much of this nuisance was attributed to Anglo-Indians attending dances with American men. An article in the December 1944 issue complains that "scores of A.I. [Anglo-Indian] girls are continuing to make fools of themselves by parading about cafes and dance halls having a good fling with these transatlantic Buddies who cannot marry them, and do not purport [to]. Leave the Yanks severely alone, British boys are better and A.I. boys best of all as husbands and fathers."[103] Yasmin Khan has found that problems with rape, prostitution, and other social ills coincided with the arrival of American troops, and that clubs often exacerbated these problems.[104] The US Army eventually banned the marriage of US military personnel to British subjects in 1944.[105] Music store owner Braganza asserted that Americans brought both good times and transgressions: "Good days, those days, but [there was] gambling, drinking, boozing."[106]

Conclusion

The military strategically deployed entertainment as a weapon to serve the interests of its leadership and to promote military identity in the city at large. Policymakers and support organizations such as the USO in the United States and the ENSA in England were stakeholders in this process and programmed music around the world to encourage a sense of global allegiance to the war effort and to serve ordinary troops who sought permitted entertainment. American popular music did not always follow strict economic aims, as seen in the impressive network of social clubs for the military, yet at least partially depended on commercial enterprises. Gramophones, radio broadcasting, Hollywood films, and jazz venues informed interest in the newest music and facilitated opportunities for profit. The entertainment economy was vast enough to support tens of thousands of Allied military personnel in Calcutta during these few short years, and operated between local entertainment commerce and the interests and dictates of the Allied military. Both were dependent on existing entertainment infrastructures in Calcutta.[107]

The next chapter focuses on Lucknow, a small city in the interior of North India. As a landlocked urban center, the growth of jazz took on a different character. The British in Lucknow dominated most of the jazz scene in the 1920s and 1930s, but by the late 1930s Anglo-Indian and Goan residents of the city became avid enthusiasts and performers. As I have discussed above, jazz is not fixed or bounded, and it influences people differently through a dynamic process that involves negotiating resource availability, adequate density of consumers to facilitate interpersonal inter- action, and consistent flows of entertainment money. The next chapter addresses these issues in the context of Lucknow.

Chapter Four

The Case of Lucknow

This chapter presents a case study of Lucknow, an interior capital city in the northern state of Uttar Pradesh. Lucknow is smaller than Bombay, Calcutta, and New Delhi, yet by the mid-1930s new entertainment enterprises facilitated a market for jazz in Hazratganj, a commercial area known for the exchange of European and British goods and services. By World War II, cafe and cinema hall proprietors were building dance floors and local entrepreneurs had established new performance venues on a thoroughfare in Hazratganj now called Mahatma Gandhi Marg. These venues included the Ambassador Club (previously a skating rink), the Mayfair Ballroom, the Soldier's Club (built for Allied troops), the Silver Slipper, the Blue Haven, and many others. This chapter explores how a small city in interior India enjoyed a lively jazz scene by the time of World War II. It emphasizes personal history narratives that I collected from now elderly individuals in Lucknow, and focuses on Mahatma Gandhi Marg and its smaller adjacent streets in the 1930s and 1940s. I cite oral histories collected from Anglo-Indian and Goan dance organizers, venue proprietors, community leaders, and musicians. Sometimes I include narratives from avid enthusiasts. The Anglo-Indian and Goan communities represented a large slice of the market for jazz in Lucknow beginning in the mid-1930s, and they regularly patronized the Mayfair Ballroom, Ambassador Club, and other venues.

Indian Civil Service (ICS) week in Lucknow in the early and mid-1930s supported the early proliferation of jazz. This weeklong festival featured a wide variety of entertainment and sports, and the British were probably the largest community in attendance. The first ongoing performances of jazz were organized during this week in a small number of venues catering to ICS week participants, including Valero's, the Mahomed Bagh Club, and the Racecourse bandstand.[1] Tourism associated with ICS week stimulated commerce in Hazratganj, and the flow of cash into the pockets of music venue proprietors and musicians during the festival was crucial to the spread of jazz in Lucknow throughout the course of the year. I finish the chapter by outlining the role of American troops in broadening the scope of jazz performances in Hazratganj during the last two years of the war.

Lucknow did not have a jazz entertainment economy at the level of Calcutta, Bombay, or Delhi, but music commodities, venue space, and sound technologies were pervasive enough to support residents who wanted to follow jazz trends in larger urban centers. I refer to Lucknow jazz guitarist James "Jumbo" Perry a number of times in this chapter. Perry was not from a wealthy family, and he told me once that he could not afford to buy a radio as a child and young man in the 1930s and 1940s, so he and others made their own radios and, as he put it, "listened to what [they] wanted."[2] He listened to jazz and paid particular attention to improvisation, learning from broadcasts out of Calcutta, Delhi, Bombay, and elsewhere, and he was especially enthusiastic about live broadcasts of Teddy Weatherford from the Grand Hotel in Calcutta and Ken Mac in Delhi. The capacity of Lucknow musicians to learn jazz was no more clearly seen than in Perry's musical development. He learned jazz on his own, watching foreign films—often by sneaking into local cinema halls—and listening to handmade radios and secondhand gramophones for guidance. Ultimately he learned just like anyone else—by practicing, listening, watching, and performing. Jazz enthusiasts in Lucknow experienced unequal distribution of opportunities, media access, and technologies, yet jazz proliferated. This chapter also reinforces the important role of economics and the commercialization of entertainment commodities in the development of jazz, especially patterns of dissemination via Hollywood films, gramophones, and radio broadcasting.

Jazz enthusiasts in Lucknow imagined that through music they were participating in an historical moment that crossed national and regional boundaries. Since Lucknow was far from the global commodity exchanges seen in larger port cities, its presence was not considered unidirectional from the United States. In fact, Perry said that musicians sought to mirror the jazz scenes of Calcutta and Bombay more than those in the United States, Britain, or Europe.[3] Thus, jazz in this instance should not be considered a metaphor for globalization or America's influence in the world, and I embrace E. Taylor Atkins's appeal to researchers to avoid considering jazz exclusively American.[4] Jazz took on unique affiliations in Lucknow based on resource availability, commercial infrastructures, religion (most audiences were Christian), ethnicity, race, and class—and it inspired meaning and purpose among motivated youth, including many who rarely traveled outside of Lucknow.

Across the globe, narratives about jazz have often centered on historically defined experiences embodied in the lives and history of African Americans,[5] which has contributed to the meaning and appeal of jazz. Scott DeVeaux makes clear that jazz's association with black Americans has often been central to discourse about its proliferation, which Randall Sandke has more recently called the "active ingredients" principle[6]—that is, jazz's roots and its association with black Americans often contributes to its aesthetic appreciation. In this light, Sandke cautions us to avoid viewing nonblack musicians as appropriators, unable to fully master jazz's component parts or appreciate it with full passion. Throughout this book, I have made it clear that audiences were often attentive to the black origins of the music, and many musicians I interviewed in Lucknow were similarly attentive. But in this chapter, I focus on a narrative about jazz that gives voice to Anglo-Indians and Goans who found significance and inspiration in its local proliferation, both individually and collectively.

Calcutta and Bombay were port cities with efficient transportation and commercial links to Europe and the Commonwealth. By contrast, Uttar Pradesh was a comparatively poor state, and Lucknow is landlocked and a considerable distance from both Calcutta and Bombay. Yet a sizable demand for Western music and commodities compelled entrepreneurs to develop Hazratganj into an entertainment center for jazz. Furthermore, the Lucknow Racecourse in the cantonment commanded a reputation throughout India as a lively venue for horse racing, tea parties, and bandstand performances. The racecourse drew large numbers of vacationers to Lucknow, especially during ICS week, and its races attracted thousands of participants and featured regular entertainment productions. Hazratganj, the racecourse, and other venues in the cantonment together supported an expansive consumer market for jazz.

Dances in the 1920s

Christian Goans probably started the first jazz orchestras in Lucknow. These instrumentalists were typically trained in Western music in private schools in Goa, where music instruction was an important part of the curriculum of many Catholic educational institutions. Goa was economically sluggish in the years before World War II, which compelled musicians from

Goa to travel to Lucknow and find work. Peter Antunis was one of the earliest drummers to live and work in Lucknow in the 1920s. He left Portuguese Goa for Uttar Pradesh at the age of ten, and when he arrived in Lucknow the Coelho brothers, two siblings also originally from Goa, taught him to play the drums. The Coelho brothers owned a music shop and sold sheet music, instruments, and gramophone discs obtained through commercial distribution networks originating in Calcutta. They also offered private music instruction.[7] They started the Coelho Brothers Orchestra in the 1920s and over the years performed at the railway institute (in the railway colony), the Mahomed Bagh Club (in the cantonment), the Gymkhana, and the United Services Club. These venues were members-only social clubs and featured areas for orchestras and dancing. The railway institute catered to railway employees, especially Anglo-Indians, and the other venues served the British and officers in the military. The Coelho brother's music shop was in Hazratganj in an area referred to as Maqbara adjacent to the tomb of Amjad Ali Shah, a nineteenth-century king of the Awadh region. Many Christians lived in this residential area and from the 1920s it was a center for forming and hiring out bands in Lucknow. Photos indicate that Antunis's drum kits mirrored those found in the United States, complete with a large bass drum struck with a pedal, temple blocks, a tambourine, and mounted cymbals (fig. 4.1). He initially obtained regular gigs with the Coelho Brothers Orchestra, but he eventually performed on his own throughout Uttar Pradesh. Peter Antunis and a handful of other musicians were able to support families through their work as musicians. His daughter Barbara, who was a child at the time, told me in 2001 that her father was the sole breadwinner of the family and that she and her siblings were "comfortably off" and "well-educated" in private schools.[8]

The Coelho brothers' music store was one of the earliest businesses in Lucknow to establish distribution links to the more vibrant music economy of Calcutta. (The other store was Bevan and Company.) At first the Coelho brothers managed the Britannia Restaurant in Hazratganj to supplement their income, but later they supported themselves through profits from their music store and paid performances.[9] Personal history narratives I collected in Lucknow suggest that the Coelho Brothers Orchestra may have been the first local group to perform jazz in Lucknow, though they probably emphasized military or ballroom repertoire more than jazz. These brothers created the support system and economic mechanisms necessary to catch the interest of others who wanted to learn jazz, including Lucknow residents and musicians arriving in the city.

Figure 4.1. Savoyans Orchestra from Lucknow, 1930s. Photographer unknown. Personal collection of Barbara Antunis.

Indian Civil Service Week in the 1930s

As noted earlier, an important reason for the growth of jazz in Lucknow was Indian Civil Service week, a weeklong festival organized in January or February each year. Some of the first documented jazz performances in Lucknow were associated with this week, and festivalgoers came from all of North India. Tourists attending the festival helped build Hazratganj's reputation as a European shopping and entertainment center. Writing about this event during the 1930s, A.I. Bowman stated, "Everything carried an aura of the great days of the Raj, when the stamp of Victorian upper-call society was set on the British in India."[10] The festival included horse racing, ballroom dances, cocktail dances, formal dinners, polo, air shows, dance competitions, dog shows, tea parties, sports, air circuses, theater shows, and film screenings. Y. D. Gundevia, an Indian ICS officer, attended his first ICS week in 1932 and remembers that "ICS Week was a veritable gala event year after year" and that participants "really beat it up." He also suggests that most entertainment functions during ICS week were segregated. Indian festivalgoers organized separate evening engagements during which Gundevia claims that the "song and dance were different . . . [and that] men appeared in formal evening dress and women in their gorgeous saris and jewels." The Governor's Ball was an exception. This event showcased high society and was the crowning event of the week open to all festivalgoers. According to Gundevia:

> The piece de resistance [*sic*] was the ball at Government House. Tail coats and white coats, and women attired in their best dresses and gorgeous saris and jewelry. Here's where everybody met everybody and everybody danced with everybody, and for once Rudyard Kipling was forgotten. At midnight . . . a voice would propose the toast: "The King!" Most of the guests would be on their second round of champagne within moments after the toast, and the gaiety would be resumed, gathering momentum with every glass of champagne, as people toasted one another, and laughed and danced till the early hours of the morning.[11]

An anonymous article in the *Pioneer* described Hazratganj during this week as "almost like Camberley High Street, full of cars and people hurrying in and out of shops buying things they can't find in their Home Towns."[12] Many activities centered on the Lucknow Racecourse, which boasted informal dances on race days.[13] The highly regarded band of the 10th Royal Hussars performed much of the military music there, as did the King's Own Scottish Band and the Band of the 1st Battalion the Cameronians.

The character of ICS week changed between 1934 and 1935. In 1934 the events began on Monday, January 28. A review in the English-language newspaper the *Pioneer* on February 2, 1934, lamented that the Lucknow Racecourse could not hold its daily activities because of rain, so the dog show was the primary attraction.[14] The evening was more jovial, and many participants patronized Valerio's, a for-profit venue in Hazratganj. On Tuesday, January 29, the King's Own Scottish Band added a festive note to the cold and rainy Lucknow racecourse. Many large dinner parties followed and the day ended with the 10th Hussars Band playing to a large crowd of dancers until 3 a.m. at the Hog-Hunter's Ball in the Mahomed Bagh Club. The Mahomed Bagh Club was in the cantonment and catered to military officers or other high-level administrators, but it opened its doors to all festivalgoers during ICS week. The ball was a success, and the *Pioneer* boasted that the "dances were up to time and did not drag and everybody went away wishing for more."[15] On Wednesday, some chose to attend a theater show graced by the presence of the governor, while others attended a party at a private residence. On Thursday, the day's activities were held at the racecourse and in the early evening revelers retreated to "clubs and places where they drink."[16] At 9:00 p.m., invited guests convened at the Government House Ball, where the band of the 1st Battalion the Cameronians performed for the entire evening. The dresses and jewelry of forty-two women at this ball were described in detail the next day in the *Pioneer*.[17] On Friday numerous polo games were followed by "so many cocktail parties . . . that a good deal of the evening seemed to be spent on the road."[18] On both Friday and Saturday the horse races were in full swing, and the United Services Club in the Chattar Manzil (Umbrella Palace), just off Hazratganj, held dinners and dances in the evening.

We see a slight—yet significant—shift in the entertainment lineup of the week in 1935. Fred Little's Rhythm Aces, described in one advertisement as "The Sultans of Modern Jazz Music," performed at Valerio's, and the event was heavily advertised.[19] Not much is known about this group other than that Roy Butler may have performed with an earlier version of the band while traveling briefly through Lucknow. Valerio's was a for-profit club-café and caterer in Hazratganj; it was not a social club. The proprietors built a small open area for dancing, and in the mid-1930s it booked jazz performers and cabarets. The reviews of ICS week during this time indicate that Valerio's was a primary venue in which to hear jazz.[20] As a private business open to all paying customers, it largely sidestepped the segregation that Gundevia mentions as typical during the week.

ICS weeks in Lucknow after 1935 were similarly programmed, and jazz was booked more frequently each year. The festivities were tempered in 1938 by the potential for war in Europe and an increase in the number of young noncommissioned military servicemen who considered formal ballroom dances and horse races somewhat old-fashioned.[21] On January 30 that year, the Pioneer griped that the Civil Service week was "not quite as gay as usual."[22]

Dances in the 1930s

Before beginning a discussion of jazz, it is important to note that, with the exception of ICS week, jazz was rare in the early 1930s, and was limited to small groups of enthusiasts. English residents typically preferred ballroom or military music. Even blithe New Year's Eve dances limited the repertoire to these styles. For example, the music at the New Year's Dance in the cantonment on December 31, 1933, included the foxtrot, a Boston two step, the Pride of Erin waltz, a rumba, the valeta (a dance to waltz music), an eightsome reel, and a schottische, all performed by the 1st Battalion the Scottish Rifles.[23] These are styles of traditional ballroom or country dances. Cantonments are defined areas set apart from other civilian areas. Beginning in the early eighteenth century they were limited to military or other official government purposes.[24] They included amenities such as churches, housing, racecourses, clubs, mess halls, bazaars, libraries, areas for polo and cricket, and cemeteries. Many British lived, worked, or socialized in the cantonment, and regimental music was central to its military culture. The 1934 New Year's Day parade in and around the cantonment the morning after the dance included the 10th Royal Hussars, Skinner's Horse, the 6th Field Brigade Royal Artillery (69th, 74th, 77th and 79th batteries), Artillery Signals, the 1st Battalion the East Yorkshire Regiment, the 1st Battalion the Cameronians (Scottish Rifles), the 3rd Battalion the 1st Punjab Regiment, and the 2nd Battalion the 16th Punjab Regiment—some three thousand troops with many bands that performed military music on procession.[25] Parades with military bands proliferated in the cantonment throughout the year, and these instrumentalists also provided music at sporting events, commencements, private functions, and social clubs, among other occasions.[26] With rare exceptions, jazz was not part of the entertainment lineup of the cantonment until the late 1930s.

The music culture of Hazratganj was different. In 1935, live radio broadcasts of domestic jazz performances and music from foreign films screened at the Elphinstone Theatre and the Plaza Talkies increased interest in jazz. Private clubs and cafés changed their entertainment lineups to profit from this growing local market. With the exception of the Railway Institute, most jazz was heard in and around Hazratganj, and musicians trickled into Lucknow to find employment and to take advantage of the profit potential. Nawab Saadat Ali Khan, ruler of Avadh between 1798 and 1814, is typically considered to have initiated the process of shaping the area that is now Hazratganj. Decades before it became a center for jazz, a number of European memoirs and travel logs compare the buildings and street design to England or Europe. Walter Hamilton wrote in the *East Indian Gazetteer* in 1828 that it "consists of one very handsome street, after the European fashion," and that the houses and palaces owned by the king along the street "are for the most part in the English style, but with a strange occasional mixture of Eastern architecture [and] are filled with European furniture and pictures, and may rank with comfortable

English houses."[27] Reginald Heber, the Bishop of Calcutta, wrote in 1828, "Lucknow has more resemblance to some of the smaller European capitals (Dresden for instance), than anything which I have seen in India." He describes the area of Hazratganj as "wider than the High Street at Oxford, but having some distant resemblance to it in the colour of its buildings and the general form and Gothic style of the greater part of them."[28] Historical references to Hazratganj often attest to its symbolic role in demarcating Lucknow as a cosmopolitan city acceptable to Europeans.

A number of venues featured jazz in 1935. Valerio's, the Lucknow Club, the Blue Room, the Railway Institute, and the Silver Slipper booked jazz performances. The Carlton Hotel, located on the edge of Hazratganj, hired a group of musicians to form the Carlton Rhythm Orchestra in 1935. They performed daily jitterbug dances.[29] Some venues occasionally advertised Lindy Hop and Shim Sham dances. Agabeg's Amusement Hall booked the early jazz group Godfrey's Band; advertisements called their performances "crazy dance[s]."[30] Entrance restrictions continued at these for-profit venues, but most were considered open to the paying public. The British-owned Valerio's introduced one of the first cabaret evenings in Lucknow on January 25, 1935. The highlight of this production, advertised as a "Cabaret and Dance," was Miss Mae Roach, the "Celebrated Danseuse,"[31] and represented the beginning of a trend in Lucknow that required patrons to book tables in advance for intimate cabaret dinners. With the influx of tourists attending horse races Valerio's was able to fill its entertainment space to capacity and engage in the profitable cabaret movement that began years earlier in Bombay and Calcutta.

Many new venues in Lucknow featured stylish names and modern amenities. For example, in 1934, the Blue Room adjacent to the Prince of Wales Theatre boasted "Electronic Sign Flashers."[32] The name "Blue Room" elicits links to notable foreign jazz venues, including the Blue Room at the Lincoln Hotel in New York City, which hosted big-name jazz groups and regular radio broadcasts. In this instance, using the name "Blue Room" in Lucknow was an effective strategy to promote a new urban topography with links to New York City, a hotbed of jazz. In the 1930s and 1940s, Blue Rooms could also be found in a number of cities including the Roosevelt Hotel in New Orleans, Louisiana, and the Normandy Dance Hall in Manitoba, Canada. By building the Blue Room, the Prince of Wales proprietors were following the global trend of opening auxiliary venues adjacent to a larger cinema hall to accommodate music and dancing.[33]

By the mid- or late 1930s, Anglo-Indians in Lucknow probably constituted the largest portion of the total audience for jazz. Though the Anglo-
Indian community organized dances with great fervor from the early
twentieth century,[34] the character of dances changed when jazz became
part of the social life of the youth. The Lucknow Club, considered a
venue for Anglo-Indians located just off Mahatma Gandhi Marg, regularly
booked dance bands during the summer, including the Rhythmites Dance
Band once a week in 1935.[35] With the arrival of the Rhythmites, the club
became associated with jazz and a new approach to dances that included
the most up-to-date transnational repertoire. The Lucknow Club boasted
events of all kinds in addition to daily dances, and was often filled to capacity. During World War II, the Christmas and New Year's dances drew crowds
of over a thousand.[36]

Why such an interest in jazz among the Anglo-Indian youth? A brief
exploration of contemporary attitudes toward the Anglo-Indian community between the 1920s and 1940s might help in answering this question.
As I mentioned earlier, my definition of Anglo-Indian in this book includes
individuals born and raised in India who have both European and Indian
ancestry. Most are Christian, a minority religion. Racially mixed communities, or any group considered as existing between two distinct and separate
dominant cultures, were termed "marginal" in much of the scholarship of
the 1920s and 1930s. According to Robert Park, one of the first to introduce the expression "marginal man" in a 1928 article, when an individual
"finds himself striving to live in two diverse cultural groups . . . the effect
is to produce an unstable character," one that more specifically arises
from "conflicting cultures [that] meet and fuse."[37] Everett V. Stonequist
notes that contempt for the marginal man made it impossible for Anglo-
Indians to "enter either of the parent-groups . . . [because] each of the
two main races is contemptuous of mixed individuals." He also asserts that
the Anglo-Indian community "clings to the coat of the aloof but retreat-
ing Englishman, despises the Indian, and is heavily despised in return."[38]
Elmer Hedin claims in 1934 that the Anglo-Indian is in some respects a
"parasite whose hold on its host is none too secure . . . [who] lives his separate life on the border of the official community, which supplies him with
sufficient employment to keep up his shabby and pathetic Britishness."[39]
Hedin observes that the British provided Anglo-Indians with employment
support that increased social standing. The Indian government gave job
preference to Anglo-Indians in the railway and telegraph employment sec-
tors, which provided financial stability and empowered employees with a

feeling of working-class solidarity.[40] Ann Baker Cottrell writes that Anglo-Indians were considered subordinate to the British, and though "resenting the British, Anglo [-Indians] remained loyal, identified strongly with the British and followed their cultural patterns as closely as financially possible." She also stresses that identifying with the British brought "power and prestige," at least in some periods.[41]

Cedric Dover, an Anglo-Indian scholar active between the late 1920s and 1950s, contested what he viewed to be deleterious ideas about the marginal status of Anglo-Indians, and responded to the above literature by promoting positive artistic and racial affinities between Anglo-Indians and African Americans through the common experience of marginality.[42] Dover expressed a need for "marginal" communities in India to identify with African Americans, including black musicians, who he claimed have achieved noteworthy levels of artistic expression.[43] (These claims are similar to beliefs about the innate musical abilities of African Americans discussed in previous chapters.) Such assertions of musical capacity suggest that through heredity, mixed races have access to black musical aptitude and white social status, the best of both worlds. But in contrast to Dover's view, Anglo-Indians were often seen to combine the worst vices of Indians and Europeans, and sometimes deemed socially inferior to both.[44] Attitudes and official strategies toward Anglo-Indians were sometimes contradictory, destabilizing, and undermining, and at other times empowering and solidifying. Many youth of the community considered commercialized jazz as transnational and as functioning outside these labels and biases.

Radios, Gramophones, and Hollywood Films

Cinema halls screened blockbuster Hollywood films as early as 1933, and multipurpose venues such as the railway institute screened sound films even earlier. In 1933, movies such as *Gold Diggers of 1933* and *The Kid from Spain* were infused with grand choreographed performances that inspired, entertained, and created a demand for live performances. Advertisements for the *Gold Diggers of 1933* at the Federal Talkies in Lucknow emphasized its "300 most beautiful girls, 5 pulse quickening songs, [and] 7 big sumptuous Spectacles."[45] These film productions effectively linked jazz to staged spectacles and dazzling Hollywood excitement. Hollywood films shaped an interest in dance crazes, including the Carioca dance from the film *Flying Down to Rio* with Fred Astaire, Ginger Rogers, and Dolores del Rio, screened to enthusiastic crowds in Lucknow in 1934 and 1935. The *Pioneer* newspaper featured full-page advertisements for *Flying Down to Rio* in art deco design, and dance halls featured Carioca dance instruction.[46] Energy and excitement from Hollywood roused thoughts about the potentials and possibilities of live performances, and new cinema houses in Lucknow facilitated this enthusiasm to a large scope of audiences. In the early 1930s, Lucknow had about four cinema houses, many of which served as multipurpose venues, but by 1939, at least eight were screening foreign films regularly. Many borrowed names from venues in Europe and North America such as the Prince of Wales Cinema (later referred to as the Prince), Universal Theatres, the Mayfair Cinema, and the Regal Cinema.

Instruments, sheet music, and gramophone discs were available by post from large urban centers in India, and their availability increased over the course of the decade. The L. M. Furtado & Company in Bombay was one of a number of companies that sold mandolins, ukuleles, guitars, classical and dance music as well as the latest song and dance albums. Low-end violins and mandolins were priced between 13 and 20 rupees, including instrument cases and strings, which was expensive but not entirely prohibitive for specialized consumers. In 1934, S. Rose and Company advertised albums for As. 13 including postage, a reasonable price for interested consumers at the time in Lucknow.[47] Sheet music arrangements for piano and ukulele were often packaged with albums. Other music commodities were available. In 1933, the Sirdar Gramophone Company in the Aminabad area of Lucknow sold gramophone discs in several languages for 1–4 rupees each, more expensive than mail order catalog listings.[48] By 1939, Ghosh and Brothers in Lucknow sold, serviced, and rented pianos and other instruments, and Godino's music shop in Hazratganj sold instruments, sheet music, and gramophone discs.[49] Gramophone discs of songs from Hollywood films increased in popularity every year, as did the frequency of newspaper advertisements promoting their availability in Lucknow.

Broadcasting in the city flourished in 1934. The number of broadcast stations increased and radio unit sales expanded. Radio owners received signals from the BBC Empire Service on shortwave and the Indian State Broadcasting Service from Calcutta and Bombay. Indian music dominated the programming on the Indian State Broadcasting Service stations, but Western music, mostly military marches and classical pieces, was programmed for short periods daily, as was jazz, though more rarely. The BBC Empire Service's charge during these years was to facilitate "home ties with British expatriates overseas,"[50] which included a small amount of jazz programming. Both the BBC Empire Service and the Indian State Broadcasting Service occasionally relayed jazz from the Grand Hotel in Calcutta for a half hour each, including performances of Herb Flemming's International Rhythm Aces at the hotel in early 1934.[51] Because of these broadcasts audiences learned that foreign bands composed of American and European jazz musicians were working in India.

Radio audiences throughout North India demanded better reception and more comprehensive programming in 1934. A 1940 report from the Office of the Controller of Broadcasting claimed that listening audiences had increased significantly in 1934 and that "interest in broadcasting was quickening apace."[52] Growing attention to radio compelled government administrators to initiate a policy of development that included building additional transmitters in Lucknow and elsewhere. Yet complaints about the poor quality of broadcast reception were frequent.[53] A 1934 article in the *Pioneer* newspaper mentions that the "Empire Short-wave station has not come up to expectations chiefly because of the uncertainty and the inherent difficulty of tuning with short waves" and that "the two Indian Broadcasting stations . . . can hardly be called enjoyable [because of the] many atmospherics present."[54] These complaints illustrate the importance placed on the need for functioning broadcast infrastructure.

To the best of my knowledge, details are unavailable about the number of radios in Lucknow or the demographics of radio owners, but units were available through several retailers. By 1938, Lucknow had its own transmitter under the auspices of All India Radio (AIR), which emerged from the Indian State Broadcasting Service administrative structure in 1936.[55] The manager of the new Lucknow radio transmitter, A. A. Advani, asserts in an article in the *Pioneer* newspaper that the station was "modern to the minute . . . [with] all the resources of the latest machinery and acoustic treatments."[56] The majority of the music on AIR in Lucknow was Indian vocal and instrumental music. Between 1938 and 1939, European music constituted about 13.5 percent of the total programming on all AIR stations.[57] According to the Office of the Controller of Broadcasting, the policy of AIR through 1939 was to transmit "one hour of European music at lunch for which there is a very definite demand" and one hour from ten to eleven in the evening.[58]

In the late 1930s, jazz bands in Calcutta, Delhi, and Bombay regularly relayed live broadcasts of their performances. These live radio programs featured orchestras based in large urban centers, highlighted celebrity musicians such as Ken Mac and Teddy Weatherford, and brought attention to the vibrant domestic jazz scenes in Bombay, Calcutta, and, to a lesser extent, Delhi. Performances by Ken Mac and His Orchestra and Peter Mendoza and His Orchestra were transmitted from the Bombay station in the evening in 1937.[59] By 1938, the Bombay transmitter was relaying regular live performances by Crickett Smith and His Boys for a half hour in the evening just before going off the air.[60] Ken Mac's Astoria Dance Band broadcast from the Delhi station in the evening that year.[61] These musicians were highly regarded, and their broadcasts proved to listeners in Lucknow that jazz was a domestic activity. By 1939, residents in Lucknow had access to around nine official Indian broadcasting signals; programs were transmitted from Delhi, Bombay, Calcutta, Madras, Lahore, and Lucknow. Live relayed broadcasts of dance bands in Bombay, Delhi, and Calcutta continued, sometimes with Teddy Weatherford and His Band between 10:00 p.m. and 11:00 p.m. on the Bombay transmission.[62] Elderly Anglo-Indian jazz enthusiasts in Lucknow still remember Weatherford's transmissions after more than seventy years, and speak about them with nostalgia and joyful reminiscence.[63] Thus, jazz enthusiasts in the late 1930s in Lucknow were aware of the most popular jazz orchestras in India and expected to hear live performances on the radio.

As I noted earlier, musicians in Lucknow listened to the radio to develop music skills. Guitarist James Perry performed with drummer Peter Antunis, jazz violinist Ken Cumines, and the jazz group Boris and His Swing Boys (fig. 4.2) during World War II. Perry asserts that the radio was an important instructional tool. He relates with delight that his father bought a first-rate radio in Lucknow, and boasts that his family listened to the BBC frequently.[64] His father played the ukulele and violin, and although he encouraged Perry to learn a musical instrument, he did not consider jazz an appropriate genre for a serious musician. While learning the ukulele as a child, Perry lamented that his father only taught him "all the old waltzes"[65] a reference to classical or traditional song-and-dance music. In spite of his father's resistance, Perry made his own radio and listened to jazz to study style and technique. He claims that the radio was empowering and pivotal in his musical development:

> You see, my father used to play classical violin. He had a perfect ear. I don't know where he got it from. My father used to play the oldies. His ukulele was tremendous. He bought it from an Italian. He taught me how to play. He gave me a rupee after every time he showed me something. A rupee was a thousand bucks at the time. That was the Ukulele at the time, not the guitar. . . .

Figure 4.2. Advertisement for Boris and His Boys at the Ambassador, *Pioneer* newspaper (Lucknow edition), February 24, 1945.

> Then what happened? We started to improvise. My father didn't like this. Then what happened was that we made our own radios, and listened to what we wanted. My father didn't like it. Then after that gradually we learned to play the real jazz, I mean the "improv."[66]

To this day he speaks with pride of his self-made musicianship, and explains that because he improvised his music preferences contrasted with his father's. Radio broadcasting and jazz improvisation inspired musicians such as Perry to cast off the music of previous generations and in some respects to reject pre-jazz genres of Western music. On the radios he built himself, James Perry remembers hearing the broadcasts of Ken Mac and His Dance Band on the AIR Bombay II signal at 9:50 p.m. According to Perry, Mac's broadcasts proved that Americans were not the only successful jazz performers in India. In rare instances of live relayed broadcasts within Lucknow, the Lucknow station sometimes transmitted live signals of performances of the Mayfair Orchestra from the Mayfair Ballroom in Hazratganj.[67] Perry was captivated by these broadcasts, and aspired to play jazz equally well.

Several stores sold radios at this time. Retailer A. Gosh and Sons in Hazratganj sold new "Tropic-Proof" radios from General Electric, while the British Radio House specialized in cheaper refurbished radios. Some new stores focused on radio repairs, such as R. N. Bhattacharji and Company in the Lalbagh area of Lucknow.[68] Not everyone considered the radio a lifestyle improvement. Shelia D'Costa, an avid jazz enthusiast in Lucknow during the war, remembers that her father did not like the radio, and that he initially refused to have one in their home: "I remember when radios came out. My father was so much against us keeping a radio. [He said,] 'It's rubbish.' [I said to him,] 'Daddy you can hear the news.' [He said,] 'you can read it in the newspaper.' Oh, he was so adamant that we should not get a radio, and after a lot of persuasion and this and that, then we could."[69] In this instance the radio shaped and reinforced generational divisions.

A number of elderly residents of Lucknow articulated the importance of gramophones in their home, and purchasing current tunes on gramophone discs were sometimes part of the family routine. Dorothy McFarland, a longtime resident of Lucknow, organized dances for Anglo-Indians at the Lucknow Club during World War II (and after), and claims that a traveling salesman used to come to her home in the 1940s to sell gramophone discs:

> We had an old fellow. And once a month he came on his cycle. A big box of records . . . boxes and boxes of records. And we'd tell him what we wanted, what song we wanted or what artist we wanted. He used to come in the morning, about half past nine, quarter to ten. My mother knew his habit. She would throw out a cotton carpet for him. He put it on the end of the veranda and he'd lie down. And we'd play them one after the other all day long and he's sleeping! Piles of them. [We would] throw out the old ones. They were old-fashioned. [We bought] Dinah Shore . . . "Forces Favorites" . . . Vera Lynn . . . "Keep the Home Fires Burning" . . . songs for soldiers to come back to.

This traveling salesman was part of the domestic routine. At the end of the day, they purchased the discs and sold their outdated inventory. According to McFarland, the discs were the latest available in India and she says that they were inexpensive because the stores and salesmen "were always competing."[70]

Similarly, Shelia D'Costa, a member of the Women's Auxiliary Corps (India) during the war, remembers that her family had a number of gramophones when she was a young woman. She suggests that her tastes included "all the oldies [such as the] Boomps-a-Daisy and the Lindy Hop."[71] She also relates that her favorite songs were those that had been popularized in Hollywood films. Some of her father's gramophone players were powered by hand cranks and others were electric, and they listened to jazz constantly in the home. She regularly listened to these songs until her death in 2009, and she showed me piles of records given to her by her father.[72] A survey of her 78 rpm disc collection reveals that she listened to Bing Crosby, Frank Sinatra, Gracie Fields, and Nelson Eddy. Gracie Fields and Nelson Eddy were in several Hollywood films. Frank Sinatra and Bing Crosby were popular singers and actors. The Boomps-a-Daisy was a stylized dance with predetermined moves popular in 1939 in London Dance Halls and ice shows and quickly became trendy in the United States.[73] It was also seen in the Hollywood film *Hellzapoppin'* in 1941. D'Costa also mentions dancing the Lambeth Walk and its spin-off, the Palais Glide; both were social mixing dances popular in London in early 1939. D'Costa and others saw these dances in foreign films and learned from instructions that were printed on sheet music.[74] These high-energy social mixing dances consisted of body movements with no one leading.

The opening of the Mayfair Cinema and Ballroom in 1939 was perhaps the most significant addition to the jazz scene of the late 1930s. For its grand opening on January 28, it screened the Stan Laurel and Oliver Hardy comedy *Block-Heads*, thus establishing its reputation as a venue for foreign films, although it also screened Indian productions. The ballroom was part of the urban, market-driven dance band economy of Hazratganj, and quickly became one of the most popular places for jazz. Advertisements portrayed it as "a theatre different in almost every fundamental respect from all the other cinema houses in Lucknow."[75] The main entrance to the building featured a large and elaborate art deco foyer and lavish stairs leading up to a cinema hall, but the stairs to the ballroom were inconspicuously constructed toward the back and off to the side of the foyer. Ballroom patrons circumnavigated the grandiose entrance to the cinema hall to get to the ballroom upstairs. A regular entrance fee required patrons to have a reasonable level of finances to attend dances, and an elaborate bar with expensive foreign liquor enhanced its sophistication. A small stage ran along the end opposite the bar. A large outdoor balcony on the second floor faced Mahatma Gandhi Marg. When the ballroom was overcrowded, dancing moved to the balcony where patrons could watch street life and enjoy the night air. According to Ram Advani, a bookseller and prominent businessman in the city, who attended dances at the Mayfair during the war:

It stayed open till five in the morning on weekends. The entrance charge was not too high but the ballrooms made enormous profits from the sale of liquor. Anyone could enter as long as they were properly dressed. Women were mostly dressed in European style though some came in saris. There were more men than ladies and many of the women who came there used to smoke and drink. This ballroom was a great opportunity for many men to learn dancing and to mix with ladies. I myself learnt to dance the Waltz, Fox Trot and Tango from an American lady who was a great Tango dancer. People would go out on to the terrace from the ballroom and later at night the revelry would sometimes spill over into the streets with drunken soldiers and their lady friends dancing on the street. But, by and large discipline was expected and maintained in areas like these. The Mayfair Ballroom used to have the tambola nights and organize music shows.[76]

Advani paints an image of gaiety during weekend performances and emphasizes the vivacity that came with foreign troops.

Finally, summer jobs at hotels in hill stations were an important source of income for bands performing in and around Hazratganj. During the summer months, many wealthy residents of the city traveled to hill stations, especially to Ranikhet, Simla, Nainital, and Mussoorie. The Carlton Rhythm Band traveled to Nainital from the Carlton Hotel in Lucknow and played jazz in a number of hotels there. The Antunis Band journeyed to Mussoorie in the summer, where they performed daily at the Savoy Hotel and temporarily changed their name to the Savoyans Orchestra.[77] The Savoy Hotel boasted contemporary amenities, and advertisements claimed it was the "most up-to-date modern hotel in Mussoorie."[78] Musicians and orchestras made a good amount of their yearly income performing in these hill station venues, and the viability of the commercial market for jazz in Hazratganj was linked to the summer jazz economies of hill stations. In addition, residents of Lucknow traveling to hill stations in the summer heard some of the best orchestras from across North India, which increased expectations that proficient musicians would come to Lucknow in the winter months. Betty Dignam lived in Lucknow, attended dances during the war, and traveled to the hills every summer as a young woman. She claimed, "In Mussoorie at that time [we] had a Parsi man Rudy Cotton, and another Jew who had a beautiful singing voice, Sollo Jacobs, he used to play the piano, very good bands, and not just three- or four-piece band, twenty-four pieces in the band. It was their livelihood."[79] Rudy Cotton and Sollo Jacobs were popular jazz performers in North India, and Dignam suggests that she was able to distinguish between skilled and unskilled musicians. Jacobs, Cotton, and other musicians in hill stations increased the demand for accomplished musicians and large orchestras in Hazratganj during the winter months.

Troops

Foreign military personnel were plentiful in Lucknow during the war. They frequented a number of clubs, and evidence suggests that they spent large sums of money on public entertainment. As mentioned in chapter 3, Allied forces in India numbered in the tens of thousands. They resisted Japanese attacks in India, staged counterattacks against Japanese forces in Burma and Southeast Asia, and helped supply nationalist China.[80] The Allied powers constructed about two hundred new airfields, built numerous roads that allowed quick mobilization in and out of Calcutta, and seized private land for defense purposes.[81] I found no official records accurately indicating how many Allied soldiers were in Lucknow, but some local residents suggested that they numbered in the hundreds or even thousands. This number is feasible because Lucknow was a staging area for the Eastern Command in Calcutta, which was under the constant threat of Japanese bombing campaigns. In 1942 the US Army set up a station in Lucknow that likely provided support for a military aerodrome just outside the city.[82] In addition to troops stationed in Lucknow, soldiers on leave from Calcutta and elsewhere traveled there to attend horse races, and most stayed in the Carlton Hotel.[83] Thousands of Italian prisoners of war were sent to India and many were posted in Lucknow. By one account, these Italian soldiers were permitted to attend dances in Hazratganj with a chaperone.[84] Though it is difficult to know how many prisoners were in Lucknow, according to US serviceman Eric Burrell, a large prisoners' barrack existed there and he was asked to escort prisoners to and from the city while stationed in India during the war.[85] These prisoners added another flavor to the vibrancy of the war effort in Lucknow.

Many senior residents of Lucknow speak about Hazratganj with particular significance and special meaning. It was a space for carefree strolls, shopping, and meetings with friends, and was collectively referred to as "ganjing." By the time of World War II, Hazratganj was lined with clubs and cafés within walking distance of each other. It contrasted with much of the rest of Lucknow in terms of type and availability of merchandise, style of music, architectural design, and historical character. It was exclusive and segregated because it did not always welcome lower classes, but for many it was a gateway to the wider world beyond Lucknow. Ram Advani remembers:

> The outbreak of the war and the influx of soldiers invigorated Hazratganj. The cinema halls had two shows a day: at six thirty and nine thirty. The

popular notion of having fun was to come to Hazratganj: have a drink, eat at a Chinese restaurant and see a movie or go to one of the ballrooms. Mayfair was the first commercial ballroom but the Ambassador Skating Rink next door was converted in to another ballroom too. There was also the Lucknow Club at Lawrence Terrace for those who found the other two very expensive.[86]

Young US personnel in Lucknow occupied social spaces previously claimed by the British and partially reconfigured prevailing norms at dances in Hazratganj. They created additional revenue for private clubs and spent large sums of money on entrance fees and alcohol. Similar to the personal history narratives I collected in Calcutta, those in Lucknow noted the tensions between young American and British military personnel, which caught the attention of "ganjing" residents. Peter Antunis Jr., son of the bandleader Peter Antunis Sr., accompanied his father to performance jobs in Hazratganj during the war and jokingly observed that "the Yanks had all the money" and that as a young man he was "scared of those boys." He also jokes that, "on the streets you could see them fighting . . . with the Britishers" and that the military police would "throw them in the truck, one after the other."[87] Americans supported the market for dances bands at the Ambassador Club, the Mayfair Ballroom, and the Soldier's Club in Hazratganj.

Allied troops not only expanded the audience base and increased demand but also reinforced the stirring notion that Lucknow was involved in world affairs. Many individuals I interviewed were careful to avoid minimizing the seriousness of the war, but at the same time they claimed that witnessing the war effort firsthand was exciting. Observing confrontations between American and British troops with such immediacy left many with the feeling that the British could be effectively challenged. Moreover, a number of people I interviewed, including Shelia D'Costa, stressed that many young British soldiers were friendly but seemed uneducated, disputing the commonly held notion of British educational superiority. US troops also challenged previously held beliefs that only certain European or wealthy Indian communities could frequent expensive venues in Hazratganj. This was a period when England was losing major battles in Europe, and by 1942 the efforts of the United States were considered integral to winning the war. D'Costa recalls recognizable distinctions between American and British troops:

I was in the army [WAC]. I was in school when the war broke out. There was all this flurry that war had been declared. Lots of British and Americans. . . .

They used to come in small groups. Mostly troops. They mixed with the Anglo-Indians. [Americans] . . . had more money than the British had. They had a tendency to smashing about a bit. Some of those boys were very nice. They were very generous. Their uniforms were smarter. They were better paid. They were popular. They were all right. The British Tommy, they were more homey. You could say anything to them.[88]

Although Americans were not necessarily always seen in a positive light, most of the residents I interviewed in Lucknow claimed that the Americans were friendly, approachable, and curious about India.

Betty Dignam associates the popularity of jazz during the war with the American presence: "Alongside the Mayfair [was] the Ambassador Ballroom. It's not far from the Mayfair Ballroom. That was very popular at the time when the American troops were in Lucknow, I think they preferred that place. To do all their jiving . . . and all that. But the music was Harry James, Tommy Dorsey, Glenn Miller, all that kind of music was very popular."[89] The jive is an energetic swing dance, but Dignam could also have been using the term *jiving* to refer to jazz or swing style. Either way, she suggests that Americans expected lively music and dance styles in Lucknow, and that clubs such as the Ambassador Ballroom largely catered to Americans.[90]

Amateur nights and singing competitions at the Mayfair Ballroom were particularly lively with the arrival of soldiers. Archie Frank, a retired music teacher who had lived in Lucknow for eighty-six years when I interviewed him in 2000, participated in singing competitions with American troops and others on Sundays during the war at the Mayfair Cinema and Ballroom. By popular demand he sang mostly songs from Hollywood films: "I used to sing at the Mayfair Ballroom, that was full of Anglo-Indians mostly . . . I was singing film songs at that time, western films. There were troops also [during] the Second World War. There were soldiers from America and Britain; they also joined us in the competitions."[91] According to Frank, the ballroom was packed in the final two years of the war because of the Allied troops. He learned songs by reading sheet music and watching English films at the Mayfair, Prince of Wales, and Capitol Cinema.[92] Barbara Antunis, a longtime resident of Maqbara, remembers: "I sang there when I was thirteen. On Saturday they would have an amateur night at Mayfair. It was during the war and the ballroom would be full of soldiers. I would sing my song and come back to our table where my mother would be sitting. Once I sang 'Moon Over Burma.'"[93] Like Frank, Barbara Antunis sang songs from Hollywood films. "Moon over Burma" was from the 1940 film

Moon over Burma starring Dorothy Lamour. Frank said that sheet music of songs from Hollywood films was easily available in Lucknow. I once asked him where he bought the music, and he responded, "at that time I got sheet music from Bevan and Company [in Lucknow], and then from Delhi and Bombay. Mr. Antunis, he used to get music. He was Goan from Goa. He and his team used to get sheet music from Bombay or Calcutta. Delhi not that much."[94] Bevan and Company had been operating in Lucknow since at least the 1910s to supply the musical needs of regimental bands in and around Lucknow.[95]

James Perry attributes much of his enthusiasm for playing jazz during World War II to the young British and US military servicemen stationed there. He claims that "a lot of the Americans used to come [to Lucknow] . . . and they used to go here and there in the clubs." He states with pride: "I'd dress up, put my shirt on, and play solid bloody numbers [for them]. I used to yap and chat with them. They were nice. They all had bicycles, and I used to roam around with them. I used to play solid bloody productions for them. I practiced and practiced and I had the highest quality jazz for them." A number of elderly Anglo-Indians I interviewed narrated similar stories about the enthusiasm created by foreign servicemen. Perry was adamant that, as he puts it, "we had a cosmopolitan bloody race [*sic*] here," pointing to the role of foreigners in creating interest in jazz during the war.[96]

Perry played the drums in his first major music job in Lucknow. Jazz violinist Ken Cumines, a prominent bandleader in Lucknow during the war, asked Perry to play a performance in the Mahomed Bagh Club in the cantonment because his regular drummer was sick. Cumines, an Iranian violinist, maintained a band in Lucknow with fifteen to twenty members. The Mahomed Bagh Club catered to military officers and their families. Perry recounts: "His drummer took sick. [He] came to my dad. [My Dad] said, 'No, he's not allowed [to play].' [Cumines] had really done so many shows . . . when [he] came in the morning . . . he was very friendly with my dad. He said, 'C'mon, Sir, help me out with this.' This is the first time I started on the drum set. He showed me how to operate it."[97] Perry and others often claimed that their parents did not like the music. His father tried to prevent him from going to clubs, but the demand for dance bands during the war increased the need for proficient musicians, and Perry would eventually help satisfy the demand. Perry also revealed that orchestras and cabaret performers were treated well during this period. Many venues had backstage rooms in which the bands could relax when not performing. He was attracted to the lifestyle and special treatment.

Perhaps ancillary to my discussion, but interesting to consider, are Perry's thoughts on Indian music. To this day Perry asserts that a jazz culture in Lucknow developed because of the popularity and integrity of Indian classical music in the city.[98] Because of a high level of musicianship and patronage in the arts, Lucknow became a center for semiclassical styles such as *ghazals* and *thumris*. For Perry, two musical genres—Indian music and Western music—occupied a city that was considered to be musically genuine, aesthetically wide-ranging, and technically virtuosic. Jazz was situated at the modern end of the spectrum and existed within the context of a Lucknow-specific value schema that Perry and his contemporaries mapped between the antiquated music culture of India (and the empire) and the modernity of jazz. Perry does not listen to Indian classical music.[99] Yet he expresses great pride in the musical effervescence permeating the city, calling Indian classical and semiclassical genres the "real origins" of music in Lucknow.[100] Part of the inspiration for performing jazz came from the integrity of these Indian traditions. Claiming that the whole of Lucknow is musically exceptional is not unique to Perry. Lucknow historian Abdul Halim Sharar maintains that in Lucknow a "feeling for rhythm is ingrained in everyone, including children" and even "bazaar boys have been heard singing . . . ragas with such excellence that those who heard them were entranced and the greatest singers envied them."[101] According to Sharar, a large segment of the city understood the complexity of classical music and knew the repertoire.

Jazz was not always the Western genre of choice during the war. An invitation-only courtyard with a bandstand at the Lucknow Racecourse in the cantonment typically featured regimental or European classical music, even though young soldiers regularly attended. Mrs. Singh, a Lucknow socialite and wife of a high-ranking military officer, organized social events at the racecourse, and told me that race days just before Independence were "like a fashion show [with] best clothes, and best jewelry [and] umbrellas [and] all of the elite of Lucknow used to be there." She relates that the music on the bandstand was mostly regimental repertoire or "a few strains from Beethoven or Strauss." Troops traveled to Lucknow from across North India to watch the races. Spanning a large part of the cantonment, it boasted a souvenir and snack shop, a food catering service, horse betting, and plenty of space for milling around and dancing. She used to go often when she was young, and asserts that the bands were proficient and played often: "They were professionals, not amateurs. Whenever we went, even if it was a tea party, with tables and snacks . . . the music was playing in the background."[102] The racecourse was popular throughout the year, even during the first few years of the war when other venues reduced the frequency of live entertainment.

Audiences

During the war, British social clubs in Lucknow restricted access, and entrance criteria were often arbitrary and inconsistent.[103] The door-keepers of new for-profit clubs and cafés beginning in the late 1930s in Lucknow were often Anglo-Indian men who established entrance criteria that included easy and unquestioned access for their community. This was the case at the Mayfair Cinema and Ballroom. I once asked Ram Advani to describe the atmosphere of dances at the Mayfair Ballroom during this time, and he asserted that "Anglo-Indians were the gatekeepers," suggesting diverse clientele and substantial Anglo-Indian participation.[104] Amaresh Misra proposes that Anglo-Indian jazz consumers in Lucknow were "caroused to the beat of the swing and the jive, playing out latest jazz numbers." He further suggests that the international character of jazz created a "non-colonial" presence in Lucknow,[105] and that Anglo-Indians did not consider jazz to be restricted-access entertainment.

Hollywood films were available to all paying customers, and many Anglo-Indian women closely followed the styles worn by American and British film stars. Fashion magazines were cheap and abundant in the 1940s, and included *Vogue, Woman's Home Companion,* and *Seventeen.*[106] These magazines, especially *Vogue,* significantly influenced popular fashions during the war. Numerous tailors in Lucknow were skilled in making European and American dresses, skirts, and other fashion apparel. D'Costa chose to wear gowns at evening dances, and for more informal afternoon tea dances she sported a skirt, which was unacceptable in most circles outside the Anglo-Indian community at the time. She wore a different dress each time she attended a dance.[107] Moreover, local hairdressers were skilled in reproducing contemporary European and American hairstyles.[108]

Indians not associated with the Anglo-Indian community attended dances, but their total numbers were smaller. Ram Advani frequently attended performances at the Mayfair Ballroom, but he stresses that, as an Indian patron, he was the exception. He dressed in a jacket at events, and he made it a point to take dance lessons from Doris Cumines, the wife of orchestra leader Ken Cumines. Advani made sure to dress and dance in a manner that followed contemporary trends because he considered the Mayfair Ballroom a "very novel" establishment.[109] Sometimes wealthy Indians organized dances in their homes with music played on gramophones, and the very wealthy often hired a live orchestra. These dances were frequent during the war when organizers invited military personnel. According to Singh:

> We used to have private dancing only on the [gramophone] disc. In my house, in another house, every second day third day there was a dance party, very private dances, so I mean in most of the houses if there was a slight bit of the western culture, and in most of these rajas [royal class], they used to have them. They used to have Indian music also, they used to have dancing girls, and along with that they used to have dances at the house, tea parties, cocktail parties. Some people who could afford, like these rajas and all that, they used to have [live orchestras].[110]

These dances most often featured ballroom dance music, probably to maintain an atmosphere of formality, but Singh claims that showcasing jazz was sometimes important to demonstrate a knowledge of contemporary trends.

The War

Jazz and cabaret performances in Lucknow were sporadic during the first three years of the war with the exception of the Mayfair Ballroom, which regularly organized cabarets with reservation-only dinners, intimate table settings, and lively dance bands. Patrons were required to book tables in advance to ensure availability. Most cabarets at the Mayfair during these years charged 2 rupees for men and 1 rupee for women plus the cost of dinner. The first cabaret group to remain in residence at the Mayfair for more than a few days was the Russian dance duet "Lantzoff & Svetlanova."[111] They performed during the first months of 1940, and their routines featured Russian-themed material. Traveling dance duos, solo cabaret dancers, variety troupes, and other entertainers graced the halls of the Mayfair Ballroom.

An increasing number of venues booked cabaret groups and performance artists in 1942. The Mayfair Ballroom hired cabaret artists "Laperi & Jeanvar" for about two months early that year.[112] This duo promoted a

Latin American theme and were probably popular because of the Carmen Miranda film *That Night in Rio* screened at Plaza Cinema at the same time.[113] In January, a new club called Blue Haven organized "Hawaiian Night" cabarets and booked Francisco, Miss Franks, and Conchita, described as "Real Filipinos."[114] The military opened the Soldier's Club in January for Allied troops on leave in Lucknow. It was especially popular with American soldiers, and the widely circulated US military publication, the *CBI Roundup*, advertised and reviewed performances. Military patrons from across the CBI theater of operations attended its nightly dances.

Hollywood films continued to draw large crowds to cinemas. At least nine cinema halls were screening both foreign and Indian films in early 1943, including Capitol, Prince, Plaza, Mayfair, Sudarshan, Royal, Elphinstone, Jagat, and Nishat. Archie Frank once told me that bands—for example, Peter Antunis at the Mayfair—played during film intermissions. He related that "[Antunis] played the piano to keep [the audience] quiet, that's why they played the music. They had piano, violin, bass violin, cello, . . . and piano."[115] These performances brought visibility and extra income to bands.

Troops became more confident of Allied victory in late 1944, and cabarets and dances increased exponentially. The Mayfair Ballroom proprietors re-formed the resident Mayfair Orchestra, which performed twice a week, along with Boris and His Swing Boys, Ken Cumines, Peter Antunis, and Cardoza's Band. The Ambassador Ballroom opened on November 1, complete with a ballroom, tea room, dining room, and cocktail bar. Boris and His Swing Boys frequently performed there, and advertisements in the *Pioneer* referred to them as the "biggest band Lucknow ever had."[116] James Perry played with Boris on occasion that year at the Ambassador. Cabarets at the Ambassador Ballroom promoted themes such as "Hawaiian Night" on December 10, "Monte Carlo" night on December 14, "Great American Night" on December 16, and so on.[117] The Ambassador advertised late afternoon dances, tea dances, night dances, and dinner dances; all required formal or military dress. The Lucknow *Pioneer* wrote that a new "feast of good things" was overtaking Lucknow this year, and Boris and His Swing Boys band was "fast becoming the most popular pastime in Lucknow."[118] On the radio, the "General Forces Programme" broadcasted everyday on the BBC, with daily programs designed for Allied forces in India.[119]

The first half of 1945 was even more vibrant. Daily dances, cabarets, and dinners were booked at the Mayfair Ballroom, the Ambassador, Blue

Haven, Soldier's Club, the Lucknow Club, and less frequently the Railway Institute, and the Silver Slipper. Many venues featured two performances each day, one in the afternoon and one at night. Evening cabarets were typically booked by table, rather than by an entrance fee. Dinners accompanied elaborate cabarets. One of the most popular groups was "Lara, Pau, Kay and Olga"; Pau and Kay were hired from the Taj Mahal Palace Hotel in Bombay. They performed daily with the Streamline Rhythm Masters dance band and featured a variety of styles in a number of entertainment mediums, including Russian ballets, acrobatic dancing, and juggling acts. They even performed the cancan.[120] The Mayfair also booked performers of Indian dance, both solo classical and choreographed. The local market for cabarets was expansive during these months, and hiring performance groups from outside Lucknow increased a venue's reputation.

A fourteen-piece American dance band performed at the Mayfair Ballroom and Ambassador Club for a few months that year (fig. 4.3). They often accompanied the cabaret artist Ramonde, a Carmen Miranda impersonator, at the Mayfair Ballroom,[121] and the band frequently performed at jitterbug competitions with the Mayfair Orchestra. (Miranda impersonators were booked through the late 1940s in Lucknow.) Many military units, both British and American, started ad hoc swing bands, and the American Swing Band was likely composed of US servicemen stationed

Figure 4.3. Advertisement for the American Swing Band at the Mayfair Ballroom, *Pioneer* newspaper (Lucknow edition), May 2, 1945.

in or around Lucknow or the nearby city of Kanpur. They were in high demand, especially at the Ambassador Club, and were often accompanied by the British tap-dancing duo "Pete and Repeat." They featured an American bandleader, Lee Connelly. Little is known about Connelly or the band, but they drew sizable audiences, and local newspaper advertisements frequently recommended that patrons book tables early for these performances to avoid disappointment.[122]

Cabaret designers created themes that were often described in marketing and advertisement publications as "enchanting" or "fantasies." One cabaret on March 9, 1945, at the Ambassador in Hazratganj was titled "A Night in India." Advertisements for this event boasted "enchanting Indian cabaret items" with "Indian Rhumba tunes" and an "Indian Dinner Menu," including roast chicken "Indian style." Prizes were awarded for the "best and original Indian female get up" and for the "best male Indian Dress."[123] Since troops were largely segregated from others, cabarets featuring Indian music and dance were perhaps their only exposure to Indian entertainment. Russian cabarets were also fashionable. Dimitri and Xenia, a cabaret duo, performed regularly at the Ambassador Club, and promoted a "Russian Nights" theme.[124] Russian themes may have been popular in part because of the large number of Russian variety groups that toured North India.

Anxieties about the war almost disappeared in May 1945 with the announcement of Allied victory in Europe. A musical inertia began that lasted about three months, and entertainment advertisements in the *Pioneer* newspaper beginning Friday, May 10, 1945, increased considerably. The Mayfair Ballroom boasted daily dance competitions with prizes, and even hired a master of ceremonies (MC) to organize events, coordinate themes, and accommodate the needs of the performers. The MC received a substantial salary.[125] The Ambassador Club held daily dances from May 10 to May 14, with victory dinners, cabarets, amateur nights, and victory balls. Boris and His Swing Band played the music at these events. Victory activities were organized throughout Lucknow. A parade on August 20 included a large military procession, complete with airplane bombers dropping leaflets and Allied flags. Military and police bands performed in parks along the parade route.[126]

Postwar

This vibrant entertainment economy did not last. After the war, daily performances continued until 1947, but the number of dances declined dramatically, with most organized at the Lucknow Club or the Railway Institute. Ken Cumines, the swing violinist, disbanded his orchestra just after the war and launched a solo career performing in orchestras across North India and recording film music. Before leaving Lucknow he occasionally performed with the Antunis Band and Ronnie Orsmonds and His Band, a new group. It is likely that Cumines could no longer support his large orchestra and decided to work under solo contract. Sollo Jacobs, a pianist who often performed with Boris and His Boys, relocated to Bombay, where he built a career as a pianist. Risbert and His Band, a much smaller group with four or five musicians, took over the Mayfair Ballroom and they often played with Cumines at the front. Most evening events were dances with no dinners or cabarets. The Mayfair ended its strategy of maintaining a resident MC, instead hiring a manager to organize events. Gramophone discs of domestic jazz groups were no longer advertised in Lucknow. One of the last advertised events for swing music was the New Year's Eve Ball on December 31, 1947, which offered "Novelties, Caps, Balloons, Streamers & Fun Galore" from 9:00 p.m. until dawn, with a morning swing session on January 1, 1948, at 11:00 a.m.[127] No cabaret, food, MC, or local celebrity performers were part of this event. The Ambassador closed soon after. The Soldier's Club closed after the war. The Mayfair Ballroom continued booking events through the 1960s.

The Antunis Band performed again at the Mayfair Ballroom and the Ambassador Ballroom after the war. They also played for many events requiring regimental or ballroom music because military bands made up of uniformed soldiers were considered potentially inflammatory between 1945 and the Indian Independence of 1947. Peter Antunis maintained a close relationship with officers of the British military stationed in the city during and after the war. Though he played swing music in public venues in Hazratganj, he focused on the traditional ballroom dance repertoire at the restricted-entry Mahomed Bagh social club in the cantonment through 1947. The management of the club considered his music a morale booster for soldiers after the war.[128] The band performed in Lucknow until 1964.

Jazz in Lucknow was profitable and pragmatic. Indians, Goans, and military troops in Lucknow embraced commercialized music as a form of cosmopolitan capital,[129] and jazz facilitated interaction among a diverse group of people. It was empowering, a source of pride and self-identification. Mrs. McFarland once told me that she and other Anglo-Indian women used to try to "dupe the British"[130] at jazz dances with fashionable hair and stylish dress. The British in Lucknow, as a whole, had more money and power, but Anglo-Indians and Goans, in this instance through the public consumption of jazz, could be more chic and cosmopolitan. These reconfigured relationships had sway. But after the war, foreigners departed, access to Western music and media declined, many cinema halls gradually stopped screening English-language films, and gramophone discs of jazz were much less available. Furthermore, prohibition in 1947 negatively affected the nature of entertainment in Hazratganj, and a brewing economic crisis and stricter regulations placed on entertainment venues tempered much of the gaiety.[131] The next chapter broadens the scope of study to all of North India, and addresses the role of Hollywood film music in Hindi film songs.

Chapter Five

Cabaret Sequences in Hindi Films

This chapter focuses on songs from a select cross section of cabaret scenes in Hindi cinema between 1943 and 1951, when a stylistic continuity in film music called *filmi*, or "film-style," took shape.[1] It will concentrate on the work of four composers—Naushad Ali, C. Ramchandra, and the composer duo commonly referred to as Shankar-Jaikishan—and explore their compositional approach to cabaret song-dance sequences, especially their exploration of Hollywood film music. It is well-known that Hollywood influenced some early composers working in Hindi films. Thus, rather than contextualize a broad relationship between the music of Indian and American cinema, this chapter analyzes the stylistic approach to sixteen songs from twelve Hindi films and focuses specifically on elements whose origins probably come from commercialized American music. Here it suggests that much of the acclimatization of Hollywood film music into these songs involved musical exchange between composers, composers and producers, and composers and local jazz musicians—an ongoing process in which these and other stakeholders in Hindi cinema borrowed identifiable musical material from each other, not just from Hollywood. In this process, it briefly explores the character of live cabarets in Bombay and details a correlation between their overarching thematic structure and the development and originality of on-screen cabaret productions. The chapter focuses on cabaret segments in films with a separate performance area and audience, typically in a club or other formal venue with food, drink, or dance. It does not address symphonic-style music heard outside of these cabaret scenes.

Before beginning, it is important to note that the film song industry has long been translocally oriented, embracing material from the subcontinent and beyond.[2] I follow Hindi film music scholar Jayson Beaster-Jones's suggestion that film songs are cosmopolitan in nature, rather than ostensibly Westernized, and I support his argument that film songs embody "mediated musical material within and beyond the local, in whatever way the local is constituted by producers and audiences."[3] Media, technologies, and other commercial and noncommercial resources that supported the proliferation of American music that I have discussed in previous chapters constituted at least a small part of the historical development of cabaret song-dance sequences in Hindi films, especially Hollywood's film industry and Bombay's jazz economy. However, this chapter is not a study on the Westernization or Hollywood-ization of film songs, nor is it a study on the extent to which Western music influenced film songs more or less than any other style. It is aimed at gaining an understanding of the capacity of compositional practice to transcend borders that define genre or style, and argues that as Hindi film songs developed during this era, characteristics previously designated "American" (or "Western") eventually lost many of the identifying markers that linked them to these very designations. The argument is built on concrete musicological analysis of a handful of songs.

Eclecticism and Stylistic Continuity

Bernard Herrmann, the American composer known for his work in mid-twentieth-century American films, once said, "No one person has complete expression because film is a mosaic art, and if you work in films, you have to partake of a community expression."[4] The economics of film music markets, like the economics of other creative industries, is such that a diversity of stakeholders—musicians, composers, writers, editors, producers, audio and film technicians, and so on—support a value chain of creativity and imagination to shape music into a commodity item.[5] A number of composers in Hollywood, including Herrmann, have emphasized the importance of teamwork and collaboration between composers and production teams, and have stressed that music must make sense to the whole film production.[6] But it must also have stand-alone value to increase the film's multiple artistic dimensions, and ultimately its profitability. Songs in Hindi cinema were typically sold as separate commodity items on gramophone discs, which required that they achieve popularity in their own right, and entire teams were involved in their success, generating input from numerous music makers and stakeholders.

In Hindi films, song-dance sequences support on-screen spatial proxemics, plot development, and narrative logic. The sequences I discuss in this chapter routinely combine material from jazz, Western classical music, and Indian theater or classical music, among other genres, and the music effectively and unobtrusively modulates among these genres to support narrative structures and meanings. For example, Latin American music was sometimes featured in cabaret sequences in the 1940s because these scenes often evoked foreign or Westernized images and interpersonal interactions. Actors wore Western dress, men and women danced and sat together at small tables, and choreography frequently showcased a mix of global forms. In this instance, the character and context of Latin American music and dance reinforced scene structures meant to evoke exotic, Westernized appearance and demeanor. This musical eclecticism conjured up distinct sounds and images among film audiences, the overwhelming majority of whom did not have access to cabarets or similar entertainment. Yet the music was decisive and its influence was critical. Herrmann once claimed that music "can tell you what people are thinking and feeling,"[7] implying that it influences audience perception of the pacing of events, on-screen action, and character development, among other elements, and suggests that music is closely connected to the whole production and, ultimately, to the audience's response to the film.[8] Thus, it is understandable that Latin American music, dance, and dress might evoke special meaning in cabaret scenes.

Music is almost always in transition, susceptible to outside influences and subject to tensions between continuity and change, traditionality and novelty.[9] Composers of Hindi film music embraced global music during this era, yet they continually gathered material from more localized styles.[10] In fact, local and regional Indian theater industries significantly influenced early film music, especially during the years before these four composers began working. V. N. Arora, Sangita Gopal and Sujata Moorti, Anna Morcom, and many others have identified some of the early musical borrowings from the Parsi theater in Bombay, regional theaters in Bengal and Maharastra, and traveling theater groups.[11] Almost every scholar of India's film history has noted Indian cinema's linguistic diversity and its long-standing adherence to music drama as a narrative form.[12] In early films such as the 1931 features *Alam Ara* in Hindustani and *Kalidas* in Tamil, and the 1932 film *Ayodhyecha Raja* in Marathi, actors were often former stage performers.[13] At various points composers asserted their creative perspectives by moving stylistically (and aesthetically) away from music theater. As an art form in its early years, Hindi film music composers sought to achieve a tenuous balance between continuity and change, conformity and rupture, which required responding to the challenges of successful innovation beyond dramatic musical traditions.

In popular music, innovation and productivity often mean survival for entertainers who must rethink stylistic compatibility and originality to successfully achieve stable profits.[14] To make money, entertainers must find their own voice that others appreciate, and in film music they must do so with a production team. Indian film music witnessed a high degree of innovation and productivity during the years this chapter discusses because, among other reasons, it needed to appeal to as large an audience as possible to bring revenue, no easy feat in a country with multiple languages, dialects, and musical genres. Film studios often sought to pioneer musical styles that appealed to a national audience rather than smaller regional markets, and Western music helped to create an additional degree of acceptability among the masses of filmgoers. Cinema scholar Sheila Nayar claims that early Indian films "came to rely, ironically, on the uniformity of the West (or, rather, what it *chose* from the West) to provide its films with a generic coat of All-Indianness."[15] Some Hindi film music composers saw significant possibilities in Hollywood film music,[16] part of a process that reached a stylistic plateau around the late 1940s when songs of these four composers appealed to a broad range of audiences across India.[17]

In what way did these composers innovate beyond dramatic styles? Their music was not passively hybrid, nor was it characterized by a series of eclectic "cosmopolitan imposters."[18] That is, composers did not necessarily insert Western elements willy-nilly to make the music more cosmopolitan or foreign sounding. They took into account contexts and larger narrative and metanarrative meanings in the film and nuanced the music accordingly. Furthermore, film song composers did not always seek to make the music more "Western." Some film song scholars, including Alison Arnold, theorize that Western music in Hindi films tended to be compartmentalized or partitioned in a manner that was distinct from the totality of the *filmi* character of songs, yet tweaked so that it still fit nicely into a *filmi* stylistic approach.[19] In this respect, certain components of the music, sometimes called sonic hooks, caught the listener's attention without conveying a sense of dominance or obtrusiveness. These sonic hooks were sometimes a muted trumpet playing improvisatory licks between vocal runs, or the bongos playing a tumbao beat (a Latin American rhythm). Instruments like the Hawaiian slide guitar, the piano,

Latin American instruments such as the maracas, cabasa, shekeré, claves, or bongos, and also dance band instruments like the saxophone and clarinet were also hooks. Such an assemblage of characteristics, whether in the area of harmony, melody, rhythm, form, or timbre, was enough to appeal to the listening audience and to help construct uniqueness, but not necessarily overbearing foreignness.

A noteworthy example of a sonic hook and its stylistic development over the course of the 1940s is heard in Naushad Ali's use of claves in the song "Ek Tu Ho Ek Main Hoon" from the film *Kanoon* in 1943, and later in "Suhani Raat Dhal Chuki" from the film *Dulari* in 1949. The clave is typically considered a Latin American instrument but was frequently used in Hollywood cinema in the 1940s, and in "Ek Tu Ho Ek Main Hoon" Naushad features a two-measure pattern, the first measure is divided in three and the next measure in two, and this repeats throughout the entire piece. This is called a 3/2 clave, and is one of the first instances of a clear 3/2 clave that I found in a film score. The composer also uses instruments and musical characteristics associated with Indian folk and classical music, among other genres. A range of resources must have been available for Naushad to effectively integrate a Latin American 3/2 clave into a film song in 1943.[20] He layers a recognizable, unvaried Latin American clave rhythm over multiple lines of Indian instruments, which is no easy feat. In this song, Naushad conveys a musical totality through the use of identifiable Western and Indian source material.

The claves are two small cylindrical pieces of wood that are struck together with the hands. One clave is placed stationary in one hand and held by the tips of the fingers, and the other clave strikes this stationary clave, which creates a sharp, resonant sound. Over the course of the 1940s, the clave is featured through an assortment of means. For Naushad Ali, the timbre of the claves becomes principal, as exemplified in the 1949 song "Suhani Raat Dhal Chuki" from *Dulari*. Here he uses a prominent clave (or a clave-like timbre) without a 3/2 rhythm, but it showcases slight offbeat rhythmic ornamentation and (delicate) improvisation. Important to note is that the 3/2 clave probably had its beginnings in Indian film through exposure to Latin American music in Hollywood films, most likely films starring Carmen Miranda, including *Week-End in Havana* (1941). Naushad took a clearly identifiable rhythm played on a recognizable instrument in 1943, and six years later stripped it of its Latin American rhythm and instead emphasized its crisp wood timbre. The extent to which the clave in 1943 and 1949 is stylistically continuous is certainly debatable, but clearly

Naushad felt that the clave timbre in 1949 could add color and depth to the song without rhythmic intrusiveness. His use of the clave demonstrates a break from the tradition of adding layers of rhythm directly from Hollywood films, and instead he emphasizes timbre when rethinking ideas about the role, function, and potential of the instrument. C. Ramchandra and Shankar-Jaikishan may have been influenced by Naushad's emphasis on clave timbre and rhythm when they also used the clave similarly in their compositions a few years later.

As the Indian film industry expanded in the 1940s, a handful of composers and film musicians were influenced by jazz.[21] These composers established working relationships with local jazz musicians in Bombay and North India, including with the performers Chic Chocolate, Micky Correa, Frank Fernand, and many others who had the repertoire knowledge and musical skills these composers valued.[22] The departure of the British and the decline in war-related entertainment revenue compelled many jazz musicians to seek professional work in the film industry. Some of the most notable early collaborations occurred between jazz musician and composer Frank Fernand and music directors Naushad Ali and C. Ramchandra.[23] Fernand was important to the productivity of these relationships, later leading him to claim, "We arrangers did all the real work. They'd show off to the directors and producers and try to show that they were indispensable. But to be a music director, salesmanship was more important than musicianship."[24] Fernand performed jazz in India from at least 1936 when he traveled to Bombay to find work in one of the many dance bands at the time. His work included stints with Rudy Cotton and George Theodore.[25] In 1948 he led Frank Fernand and His All Star Band, performing in numerous cabarets and jazz performances in Bombay. He composed music for a number of films (including Konkani-language films) and arranged several jazz pieces for live performance, including the opening number for the Bombay Swing Club concert in 1948. It featured themes from Duke Ellington's "In a Sentimental Mood,"[26] and he titled the work "Prabhat," possibly an allusion to the Indian film production company of the same name.[27] His experiences composing in the local Bombay entertainment industry undoubtedly influenced his work in films. C. Ramchandra also worked with Goan trumpeter Chic Chocolate (a staple dance band musician and bandleader from the early 1940s), Francis Vaz, and Mike Machado. These musicians played jazz in live venues, and sometimes shared the stage with Teddy Weatherford and Roy Butler.[28]

Live Cabarets

The thematic designs of live Bombay cabarets may have influenced these four composers' compositional approach to film cabaret sequences. Patrons in live Bombay cabarets often wore formal Western dress. Menu items were eclectic and international. Imported alcohol was frequently available. Art deco stage designs were common. Dance and drink were encouraged. Jazz orchestras composed of musicians who could read staff notation and accompany choreographed routines and informal dancing took the lead. Many of the orchestras mentioned in chapter 3 performed in cabarets. In the 1930s, Joseph Ghislerie's Orchestra from France was one of the first foreign groups to perform in hotel cabarets. The orchestra arrived in Bombay in November 1933.[29] A year later, Crickett's Symphonians accompanied a variety of cabarets at the Taj Mahal Palace Hotel after Ghislerie's departure. Leon Abby and His Boys may have most effectively mastered the skills necessary to perform in cabarets at the hotel and carefully synchronized their efforts with stage performers in the mid-1930s.[30] In 1936, according to the *Times of India*:

> It is sometimes easier to make a first class entertainment when the material is not too rich. Among the lavish cabaret shows at the Taj, it is not always the most diverse in numbers that is the most successful. With the present Cabaret, Leon Abby and his Boys have got their ideas synchronized with the artistes (who have been here long enough to settle down) and the result is a very smooth show.[31]

Another 1936 *Times of India* article notes that cabarets were pervasive in Bombay, overtaking other popular entertainment such as the theater: "There is little wonder that few theatrical companies are seen in Bombay these last five years, for the cabaret habit must have absorbed all the available artists."[32] By the 1940s, cabarets were professionally arranged and managed with the intention of achieving commercial divertissement; they were designed to attract large audiences, not just a small circle of connoisseurs or foreign audiences.[33] To be sure, Bombay cabarets were by no means the only source for cabaret scenes in films. The film vamp dancer Helen Richardson Khan, who first performed in Raj Kapoor's *Awara* (1951), claims that the inspiration for cabaret or nightclub scenes in the 1950s came from cabarets in other countries, including the Parisian establishments Folies Bergère and the Crazy Horse.[34] Film music composers also viewed cabaret scenes in foreign films for material and inspiration. Bombay cabarets, however, provided both material and resources.

Reviews in serial publications give a general idea of the compositional character of live cabarets in Bombay, and program booklets give a sense of thematic approach.[35] Cabarets often promoted themes that drew from foreign places or cultural identity, which possibly influenced film cabaret scenes more than anything else. Latin American themes were popular in live cabarets. The June 4, 1949, edition of the *Federation of Musicians* (India) serial brochure stressed that "the public go for Latin American stuff in a big way,"[36] and that "bands all over the country would do well to study the trend and stock up."[37] One of the first bands to organize Latin American cabarets with music, dance, and design that were tightly thematic throughout an entire evening was Jose Gadimbas and His Latin American Band.[38] The Taj Mahal Palace Hotel hired the band in late 1948 to perform in the main air-conditioned ballroom. The management of the hotel claimed that Gadimbas and other foreign performers were brought to Bombay "at considerable expense" and were part of an effort to "seize the opportunity . . . to restore some of the gaiety of old Bombay."[39] They arrived direct from high-end establishments in France, were often marketed as a Latin American group even though they were from Europe, and they performed Latin American or Spanish theme cabarets in collaboration with other orchestras and traveling entertainers.

Spanish pianist Jose Morato performed at the Taj Mahal Palace Hotel after the Gadimbas Band and organized cabarets that included titles such as "A Breath of Spain" (1950),[40] "Valencia" (1951),[41] "A Spanish Fantasy" (1951),[42] as well as many fiesta themes. Spanish and Latin American themes were conflated, and distinctions between the two were often unformulated. Micky Correa's Band sometimes accompanied Morato in Mexican-themed costumes, even when the music was not Mexican. Jose Morato performed on the piano and Solovox,[43] Spanish dancer Leonor Maria provided the dancing, and Correa accompanied much of the music with his full orchestra.

French, Arab, and Island themes were also popular. Gadimbas organized the music for a French-themed "Place Pigalle" (1949)[44] cabaret that featured a cancan performance (fig. 5.1). Correa later performed French-themed events at the hotel, including one on July 17, 1949, titled the "Quatorze Juillet a Montparnasse Grand Gala Dance" complete with "Chansons D'Amour" (love songs) and a French dinner (fig. 5.2).[45] The entertainment was provided by a number of groups and cabaret dancers, including Micky Correa and His Band and Goody Seervai and His Orchestra. The 1951 film *Valentino* popularized Arab themes. The

Figure 5.1. "Place Pigalle" program booklet, February 24, 1949. Personal collection of Micky Correa. Reproduced by permission from Christine Correa.

Figure 5.2. "Quatorze Juillet a Montparnasse" program booklet, July 14, 1949. Personal collection of Micky Correa. Reproduced by permission from Christine Correa.

Ambassador's Starlit Roof Garden held a recurring "Valentino Ball" throughout December of that year, and it included Valentino costume competitions. Ken Mac and His Band performed, but were advertised as "Sheik Ken Mac and His Sheiks."[46] Figure 5.3 shows the front page of the program booklet for the "South Sea Rhapsody" dance at the Taj Mahal Palace Hotel on January 27, 1949. The inside of the booklet mentions the subtheme, "Island Dream Cabaret." The music was performed by Jose Gadimbas and His Latin American Band and Micky Correa and His Band, and the dinner featured a "Salade Hula-Hula," a "Filet de Pomfret a la Samoa," and an after-dinner "Café des Isles."[47] In this instance, the island theme was reinforced in the description of the dinner, which was done commonly in cabaret booklets.[48]

French, Arab, Latin American, and Hawaiian themes, elaborate stage designs, and foreign bands transported audiences to glitzy, sophisticated, and exotic locales. Cabaret program booklets often showcased ornate imagery to further reinforce exotic event themes. Figure 5.4 reproduces the brochure of the cabaret "A Breath of Spain" at the Taj Mahal Palace Hotel.[49] A dancer accompanies a solo instrumentalist, both are in traditional dress, and their bodies seem to flow from the music. The dull red brick building in the background contains two archways. One lists the menu in Spanish and the other includes the lineup of performers. Organized by cabaret performer Peter Sarter, the event showcased the music of Micky Correa and His New Band and Jose Morato on the Solovox, along with five cabaret artists. This design promotes an outdoor celebration amid Spanish architecture and artists immersed in music and dance performance. Another program booklet printed in 1948 for a dinner and dance at the Taj Mahal Palace Hotel (fig. 5.5) evokes a colorful cabaret image with dancers on a deep stage, fronted by two audience members enjoying cocktails.[50] It stirs up images of perhaps Indian or Latin American dance and brings to mind some of the more elaborate film songs–dance sequences with deep stages and multiple performers. Difficulty in distinguishing between the origins of costume, dance, and setting of these graphic designs is symbolic of the eclectic array of styles found in the music and dances of cabarets.

Hindi film stars occasionally performed in cabarets. One of the earliest documented instances I found occurred at the Taj Mahal Palace Hotel on May 10, 1951. Ken Mac and His Orchestra and Micky Correa and His New Band accompanied Nutan, who at the time was a young up-and-coming heroine who had acted in the films *Hamari Beti* (1950), *Hum Log* (1951), and *Nagina* (1951). She later became a highly successful actress, and is

Figure 5.3. "South Sea Rhapsody" program booklet, January 27, 1949. Personal collection of Micky Correa. Reproduced by permission from Christine Correa.

Figure 5.4. "A Breath of Spain" cabaret brochure. Personal collection of Micky Correa. Reproduced by permission from Christine Correa.

billed in the performance as a "film starlet" and an "Indian Beauty Queen" because she had won a number of beauty competitions by this date.[51] The evening was billed as her singing debut. After an opening cabaret act, she danced to music performed by Micky Correa's orchestra, and concluded the evening as the lead vocalist with Ken Mac's band, singing duos with Jean Stratham, a well-known Bombay singer. Not coincidentally, Nutan performed two song-and-dance sequences in the film *Nagina* the same year that draw heavily from swing music and dance, which I will address later. The proprietors of the Taj Mahal Palace Hotel recognized the rising popularity of the Hindi film industry and booked the entertainment accordingly. Unfortunately, no recordings exist, and events with prominent film stars were rare.

In at least one instance a film music composer composed cabaret music. Vasant Desai, whose career began in the mid-1940s, wrote the music performed by Micky Correa and Jose Morato at The Taj Mahal Palace Hotel for Republic Day on January 25, 1951.[52] The theme of the evening was "The Triumph of Life: A Ballet," and the well-known author Mulk Raj Anand wrote the story. It addressed the tension between the simplicity and morality of village life and the complicated, urbane life of the city, which

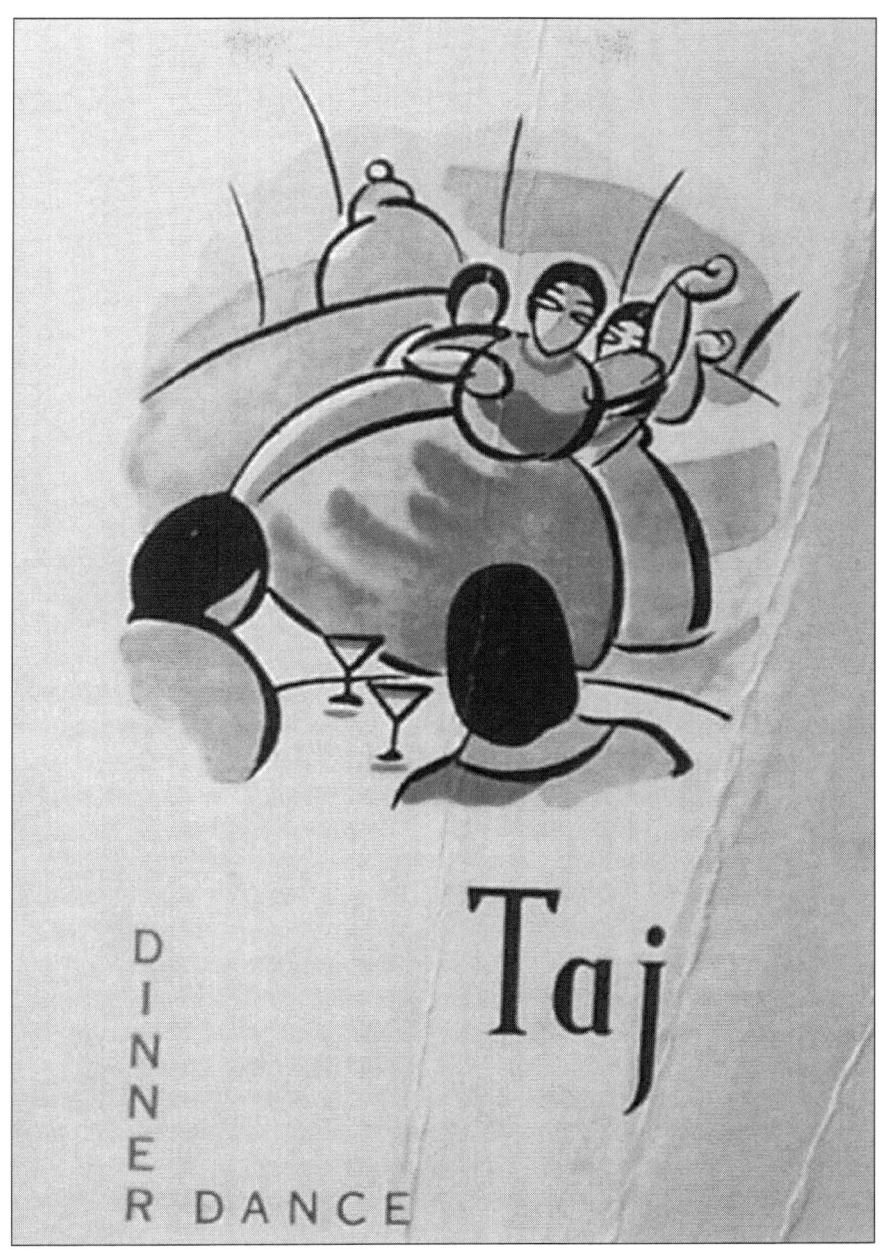

Figure 5.5. "Taj Dinner Dance" cabaret brochure, September 30, 1948. Personal collection of Micky Correa. Reproduced by permission from Christine Correa.

is sometimes a theme in Hindi films. Vasant Desai was not known for composing in a Western style.[53] Though it is frustrating that we have no recordings of these performances, the scale on which this event was organized reflects the increasing popularity of film songs across a broad spectrum of audiences.

Recording Film Music

Before the mid-1930s, film actors performed songs on a soundstage, and accompanying musicians played into the same microphones, but outside the range of the camera.[54] Early films were largely a matter of recording a single event on sets delicately choreographed to fit the needs of filmed stagecraft. By some measures, these early Indian films continued to be conceived as if actors were performing on a theater stage. These practices were framed around the demands of simultaneous recording, which followed the conventions of live music drama performances. After the mid-1930s, songs were recorded before the filming of the scene and under better quality conditions in sound studios, which separated the production of the songs from that of the films, and lifted recordings as a stand-alone industry. Gregory Booth notes that this system "became the central concept and key process in the system of use, the interwoven sets of attitudes, practices, and cultural values that defined the Hindi cinema and its music," and continued for decades.[55] At this point, film music became a critical component of the sound reproduction industry in India, and the model of recording popular songs in films for dissemination on records became standard. Films profoundly influenced the infrastructures and practices of the popular music of India and became a primary platform for the dissemination of popular music. In theory, if both the songs and the film became popular, then each lifted the sale of the other. The Bollywood music industry thus became a production center for film soundtracks, a support structure for much of the continent's popular music, and a revenue source for composers and recording musicians. Some of the most successful jazz musicians worked in both the film song business and the domestic jazz economy.

During World War II, businesses and individuals who profited from war-related industries invested in film productions. This new flow of capital caused increases in the salaries paid to artists and encouraged freelancing and competition among musicians and singers.[56] Furthermore, as the

music director began to achieve celebrity status in the 1940s, the new positions of musical assistant and arranger emerged, and according to Alison
Arnold, music directors came to rely more heavily on arrangers for "orches-
tral arrangement, copying of instrumental parts and even conducting in
the recording studios."[57] Expanded availability of jobs in the film industry,
including in gramophone studios, and a demand for trained instrumentalists and arrangers brought an increase in employment possibilities, and
some of these arrangers were local jazz bandleaders.

Jazz musicians often viewed work in the film industry in a negative
light, clearly the case among many members of the Indian chapter of the
Federation of Musicians. Local jazz and classical musicians in Bombay
organized the chapter in January 1947. Led by saxophonist Ken Keenan,
it did not typically advocate Indian music, including film music. The federation started a publication that year to disseminate information relevant
to musicians in India, especially in Bombay. The publication content and
member issues were primarily relevant to jazz musicians, at least for its first
few years. The front-page editorial of the October 27, 1948, edition claims
that the main function of the federation was to create a union-like organization to help combat the declining level of musicianship and the use of
foreign bands in hotels.[58] Sensing further marginalization because of the
increased presence of traveling foreign musicians, the federation advised,
"Musicians must make themselves so proficient as to obviate the necessity
for the importation of Dances Bands, local Dance Bands must immediately
implement a programme of self-improvement."[59] Some of this sentiment
was probably a reaction to the strategy of the Taj Mahal Palace Hotel to hire
foreign bands that were considered a better draw, more proficient, and
even more economically viable because many came from postwar Europe,
where jobs were scarce.[60] The editorial also claims that in post-Indepen-
dence India a "reshuffling of the Profession [was] inevitable," and that
musicians should band together: "With the reduction of sources of income
and without a corresponding reduction of wage earners, jungle law will dic-
tate the economic rape of Musicians by Musicians . . . and many belts will
require tightening unless all Musicians band together immediately in pur-
suit of a common goal of assured economic security."[61] The federation also
addressed prohibition and its effects on the marketability of dance band
musicians and the profitability of jazz venues. A series of restrictions on the
sales of alcohol began in 1946 and peaked in 1949 with the passing of the
Bombay Prohibition Act. Prohibition laws heavily affected the profitability
of hotels and other entertainment venues.

These challenges compelled many musicians to record with the film song industry to earn extra income. The Federation of Musicians criticized musicians who worked for film studios. Speaking about the decline in available dance band jobs in public venues in Bombay, the same editorial implied that dance band musicians might be forced to take more film studio jobs and saturate the film market with more proficient musicians: "Musicians who are employed by Film Companies' Recording Studios, and so on might smirk . . . but their present satisfaction will avail them nothing once Dance Musicians are forced to other avenues of income."[62] These strong sentiments suggest divided attitudes about respectability between public dance band musicians and film studio musicians. Many jazz musicians considered film music unsuitable material.[63] Reuben Soloman and Roy Butler claim they were asked to record film songs in the 1940s while in the studio. Soloman complained that when his orchestra went to a studio to record jazz, the management "always insisted . . . [they] play the latest film hits—very unsuitable."[64] Yet an increasing number of musicians embraced the income potential of the film industry after Indian Independence. Joe Gomes, a saxophonist working in Bombay before and after Independence, asserted that before the reorientation of the jazz economy, "Good musicians had no time for films."[65] But his attitude apparently changed in the years after 1947, when making a living performing in dance bands was increasingly difficult.

By contrast, other musicians and jazz critics appreciated the innovative character of film music and respected its creativity and popular appeal. In 1948 H. J. Collet wrote in the *Illustrated Weekly of India* that the future of jazz depended on an eclectic Indian film industry. He admitted that the outlook of jazz in India was in question and he attached its continued viability to the film industry because "young Indian musicians [are] beginning to appreciate [jazz], which has been influencing in turn the light, catchy music served up by the Indian cinema." Collet boasts that some Indian film music is cutting-edge in style and character, and contrasts it to classical music and its "older school of Indian musicians, steeped in their own tradition, [who] look upon jazz with abhorrence."[66] Viewing the development of film music in a positive light, he suggested that film songs were in their infancy, and would likely develop into a more mature style. He claimed that the possibility of the continued growth of jazz was at least partially dependent on innovative composers in the film music industry. He emphasized that dance band musicians had arranged the popular song "Sunday Ke Sunday" from the film *Shehnai* (1947) into quick foxtrots and rumbas in live performances, which were met by audiences with reserved enthusiasm. He also related the development of film music with the early development of jazz in the 1920s, which he claimed lacked serious content but eventually matured into standardized styles that appealed to large audiences. Conflating the history of film music with the history of jazz paid tribute to film music's popular appeal and innovative character, but at the same time diminished its value by linking it to notions of infancy.

Composing Film Music

This section examines a small cross section of key film songs of the four composers discussed above. I focus on songs that feature instruments such as the saxophone, trumpet, drum set, claves, maracas, guitar, conga or bongo drums, and acoustic bass. The use of swing, Latin American rhythms, the blue note, and stylistic features such as a busy or ragtime-style piano style or percussive emphasis on beats 2 and 4 (sometimes referred to as a backbeat) are also featured in the songs I examine. For our purposes, I consider these characteristics to be within the broad realm of commercialized jazz, especially as it was heard in Hollywood film music. It should be noted that Naushad Ali, C. Ramchandra, and Shankar-Jaikishan did not necessarily consume jazz outside of their work in the film industry. C. Ramchandra attended cabarets in Bombay, and program booklets and newspaper advertisements sometimes noted his attendance at performances at the Taj Mahal Palace Hotel and other venues,[67] but he was largely an interested observer. Successful film song composers did not need to be jazz connoisseurs because the masses of filmgoers determined a song's success, not jazz aficionados. The profit potential from the collective imaginaries of the masses of filmgoers was paramount. Before I begin my analysis of songs, I should mention that the Latin American popular music I reference in this chapter was typically from Hollywood films. I found no evidence that jazz musicians or film song composers extensively listened to music directly from South or Central America.[68]

Songs in the first three Hindi films I reference did not necessarily take place in cabaret or nightclub scenes, but they reveal that jazzy characteristics were heard in films as early as 1943. Some of the first such characteristics were introduced by Naushad Ali. In his 1943 film *Kanoon*, the song "Ek Tu Ho Ek Main Hoon," which I mentioned earlier, showcases a prominent Latin American 3/2 clave preceded by a busy piano introduction that hints at early piano rags, perhaps "The Entertainer" by Scott Joplin. Dense piano fills are featured in the background during much of the song, and harmonic movements emphasize exaggerated back-and-forth drive between tonic and dominant chords. Quick syncopations and full, repeating, unarpeggiated chords add harmonic depth and rhythmic inertia. The piano is out of tune. Considering the care given to piano tuning heard in other compositions at the time, it may have been deliberately tweaked, to indicate the sonic imagery of a raw, slightly out-of-tune ragtime upright piano. The quick syncopations also hint at ragtime. The song features a solo muted trumpet at the beginning that later provides background material and intermittent, brief solo breaks. These passing solos sometimes form the second half of a catchy melody introduced by the voice, creating the feel of a duet. The muted trumpet weaves in and out of the entire song, but never parallels the melodic movement of the voice, suggesting that Naushad was interested in its potential as a jazzy solo or improvisational instrument, a compositional approach that he used over the years. It may not be coincidental that Shankar-Jaikishan and Ramchandra use the muted trumpet for introductory, solo formulaic material and to provide improvisatory breaks between vocal lines later in the decade.

Anmol Ghadi (1946), also composed by Naushad Ali, features some of the most popular music in the history of Hindi cinema.[69] Similar to "Ek Tu Ho Ek Main Hoon" in *Kanoon*, the song "Man Leta Hai Angdai" in *Anmol Ghadi* also carries the pronounced 3/2 clave throughout, and begins with a solo muted trumpet fanfare. A tambourine (or some type of metal rattle) performs a Latin rhythm in $^4_4$ that emphasizes beats 1 and 3, with two eighth notes leading to each of these two beats. This pattern is often performed on the shaker, maracas, or shekeré in Latin American music in Hollywood films, and is showcased in a number of Carmen Miranda films, including the song "Week-End in Havana" from the film of the same name (1941). It is possible that Naushad borrowed rhythmic ideas directly from Miranda's songs in the film, which had been screened in Bombay a few years earlier. He uses the rhythmic pattern effectively, and it gives the piece drive. He uses Indian drums, probably the tabla drums, to emphasize beats 4 and 1, which adds a layer of anticipation to the downbeat. The tambourine and tabla drums layered together stress anticipation leading to and resolution at the downbeat, thus giving a strong, repeating ostinato-style foundation on which the strings, woodwinds, and voice can offer a memorable, singable melody. A muted trumpet break toward the beginning and a Hawaiian guitar break later hint at Naushad's continued interest in integrating improvisatory solo material into the ensemble focus. (Perhaps not coincidentally, this strategy is used in the song "The Nango" from *Week-End in Havana*.) The muted trumpet alternates between staccato and sustained notes in virtuosic melodic lines, giving a depth of technique that is pronounced, yet not overbearing. It functions largely as filler during pauses in the voice. The vocal melodies are uncluttered by instrumental contrasts or layered rhythmic material, and the instrumentation typically parallels the melodic movement of the voice. The lyrics are important to the larger narrative plot, and Naushad respects their role through a compositional strategy that gives room to the voice, yet still offers a feeling of jazz improvisation at appropriate moments.

Another of Naushad's pieces, "Suhani Raat Dhal Chuki" from the film *Dulari* (1949), showcases the melancholy hero, Suresh, strumming a small stringed instrument, heard as a guitar on the soundtrack. The guitar sets the mood with a slow V–I harmonic progression on open chords with unfretted notes (sometimes now called "cowboy chords") that lead to the downbeat. This gives the guitar sustain and volume. Claves emphasize beats 4 and 1 in a four-beat meter, a rhythmic pattern often performed on a drum in many other Hindi film songs. The clave is very pronounced, and Naushad seems to emphasize its timbre as much as the rhythmic movement. One instrumental break showcases muted trumpets and jazzy clarinets, both using heavy vibrato, and the trumpet supports recurring minor tonalities. Brass instruments, including the muted trumpet, are prominent and signal a jazzy style, and the stringed instruments take a secondary role for much of the piece. Many songs during this era use high-pitched violins or other string instruments during instrumental breaks between vocal lines, but in this song we hear either a guitar or wind instruments (usually a trumpet). The tempo is quite slow, and Naushad effectively uses the dawdling muted trumpet in conjunction with symphonic style backing and the sparse, repetitive claves to establish musical layers that evoke a gloomy sentiment. As with Naushad's earlier pieces, the trumpet does not parallel the melodic movement of the voice, but adds brief improvisatory interludes. He uses the guitar in a similar fashion. By contrast, a sitar or other stringed instrument often parallels the voice quietly in the background. Naushad again seems to use jazzy sounds and instruments such as the trumpet and guitar to emphasize or ornament through interludes or solo activity rather than integration into parallel ensemble sections. With the reconfigured clave pattern, we see new ways of thinking about the relationship between the clave and Latin rhythms, but the muted trumpet continues Naushad's strategy at evoking a brief feel of improvisation during vocal breaks.

Jazz musicians in Bombay at the time felt that Naushad had adapted well to Western music, and many applauded his use of large orchestras and efforts at eclecticism. His songs were described in an anonymous article in the *Federation of Musicians* in 1949 as "a vast improvement of the existing standard of music."[70] Not coincidentally, one of Naushad's earliest arrangers was violinist Josique Menzies,[71] who performed in a number of jazz orchestras, including with Teddy Weatherford and His Band in 1938. As mentioned above, Naushad also used the talents of trumpeter Frank Fernand, who arranged jazz and swing pieces for Bombay Swing Club performances in 1949. Fernand knew the styles of the most recognized jazz musicians of the time, a marketable skill in the film industry.[72]

C. Ramchandra employed techniques similar to Naushad's use of syncopated accents on the piano, Latin American rhythms, a muted trumpet for introductory material, and solo instruments to finish vocal lines, often with a jazzy feel. Ramchandra's song "Koi Kisi Ka Deewana Na Bane" from the film *Sargam* (1950) features a club with a full dance band accompanying the actress Rehana performing a solo piece. The stage is decorated in a cruise ship theme with art deco accents. An audience sits on the opposite end of the stage. The dance band sits on a bandstand immediately behind the singer. The male musicians are in white tuxes, and sit on a tiered stage. The instrumentation includes violins, a saxophone, a trumpet, an upright bass, a guitar, a drum set, and a piano. Rehana is positioned as if she is a crooner and a member of the orchestra. Her voice is certainly the most prominent melodic feature, and the ensemble interludes increase in density and volume only when she is not singing. The song begins with a solo voice line augmented with upward moving arpeggiated chords on the piano that span a large tonal range. These runs are layered beneath the vocal line, and add a unique timbre quality beneath her voice. Later, the piano is visually emphasized with close-up shots that focus on the pianist and showcase a syncopated rhythm on unarppegiated chords almost entirely on the offbeats, perhaps again hinting at a ragtime rhythmic feel. The volume of the piano increases during these close-up shots, probably done in post-production, and is dynamically emphasized as the cinematography dictates.[73]

Ramchandra extensively embraced Latin American music. In "Koi Kisi Ka Deewana Na Bane" he focused on the castanets, which articulate a repetitive tumbao-like progression, a pattern used in Latin dance music that forms the basic rhythm of the conga and emphasizes the last two eighth notes of a $\frac{4}{4}$ bar. The castanets are a percussion instrument, usually a pair of concave wood shells connected on one end by a string. They are played with the hands and are clicked together to create a short, sharp sound, often providing an ostinato. The pattern in this song is in a $\frac{4}{4}$ meter, with two sixteenth notes leading to beat 2 and an emphasis on beat 4 and its offbeat. The castanets are cautious and unobtrusive. Carmen Miranda's films may have played a role in Ramchandra's compositional approach at this time, at least with reference to the use of rhythmic ostinatos. A number of songs from the film *Copacabana* (1947), released in India two years before *Sargam*, feature this tumbao feel, though not on the castanets, including "My Heart Was Doing the Bolero" and "He Hasn't Got a Thing to Sell." The Latin American elements in "Koi Kisi Ka Deewana Na Bane" are understated, adding color and rhythmic support, in contrast to Naushad's earlier pieces discussed above, which were much more obvious in their Latin American influence.

We also see subtle use of Latin American music in Ramchandra's 1949 song "Pehle Toh Ho Gayi, Namaste, Namaste" from the film *Patanga* (1949). It includes Latin bongos played with sticks, a technique seen in a number of compositions at the time, including Shankar-Jaikishan's song "Patli Kamar Hai" from the film *Barsaat* discussed below. Bongo or timbale drum rolls performed during key musical moments emphasize the downbeats. Similar to "Koi Kisi Ka Deewana Na Bane," a piano plays prominent upward moving melodic runs to emphasize transitions to new sections. An instrument, possibly a tambourine, plays the Latin maraca rhythm, which is featured prominently. This example also includes a muted trumpet, which had become a key stylistic technique first introduced by Naushad.

Ramchandra explored tone color, texture, and timbre along with Latin American rhythmic characteristics. The song sequence "Sunday ke Sunday" from the 1947 film *Shehnai* composed by Ramchandra is set in a staged performance venue with a seated audience. It begins with a bluesy guitar lick with a rough tone quality, followed by a brief harmonica passage that almost blares, giving it a unique texture. The song at times emphasizes beats 2 and 4 on a drum set and includes sparse fills on the snare drum to accent some of the vocal nuances. Toward the end of the song the drum set provides almost continuous fill activity on the snare drum, perhaps mimicking the improvisational style of the drum set in jazz. A busy repetitive piano style is heard at times throughout the piece. We are also treated to bongos in the background that execute drum breaks reminiscent of drum fills in jazz; sometimes a jazzy clarinet lick provides the fill. A banjo often parallels the vocal melody. The diverse array of instruments and timbre in this piece suggest that Ramchandra was interested in tone quality, layering, and brief instrumental motifs to create an implied jazzy sound. Dance band rearrangements of this piece were briefly popular in live venues in Bombay and Calcutta at the time.

The composer duo Shankar-Jaikishan also explored the relationship between staccato and sustained notes on the muted trumpet, brief arpeggiated piano runs, and Latin American sounds in their compositions. They worked extensively with the actor Raj Kapoor, and together produced over twenty films. As Raj Kapoor's popularity increased, so did his power and influence on the content of songs in his films. Their first collaboration was in the 1949 film *Barsaat*, which demonstrates heavy use of instrumental solos and eclectic dance. The song "Patli Kamar Hai" is set in a cabaret with a large dance floor for the actress Nimmi to perform a mix of Indian and Western dance styles, including some moves loosely analogous to the style of Carmen Miranda, as well as some flamenco mixed with swing and formal ballroom dancing. She is dressed in a Latin-esque costume, while Kapoor is in a tuxedo. The beginning shot focuses on a jazz orchestra seated at a bandstand, complete with a drum set, upright bass, saxophone, guitar, violin, trumpet, and a maraca player. The music contains a prominent 3/2 clave throughout the piece, as well as maracas and bongos, strongly establishing a simple and recognizable Latin American feel, a technique similar to Naushad's compositional approach four years earlier in *Kanoon*.

The piece begins with a solo trumpet fanfare, with the camera emerging outward from the trumpet bell, a shot that occupies the whole screen. This introductory material is technically challenging, and intermixes staccato patterns with sustained tones in a descending melodic contour, effectively transitioning into ensemble orchestration. The trumpeter turns, and we briefly see his dark silhouetted profile; he then returns to the bandstand. Male patrons sit around the dance floor in tuxes, accompanied by women in formal dress. After the trumpet introduction, maracas, claves, and a drum together perform a basic tumbao rhythm, sometimes accented with syncopated, staccato piano hits in a repetitive rhythm similar to the maraca pattern. The clave is heavily accented, probably the result of conscious sound production techniques used to highlight the Latin feel. At times the timbales provide thick rhythmic fills that drive forward with sixteenth notes on rim shots. Rim shots are a technique in which the wood stick used to strike the drum hits both the drumhead and the rim at the same time, which creates a sharp accented sound. These are often done to emphasize Nimmi's dance moves, and are quick and somewhat improvisatory. Muted trumpet solos act as musical interludes, creating a transition between sections with heavy, layered orchestrated rhythms and more sparse vocal sections. To be sure, Shankar-Jaikishan used Indian instruments as well in this sequence. When the cabaret scene briefly transitions to a rural setting, which occurs from time to time, Shankar-Jaikishan add Indian instruments such as the tabla drums to sonically represent a more traditional village backdrop. *Barsaat* (1949) was one of the top five commercial successes of the 1940s. According to Gregory Booth, "The success of *Barsaat* and the subsequent ongoing success of the 'Kapoor brand' as both actor and producer/director positioned Shankar-Jaikishan to effect historical change because it encouraged other film producers to hire them as well."[74] Beginning with *Barsaat*, Kapoor helped design song-dance sequences with a strong jazzy or Latin sound, and his efforts may have inspired others to follow suit.

Cabaret scenes such as those seen in *Barsaat* often featured diverse styles from across the globe to catch audience attention, and their stylistic characteristics were influenced by any number of commercialized (or noncommercialized) music genres or performance practices, including Indian classical, semiclassical, and folk forms. Early cabaret scenes often focused on distinctions between the rich and the poor, the old-fashioned and the modern, and sometimes served as a model of comparison to traditional India through decadent images.[75] Cabaret music and images contained meanings relevant to the narrative framework of films, and jazzy sounds often reinforced these frameworks and structures. These scenes fulfilled audience expectations about class and gender relations because, in part, men and women drank and danced together in tuxes and formal dresses, and interaction between the sexes was less restricted. Film audiences did not have access to these lifestyles, so cabaret scenes were fantasies unreachable to most, which was likely part of their appeal.[76]

Shankar-Jaikishan later composed in a jazzy style without Kapoor. The film *Nagina* (1951), starring Nutan and Nasir Khan, features the song "Humse Koi Pyar Karo Ji" and an all-female dance band dressed in sailor outfits. In this sequence the audience sits to one side, the dance band is on the opposite end on a raised stage, and between both is the choreographed dance routine. The dance evokes strong characteristics of swing and stereotyped hula dancing, and both are mixed with a Latin American and classical Indian dance flair. A pronounced close-up of a maraca player ensures that the viewer sees the Latin instrument. The music features the clarinet (in a manner perhaps reminiscent of Benny Goodman) and saxophone, a strong backbeat, and a prominent double bass line.

Instrumentation includes a saxophone, clarinet, maracas, trumpet, upright bass, drum set, and upright piano. With the band members visually jamming (foot-tapping included), Nutan enters in a Latin American dress followed by a conga line of female dancers mimicking Carmen Miranda's well-known alternating hand-to-elbow visual. The music begins with a quick ostinato on the upright bass. The strings are plucked and layered with a swing rhythm on the high hat of the drum set. This ends quickly with the entrance of Nutan and a group of backup dancers. The drum set then emphasizes beasts 2 and 4 on the snare drum, and the walking bass line is made more prominent in the mix for brief periods of a beat or two. This rhythmic foundation is further layered by a clarinet playing improvisatory melodic fills with bending notes that cover a wide melodic range, emphasizing the high end at points between vocal lines. The drum set, walking bass line, and clarinet effectively create a swing feel, which Shankar-Jaikishan are sure to emphasize for brief interludes throughout the piece. Less often, the saxophone is accentuated with quick licks during instrumental ensemble sections. The song ends with a descending solo clarinet line that showcases a good degree of performance virtuosity.

Another song, "Tumko Apni Zindagi" is stylistically different from "Hum Se Koi Pyar Karo Ji," but the use of the claves, the muted trumpet, and piano runs suggest that Shankar-Jaikishan paid attention to certain stylistic attributes across a broad spectrum of songs, even pieces that were not overtly jazzy or influenced by Latin American music. This sequence does not take place in a cabaret or a setting with an audience, but it suggests that Shankar-Jaikishan gave increased attention to timbre in many of their songs. The song begins with piano chords that emphasize harmonic movements sustained over two beats in a $\frac{4}{4}$ meter, and ends with an ascending melodic run across wide-ranging notes. This introductory material introduces orchestrated strings and a voice, once interspersed with a Hawaiian guitar bend on a single note. The clave (or another instrument with a similar timbre quality) emphasizes beats 1, the offbeat of beat 2, and beat 4, with variations. This is not a 2/3 clave, but an accented pattern often heard on a tabla drum. We also hear quiet muted trumpet runs occasionally in the background. As with Naushad's music in *Dulari*, it seems Shankar-Jaikishan seek to emphasize timbre here rather than Latin rhythms. At least once we briefly hear a descending piano roll that leads into the downbeat, which in this instance creates quick ornamentation and anticipation of the downbeat rather than a jazzy sound. Shankar-Jaikishan likely reconfigured a piano run technique used in Carmen Miranda's films to emphasize rhythmic anticipation and provide embellishment.

Other nightclub scenes composed by Shankar-Jaikishan showcase less explicit jazzy sounds, but demonstrate their ability to compose through subtle use of formulaic material. In the 1951 Raj Kapoor film *Awaara*, the song "Ek Do Teen" is set in a smoky nightclub with informal interaction between men and women, intimate eye contact between a female solo dancer and male patrons, and rowdy customers. Set in an underground, somewhat seedy nightclub, the dance hints at elements from the Apache dance. The song begins with a solo trumpet, which by 1951 had become common in compositions that accompanied Westernized cabarets scenes. The trumpet features sustained notes briefly intermixed with staccato patterns, thus giving a reconfigured fanfare feel reminiscent of "Patli Kamar Hai" in *Barsaat*. The trumpet is used only for this purpose, and is not heard later in the song. Composed in a $\frac{4}{4}$ meter, a strong tambourine over a crisp clave sound create rhythmic drive and emphasize the beat. Another song, "Tere Bina Aag Yeh Chandani," contains intermittent jazz-like orchestrations at the beginning, with a prominent xylophone presence. Later, the xylophone showcases rolled notes on the downbeat played with two mallets, which emphasize unique percussion performance techniques. The beginning section also includes brief clarinet runs. Similar to *Nagina*, the clarinet covers a wide melodic range with bent notes to give a jazzy blue-note feel, and often fills spaces between vocal lines. By the time of *Awaara*, Shankar-Jaikishan were effective in the formulaic use of the trumpet and clarinet, and emphasized timbre, melody, and rhythm to give unobtrusive variety and range of sounds. By 1951, the muted trumpet had been codified as an instrument used in cabaret scenes to add a feeling of improvisation and to provide brief solo material between vocal lines. Also by 1951, the solo clarinet had been regularly used to cover wide interval ranges that filled in spaces between vocal lines, and the claves were featured in a variety of rhythms.

One of the most interesting musical relationships occurred between Goan jazz trumpeter Chic Chocolate and composer C. Ramchandra. Their professional rapport was highly productive and their collaborations resulted in compositions that featured both foreign and Indian stylistic elements. Chocolate was an important figure in the local Bombay music economy. He first played in the 1930s with the Spotlights, often at Green's Hotel in Bombay. African American trumpeter Bill Coleman, who was playing with Leon Abby at the nearby Taj Mahal Palace Hotel at the same time, inspired Chocolate.[77] He later performed with saxophonist Vince Cummine and bandleader-saxophonist Rudy Cotton in Bombay and hill stations. He recorded twenty tracks between 1943 and 1945 under the name Chic and His Music Makers with Columbia Records in Calcutta. Most were covers of Hollywood film songs, including a few rumbas such as "She's a Bombshell from Brooklyn" and "You Discover You're in New York." Chocolate's posture, demeanor, and physical appearance were also said to have resembled those of Louis Armstrong, and he was listed in program booklets and newspapers as the "Louis Armstrong of India."[78] Such comparisons to musicians from the United States were common,[79] and Chocolate consciously promoted and benefited from this evocation of Armstrong's sound and image.

The music for the film *Albela* (1951) illustrates the influence of both Hollywood film songs and local dance band musicians on a music composer's sound palate. Ramchandra wrote the music score for *Albela* with the assistance of Chic Chocolate. Cawas Lord, Chocolate's drummer at the time, provided the Latin rhythms using Latin drums he obtained from Jose Gadimbas at the Taj Mahal Hotel.[80] The music, dance, stage proxemics, and costumes in a number of sequences in *Albela* are similar to material seen in musical segments performed by Carmen Miranda in Hollywood films such as "I Like to Be Loved by You" from the film *Greenwich Village* (1944), "Batucada" from the film *If I'm Lucky* (1946), and "Tico Tico no Fuba" from the film *Copacabana* (1947).[81] Many of Geeta Bali's dance solos in *Albela* include brief yet pronounced and quick samba-style footwork. Miranda had been popular for a decade by the time *Albela* was produced, and Miranda impersonators in cabarets were active in a number of cities, especially Bombay. The cabaret duo of the time "Mirabai and Severyn" performed regular cabaret shows that included impersonations of Carmen Miranda at the West End Hotel in Bombay the same year *Albela* was released.[82]

Ramchandra uses a number of musical characteristics that mirror some of the works of Naushad Ali and Shankar-Jaikishan, such as solo muted trumpet introductory material, a 3/2 clave, and a maraca rhythm, but he also incorporates his own unique musical approach. Ramchandra's work demonstrates a strong interest in innovation grounded in stylistic continuity, especially in the song sequence "Dil Dhadke Nazar Sharmaye" from *Albela*. In a $\frac{4}{4}$ meter, the beginning of the song emphasizes the piano on the pickup to the second beat with a quick rolling melodic pattern, which gives us a Latin American feel, and is a feature heard in musical segments in Miranda's films *Copacabana* and *That Night in Rio.* Syncopated rhythms on the piano in the background of the song, especially accents on the off-beat of beats 2 and 4, mirror staccato patterns typically played on a drum in other songs of the era. These offbeats on the piano usually occur in the background, but are often amplified at key moments to add emphasis. Later, the piano accents random offbeats, often between vocal lines to add improvisatory feel, and mirror some of Naushad's early works that emphasize solo improvisatory-feeling material to fill in the spaces between vocal melodies. The song also incorporates a driving maraca rhythm on beat 2, its offbeat, and beat 3, as well as beat 4, its offbeat, and beat 1. Ramchandra uses piano rolls in another *Albela* song, titled "Mere Dil Ke Ghadi," that has antecedents in some of Naushad's and Shankar-Jaikishan's earlier works discussed above.

Albela also features Hawaiian music. The song-dance sequence "Shola jo Bhadke" begins with a close-up of a drum played like a Latin American conga. The drum rhythm is repetitive, and lines of dancers perform complex clapping rhythms. It is set on a beach with a fire that provides a strobe effect, and dancers wear Hawaiian shirts complete with leis and hula dancing. This dance sequence follows global interest in Hawaii and Hawaiian themes in films at the time.[83] Dozens of tracks of Hawaiian or Hawaiian-inspired music had been recorded by this time in India, largely in Calcutta, and Hawaiian-themed cabarets were common in Bombay by the date of the production of *Albela*.[84] Tau Moe was probably the most recognized Hawaiian performer in India. He performed in Calcutta, Bombay, and other urban centers for years. Other groups including the Aloha Boys popularized the slide guitar (also called the Hawaiian guitar) in India, which became part of the sound palette of Hindi films.

By the mid-1950s, cabaret and nightclub scenes were an important component of many successful films. Audience expectations of these scenes soared, and the sheer number from this period are extraordinary. Especially sophisticated, elaborate, and noteworthy scenes were viewed in films by Raj Kapoor, who by this time was an enormously successful actor. Regardless of composer, his films often contained at least one cabaret or nightclub segment. These sequences were elaborately choreographed and sometimes included two or more contrasting segments in a single dance, with costume changes and a shift in musical style. The song "Mud Mud Ke Na Dekh" from the successful 1955 film *Shree 420* is perhaps most striking.

Composed by Shankar-Jaikishan, it begins with a short fanfare that features the ukulele and segues into a waltz with dancers entering the stage dressed in formalwear. The Rumba Boys, a Goan group performing in Bombay at the time, are featured in the background on a bandstand. Dance choreography hints at ballet and the ballroom waltz, all performed by female dancers but focused on the actress Nadira.

About halfway through the song, a transition segment begins with Raj Kapoor unwittingly dragged onto the stage by Nadira, who begins a quasi-flamenco dance as he stands bewildered. His unsure response is brief. The lights go down. He grabs a trumpet and plays a brief solo improvisatory introduction as dancers enter in Latin costumes. The trumpet provides transitional material to this new section, and is reminiscent of Shankar-Jaikishan's technical approach to "Patli Kamar Hai" in *Barsaat*, in which he uses staccato patterns to show off technical ability and virtuosity in improvisation. Kapoor then becomes the crooner and object of the attention of flirtatious dancers. Next we hear an introductory roll on the tambourine that transitions into the Latin rhythms. This pattern is tighter than earlier compositions of Shankar-Jaikishan, with less sustained rattle and more staccato, especially on beats 2 and 4. Trumpet improvisations between vocal lines complete the display of technical ability on the trumpet, and hint at Mariachi patterns and melodies. All of these subtle characteristics are developments of key components of earlier compositions of Shankar-Jaikishan, Ramchandra, and Naushad Ali that represent a nuanced formulaic approach to unobtrusively intermixing style and genre. The sequence ends with many of the men in the audience engaging in couples dance, and we hear what seems to be a *grito*, a shout that adds emphasis or conveys excitement in certain styles of Mexican music. "Mud Mud Ke Na Dekh" draws from numerous stylistic sources, including mariachi and flamenco, and although it is difficult to differentiate between them, together they represent a singly recognizable *filmi* style.

It is clear that certain refined characteristics featured by these four composers in some of their compositions added a jazzy feel, sometimes throughout the entire piece, and at other times in compartmentalized sections, but by the early 1950s we find that they had regularly borrowed material from each other, including maraca and tumbao rhythms, rolls on the piano leading to the second beat in a $\frac{4}{4}$ meter, solo muted trumpets with quick movements between staccato and sustained notes, bongo drums with sticks, the 3/2 clave pattern, and syncopated staccato patterns on the piano, to name just a few. In addition to the composers I discuss above, O. P. Nayyar, who also composed for cabaret scenes, was possibly inspired by some of the techniques of Ramchandra, Shankar-Jaikishan, and Naushad. In one noteworthy example, the Nayyar song sequence "Babuji Dheere Chalna" from the 1954 film *Aar Paar* features a seductive dance, intimate table placements, dim lamps, and men and women sitting together in formal dress at a cabaret. Musically, this song employs a tambourine in a $\frac{4}{4}$ meter that hints at the maraca rhythm used by all four composers discussed above, but with added variation, including sections that feature a quick sextuplet pattern leading to each beat, played with impressive rhythmic precision. I mention this exactitude to note that the performer does not simply roll the tambourine before each beat, which would have been a technique of Ramchandra and Shankar-Jaikishan. Nayyar's approach uses the tambourine to articulate a repeating rhythmic idea and to add additional variation and depth, and in some respects takes the rhythmic delicacies used by Naushad, Shankar-Jaikishan, and Ramchandra to a new level with more concern for rhythmic precision.

Conclusion

Stylistic continuity is hard to directly document and observe, and we often have to interpret the nuanced musical behavior of composers to identify novel compositional approaches and practices. Composers' use of slight, yet significant, compositional material and practices, such as reconfigured ideas about the clave or improvised muted trumpet licks, can suggest compositional choice pointing to larger trends. These composers felt that Hollywood source material could enhance their work, and they sought new stylistics to modify and enhance richness and expand potential. Once a compositional choice was made, further alternatives were generated drawing from those choices, and to discern novel possibilities, these four composers seem to have been as prone to identifying and reidentifying alternatives from each other as much or more than from Hollywood. Composer temperament, creative proclivities, entrenched habits, musical experience, and the nature of creativity itself influenced their tendency to innovate, borrow, and reconfigure. But their innovations were also consistent with continuity and the skillful use of established constraints. They remained attentive to Indian classical and folk elements, as well as other trends in the *filmi* style. And to be sure, the behaviors of these composers were not monolithic; they were not necessarily innovative the same way in all elements of their compositions across time. Their openness to innovative use of Hollywood music in cabaret sequences was largely a product of their global aesthetic aspirations, the availability of local jazz musicians, and the popularity of cabaret scenes in which implied, overt, and reconfigured elements from Hollywood music seemed to fit the narrative and metanarrative framework.[85]

This chapter also demonstrates that after Independence, jazz musicians faced new challenges, and most struggled to earn a living. Their professional lives benefited from the large flow of money in and out of the Hindi film industry, and most jazz musicians understood the need for flexibility in an environment of immense audience demand for film songs. These musicians successfully negotiated the space between two performance practices, and profited from both. My claim that live cabarets partially influenced cabaret and club scenes in films does not mean that composers mimicked live-venue cabarets. Rather, I propose that the financial needs of qualified musicians and their experience in designing and executing cabarets in hotels supported the practicality of composing and performing music, choreographing dance, and designing effective costumes and sets for film cabaret productions.

Afterword

It is clear that Britain's Raj supported the commercial potentials of American music in India and played a vital role in the social, economic, and political processes embedded in the entertainment infrastructures discussed in this book. The British preference for Western music, foods, and other commodities stimulated trade and exchange with much of the Anglophone world. When their political, social, and economic authority eroded during World War II, so did a portion of the demand for Western entertainment. At the beginning of the book, I note that American black-face minstrel performer Dave Carson succeeded in 1865 in part because when the global trade balance broke down after the price of cotton shares crashed in Bombay, he used the event for performance material. Humorous references to the cotton crisis were an effective marketing strategy to appeal to European and British audiences. Yet after the crisis, the British remained in India, people eventually began to make money again, and the music continued. Eighty years later, when the economic and political authority of the Raj was operating on shakier grounds during World War II, enthusiasm diminished for entertainment in India associated with Europeans and British—two of the most visible communities to engage American popular music.

This demise left many musicians and connoisseurs disillusioned. I interviewed Lucknow guitarist James "Jumbo" Perry dozens of times, and I was able to collect a number of personal history narratives attesting that he was strongly distressed about the decline of jazz after the war in Lucknow, especially in the 1950s and 1960s. He asserted that after Independence he found the audience dramatically reduced and the market weakened. He once lamented to me that playing music for people who did not appreciate jazz was challenging: "To play my music is a crime if a person I'm playing it for doesn't understand one thing I'm playing. So I'm a bloody fool for playing it. You follow? I'm playing absolutely modern, and I'm seeing modern. And it's real jazz."[1] Perry is speaking about the 1950s and 1960s as the jazz scene in Lucknow all but evaporated, and he was especially frustrated by the lack of an audience that appreciated the intricacies of his music. After the late 1940s, Perry's musical standing weakened as he ceased to receive recognition and equity among other musicians in Lucknow. Deteriorated musical status and a reconfigured popular music scene made Perry feel marginalized and less a partner in the social and musical interaction of the city, a process that Nancy Fraser has termed "status subordination."[2] In this instance it is not that Perry was an unskilled musician, but that the musical world around him had rapidly changed. Perry was left musically hapless in a city and country in which the meaning and scope of jazz had changed.

To be sure, big-name jazz musicians from the United States such as Duke Ellington, Dave Brubeck, and Louis Armstrong toured India in the 1950s and 1960s, and their influence remained. Warren Pinckney claims that some of Ellington's sidemen played a series of after-hours performances at the Venice, a popular club in Bombay at the time, and that these late-night performances at the Venice continued for years after Ellington's tour.[3] A rock-and-roll scene also blossomed. According to Gregory Booth's recent study, several rock bands emerged in 1963 in Bombay and performed in a wide range of styles.[4] Rock has been part of India's popular music land-scape in urban centers ever since. Booth attributes the popularity of rock in part to "India's postcolonial identity vis-à-vis the cultural practices and content of the former colonial culture (Great Britain) and the hegemonic influences of the US music industry."[5] American popular music in India has carried with it all sorts of tangible as well as irresolute meanings that have varied over time. Not everyone defines American music in the same way. Not everyone appreciates it in the same way. Some feel it is an impor-tant part of the musical landscape of India, but others might disagree. These positions all carry weight. I hope to have sorted through some of these divergent ideas and meanings and added to the conversation by look-ing at one small slice of the music history of India.

At the beginning of this book I emphasize that this study is not lin-ear or comprehensive, and that I seek to address only part of the story of American popular music in India. The larger arguments about global-ized networks and cosmopolitan responses that I address are only one way of conceptualizing commercialized music in the subcontinent. And although macro-level British governmental and economic strategies, and technological progress in general, played a role in the specific mix of fac-tors that determined the course of musical transitions and developments, American music always influenced lives and created careers, and not just for the rich or powerful. For example, the availability of jazz in Lucknow influenced jazz guitarist James Perry unlike anything else in his profes-sional life, and he was not alone. Individuals approached their experience of music and culture with others in a variety of ways and in an assortment of performance contexts. The unnamed individual who sported the award-winning black mammy costume at the fancy dress dance in Nainital in 1933 (discussed in the introduction) was not only expressing creativity in cos-tume design. He or she was responding to global media and beliefs about race as well as displaying knowledge of the wider world. Finally, as John Blacking has remarked, it is continuity in music that should be noted as remarkable, not just change, and we should be sensitive to the agency of individuals.[6] Commerce, technology, and cultural globalization embed-ded in durable entertainment infrastructures such as the Indian theater industry in the mid- and late 1800s, the moving picture economy of the early and mid-twentieth century, and the gramophone trade of the 1930s and 1940s supported American popular music over the course of many decades—but empowered individuals were always agents in their evolution and sustainability.

Notes

Introduction

1. Reprinted in "The Minstrels in Calcutta," *Times of India*, July 17, 1865.
2. For additional discussion of Carson and blackface minstrels in Bombay, see Fernandes, *Taj Mahal*, 45–51.
3. The "British Raj" refers to the direct rule of much of present-day India by the British from 1858 to 1947.
4. "Eastern Command Dance," *Pioneer*, Lucknow ed., July 16, 1933.
5. Low, *History of British Film*, 203.
6. Middleton, "Mum's the Word," 108. Paul Whiteman and His Orchestra also recorded the song in 1922. An example of his original 1922 recording may be found at Library of Congress National Jukebox, accessed June 20, 2015, http://www.loc.gov/jukebox/recordings/detail/id/8972/.
7. I borrow the phrase "wider shores" from John Tomlinson's study of cosmopolitanism, in *Globalization and Culture*, 202. In another context, Leo Ou-fan Lee, in *Shanghai Modern*, comments that jazz in Shanghai during the interwar years in China represented niche access to uncommon music, and allowed those who had access to feel they were in some ways sophisticated cultural mediators between China and the West.
8. For a more detailed discussion of the format of black and blackface minstrel shows, see Londré and Watermeier, *History of the North American Theater*.
9. Carson's minstrel performance in Bombay took place in the Town Hall, built in 1833. It was a gathering space for the elite and business class in Bombay (Morris, *Stones of Empire*), and information about the financial collapse and the financial metrics that explained it flowed freely there.
10. Tomlinson, "Political Economy of the Raj," 137.
11. Many characterizations of cosmopolitanism emphasize a "world" within which composers, music makers, and others can navigate with nuance, purpose, imagination, and creative determination (see Stokes, "On Musical Cosmopolitanism," and Marsden, "Muslim Cosmopolitans?"). In the nineteenth century, the term *cosmopolitanism* was associated with new flows of money and commerce as much as increased interest in the wider world. Lauren M. E. Goodlad suggests that late nineteenth-century cosmopolitanism was, in some respects, "more likely to evoke impersonal structures of capitalism and imperialism than an ethos of tolerance, world citizenship, or multiculturalism" ("Cosmopolitanism's Actually Existing Beyond," 401).
12. Many scholars contextualizing the scope of black music over time, including Ronald Radano (*New Musical Figurations* and *Lying Up a Nation*), have warned to avoid overglorifying or overexoticizing music associated with African Americans.

13. I owe this idea to Martin Stokes's study of globalization and cosmopolitanism, "On Musical Cosmopolitanism," 5.

14. I owe some of these ideas to John Tomlinson's work on cosmopolitanism, especially *Globalization and Culture*, 202.

15. Magee and Thompson, *Empire and Globalization*.

16. Ibid., 27.

17. Richards, *Imperialism and Music*, 14.

18. Ibid.

19. Walkowitz, *Nights Out*, 5–6.

20. Frith, "Playing with Real Feeling," 48.

21. International troupes toured the theater industry of Calcutta as well (Capwell, *Music of the Bauls*).

22. Hansen, "Languages on the Stage," 382–84.

23. See Brown and Held (*Cosmopolitan Reader*) for further discussions of the role of economic circumstances in creating cosmopolitan livelihoods.

24. Misra, *Business, Race, and Politics in British India*, 68–69.

25. Ibid.

26. Yagnik and Sheth, *Shaping of Modern Gujarat*, 106.

27. Ibid.

28. Bolles, *Industrial History of the United States*, 850–78.

29. Ibid., 873.

30. Smith, "The City of London," 85.

31. *Times of India*, December 3, 1908.

32. Ibid.

33. Hughes, "The 'Music Boom,'" 447. Gramophones were played in homes, stores, along the streets, in parks, and in other public spaces. Both Western and Indian music were publicly performed. Margaret Cousins suggests that before the 1930s, "The only free public performances were provided for the Western and Anglo-Indian residents by military brass bands, which played nothing but Western music ... but nowadays [in the 1930s] it is inspiring to see whole Indian and Muhammadan families, rich and poor, flocking to the parks, maidans or marinas where these broadcasted concerts of Indian music are held several times a week" (*Music of the Orient*, 180–81).

34. For further discussion of the relationship between commerce and cosmopolitanism, see Woodward and Skrbis, "Performing Cosmopolitanism."

35. For further discussion of the gramophone industry, see Arnold, "Popular Film Song in India"; Farrell, "Early Days of the Gramophone" and *"Indian Music and the West*; Jha, "Eurasian Women as *Tawa'if* Singers"; Hughes, "The 'Music Boom'"; Manuel, "Popular Music in India" and *Cassette Culture*; Qureshi, "His Master's Voice?"; and Weidman, "Guru and Gramophone."

36. Gaisburg, *The Music Goes Round*. Regula Qureshi also notes that the gramophone was a marker of status and power. In writing about recorded Qawwali music, Qureshi argues that musical preferences were in some respects constructed "by the duality of the medium as both a sonic commodity and a sonic experience to consumers" ("His Master's Voice?" 65).

37. Farrell, "Early Days of the Gramophone," 35–36.

38. Gaisburg, *The Music Goes Round*.

39. Jha, "Eurasian Women as *Tawa'if* Singers," 281.

40. Kinnear, *First Indian Recordings*, 23.
41. A survey of advertisements in the Calcutta *Statesman* in 1905 suggests that gramophones could be purchased from Gramophone and Typewriter Ltd. for from Rs. 22 to Rs. 205. Numerous authorized dealers, especially in Bombay and Calcutta, sold a wide variety of gramophones, discophones, and phonographs. The Nicolephone, under the development of Nicole Freres (India) Ltd. (Kinnear, *First Indian Recordings*, 38), sold machines that were considerably less expensive from 1904 to 1909.
42. Barnouw and Krishnaswamy, *Indian Film*, 1–5; and Sahay, *Visual Anthropology*, 4.
43. In addressing the availability of amusements for Europeans in Calcutta at the turn of the century, Sudhir Mahadevan asserts that "European consumer culture in Calcutta aspired to the latest fads and trends in England" ("Traveling Showmen," 31). European shops in the nineteenth century sold all sorts of luxury goods, including projection technologies. Camera obscuras, daguerreotypes, and magic lanterns were early technologies that projected images on a screen, and audiences demanded access to these and other new devices. By the late 1800s, these technologies included moving pictures.
44. Hughes, "House Full," 36.
45. "Grand Opening Night of the Chronophone," *Times of India*, November 13, 1908. An advertisement in the *Statesman* on September 20, 1905, titled "What Is Chronophone," suggests that it was first introduced in India in 1905 and said it was "remarkable how perfectly the lips of the figure on the screen moved with the words from the talking machine."
46. From a survey of advertisements in the Calcutta *Statesman* in early 1900.
47. See, for example, "All Aboard, Tonight at the Taj," *Times of India*, August 28, 1936.
48. For a discussion of cosmopolitanism and provincialism, see Roberts and Arnett, *Communication Ethics*.
49. See Paul van der Grijp ("Cultural Search for Authenticity," 134) for a similar discussion of the relationship between exoticism and nostalgia.
50. Similar primitivist depictions continued through the 1940s in India. Khwaja Ahmad Abbas's accounts of dances in in Mussoorie, a hill station in the foothills of the Himalaya ranges, emphasize visceral energy and excitement, flavored with overtones of tribal energy and social transgression: "The music had come from all over the world and been syncopated into this wild and sensuous rhythm. . . . There were hot jazzy tunes from America, musical expressions of a dynamic but confused culture. . . . The wail of the violin and the blare of the saxophone were superimposed on the beating of a barbaric tom-tom calling the men and women of some cannibalistic tribe to a dance round a fire on which a human is roasted" (Abbas, *I Write as I Feel*, 291). In this instance, the author taps into the imaginary elsewhere of jazz to emphasize the excitement of dances.
51. Cosmopolitanism is not necessarily about refinement or tolerance (Skrbis, "Performing Cosmopolitanism," 136). As Kathleen Glenister Roberts and Ronald C. Arnett remind us, "We cannot invite cosmopolitanism without provinciality" (*Communication Ethics*, 2).
52. Interview conducted by Kurt Piehler and Rheka Gandhi in New Brunswick, New Jersey, in 1995. Transcript accessed via the Rutgers Oral History Archives, April 9, 2013, http://oralhistory.rutgers.edu/interviews.
53. The designation "Anglo-Indian" should not be confused with the British in India. Christian Goans were from Portuguese Goa.

54. Bronislaw Szerszynski and John Urry have called this process a "transformation of vision" ("Visuality, Mobility and the Cosmopolitan," 115). See Hannerz ("Cosmopolitans and Locals," 239) for a similar and more complete definition of cosmopolitanism as it relates to an aesthetic of openness. See Regev, "Cultural Uniqueness" and *Pop-Rock Music*, for further discussion of the impact of global media on local music.

55. American popular music, broadly speaking, was not solely in the hands of wealthy businessmen, Hindi film proprietors, or others who sought musicians to gain prosperity. In this book I seek to give agency to individual musicians and I avoid claiming that individual enterprise was engulfed by a mainstream music industry (see Sanjek "One Size," 536).

56. Bayly and Harper, *Forgotten Armies*, 363–64.

57. Jones, *Yellow Music*.

58. I found no conclusive indication that jazz in India—unlike the spread of jazz in the Chinese context—evolved into new or hybridized forms of music until the advent of the Indian sound film industry when film composers used jazzy characteristics in their cinema scores.

59. Cohen, "Sounding Out the City"; "Paying One's Dues"; and "Rock Landmark at Risk."

60. I am particularly influenced by Allen and Wilcken's (*Island Sounds in the Global City*) work on New York City, which they define in part through its musical relationship to spaces beyond the nation-state, such as the Caribbean.

61. For further discussion, see Michael Windover's study of art deco in Bombay in *Art Deco*.

62. Fernandes, *Taj Mahal Foxtrot*, and Shope "They Treat Us White Folks Fine," "From Imperial Exclusivity to Global Receptivity," and "Latin American Music."

63. American music represented more than the authority or dominance of the Western experience. See Woodward and Skrbis, "Performing Cosmopolitanism," and Appadurai, "Grassroots Globalization," for discussions of Western hegemony in the context of cosmopolitanism.

64. Woodfield, *Music of the Raj*.

65. Ibid., 145.

66. Head, "Corelli in Calcutta."

67. Woodfield, "Collecting Indian Songs."

68. Woodfield, *Music of the Raj*, 21.

69. Ibid., 18–20. Written music was widely available. By the 1800s, instrument and music companies flourished. One of the most pervasive was Soundy and Company, which by the mid-1860s served as a box office for local performance venues such as the Gaiety Theatre in Bombay. These companies also sold music, instruments, and specialty items such as table glassware, stencil plates, and copying presses, and relied on a diverse inventory to remain profitable.

70. Coelho, "Connecting Histories," 138.

71. Sebastiani, *Seconda Speditione*, 105. Translated by Coelho, "Connecting Histories," 131.

72. Woodfield, "Collecting Indian Songs," and *Music of the Raj*; Capwell, *Music of the Bauls*.

73. Woodfield, *Music of the Raj*, 158.

Chapter One

1. Misra, *Business, Race, and Politics*, 18.
2. Ibid.
3. Kling, *Blue Mutiny;* Ghosh, "Industrial Concentration," 57; Rungta, *Rise of Business Corporations*, 226.
4. Sinha, *Communication and Colonialism*, xxxi.
5. Brown, *Ordinary Man's India*, 101.
6. "India: A Market," 8.
7. Joshi, "Our Shipping and Ship Building," 180. This increase was also paralleled in the amount of seaborne trade, which increased almost tenfold in terms of rupee value.
8. Sinha, *Communication and Colonialism*, 206.
9. Wittman, *Empire of Culture*, 162.
10. Misra, *Business, Race, and Politics*, 38–39.
11. Robert Pearson claims that by the end of the nineteenth century club-land comprised gentlemen conversing in "large, depressing lounges and smoking rooms, filled with heavy leather or cane-bottomed chairs" (*Eastern Interlude*, 22).
12. Sinha, "Britishness, Clubbability," 499.
13. Rogan, "Regimental Bands," 29.
14. Herbert and Sarkissian, "Victorian Bands," 168.
15. Heathcote, "Army of British India," 362.
16. "Regimental Bands and Military Messes," *Bombay Times and Journal of Commerce,* July 19, 1848.
17. "Want of Support to Regimental Bands," *Bombay Times and Journal of Commerce,* March 10, 1847. Among other critics who commented on the specter of mortality cast over bands was Thomas Bacon, a lieutenant in the Bengal Horse Artillery. In 1837, he says, with a hint of cynicism, "It would appear that, in such a climate as that of India, the eternal puffing and blowing necessary for the wind instruments very quickly induces pulmonary diseases" (*First Impressions*, 159).
18. Herbert and Barlow, *Music and the British Military*, 136.
19. Ibid.
20. From a survey of his advertisements in the *Times of India* in the 1850s.
21. "Music for Military Bands," *Bombay Times and Journal of Commerce*, August 16, 1851.
22. "Music for Military Bands," *Bombay Times and Journal of Commerce*, August 23, 1851.
23. Ibid.
24. See, for example, "Just Received Overland," *Bombay Times and Journal of Commerce*, December 22, 1854.
25. "Music for Military Bands," August 23, 1851. By the late 1850s, Herbert and Company sold music for brass and woodwinds, brass bands, string bands, and drum and fife (regimental) bands. Based in Bombay Herbert offered music throughout India. Furthermore, steamships often housed resident entertainment companies that performed in coastal cities while in port, and often engaged audiences with short outdoor performances of blackface minstrel routines along the waterfront.
26. Braddon, *Life in India*, 144.
27. Growth in the number of women from Europe in the nineteenth century increased the frequency and scope of social ballroom dances across India (Woodfield, *Music of the Raj*, 6).

28. "Farewell Ball at the Town Hall, Calcutta," in *Speeches by the Marquis of Lansdowne: Viceroy and Governor General of India*, vol. 2, 1894, 653–54.
29. Shope, "Masquerading Cosmopolitanism."
30. Diary of Jane Maria Strachey, June 8–19, 1863.
31. Pennell, *Charles Godfrey Leland*, 387.
32. Lee, *Commerce and Culture*, 102. Indian businessmen who survived the crisis concentrated on domestic trade or invested in Indian industry and became pioneers in Indian innovation at the end of the nineteenth century.
33. Ibid., 103.
34. Ties between Parsi and European businesspeople included appreciation for entrepreneurial opportunities in Western entertainment. Parsis and other colonial elites attended English dramas in the nineteenth century, as did Indians who would often host Indian *nautch* (dance) parties in return (Hansen, "Language, Community," 65). These social and musical hospitality exchanges constituted "cultural capital" that Kathryn Hansen hints "reinforced economic collaboration between European and local mercantile communities" (ibid.).
35. The Gaiety Theatre, which had a capacity of eight hundred seats, rented to traveling minstrel and theater companies for one hundred rupees a month and became the scene of numerous minstrel shows by local and foreign traveling troupes. Less frequently, the thousand-seat Theatre Royal in Calcutta booked minstrels.
36. Daniel Bandmann, an entertainer who traveled to Madras, Bombay, and Calcutta in the late 1800s to do Shakespearean theater, described the interior of these theaters favorably, especially the venues in Calcutta, claiming that "the theatres are lofty buildings with only one gallery, and have a dress circle, stalls, and generally a considerable number of private boxes" (Bandmann, *Actor's Tour*, 126). His descriptions also point to the potential profitability of the English theater: "Stalls and dress circles are four or five rupees (two dollars or two dollars and a half), and the private boxes are from twenty to forty rupees (from ten to twenty dollars)" (ibid.). At a performance on December 24, 1881, at the Corinthian Theatre, he reports that admission revenue was $1,000 (ibid., 128).
37. Scott, *Sounds of the Metropolis*, 145.
38. *Spirit of the Times*, January 7, 1837. Quoted in Scott, *Sounds of the Metropolis*, 145.
39. Scott, *Sounds of the Metropolis*, 145.
40. Gilmore, "'De Genewine Artekil,'" 746.
41. Meer, *Uncle Tom Mania*, 15.
42. Hill and Hatch, *African American Theatre*, 94.
43. "Fun on the Bristol," *Times of India*, December 6, 1886.
44. Strausbaugh, *Black Like You*, 118.
45. "Important to Ethiopians," *Bombay Times and Journal of Commerce*, January 25, 1853. This advertisement listed a banjo for sale for 30 rupees and claimed it was only for "Ethiopians," a reference to blackface performers.
46. See, for example, "Just Received Overland," *Bombay Times and Journal of Commerce*, October 29, 1856.
47. For reviews of Mackney's work, see "Mr. E. Mackney," *The Players*, February 16, 1861.
48. Miner, *American Dramatic Directory*, 7.
49. For additional information on the structures of minstrels, see Saxton, "Blackface Minstrelsy."

50. Meer suggests that some of *Uncle Tom's Cabin*'s "most famous scenes, such as the conversations between Topsy and Miss Ophelia, can be seen to be derived from minstrelsy's end man-interlocutor exchange" (*Uncle Tom Mania*, 12). These exchanges were central to minstrels.

51. Meer, *Uncle Tom Mania*, 17.

52. Slout, *Burnt Cork and Tambourines*, 95, and Rice, *Monarchs of Minstrelsy*, 71.

53. Rice, *Monarchs of Minstrelsy*, 71.

54. Brown, "Early History of Negro Minstrelsy," n.p., quoted in Slout, *Burnt Cork and Tambourines*, 50–51. See also *New York Clipper*, May 25, 1867.

55. Bahkle, *Two Men and Music*, 87.

56. Quoted in Trivedi, "Performing the Nation, 252.

57. Ibid.

58. Trivedi, "Performing the Nation," and Kumar, *Indian English Drama*. For example, titles of skits such as "'I am going to Charleston' became 'Hum Jata Charleston,' and 'Hold your Horses' became 'Hold your Ghoras'" (Trivedi, "Performing the Nation," 254).

59. "New Advertisements: Theatre Royal," *Times of India*, November 24, 1877.

60. Parkinson, *Ocean Telegraph to India*, 58.

61. Quoted in Trivedi, "Performing the Nation," 259.

62. Wacha, *Shells from the Sands*, 351.

63. Hastie, "The Bengalee Baboo," 191.

64. Scott, "Rise and Fall," 91.

65. Sinha, *Colonial Masculinity*, 17.

66. Trivedi, "Performing the Nation," 265.

67. "The Minstrels in Calcutta," *Times of India*, July 17, 1865.

68. See, for example, "Entertainment at Lowjee Castle," *Times of India*, March 14, 1874.

69. See, for example, "New Advertisements: Theatre Royal," *Times of India*, May 10, 1877.

70. "Christy Minstrel Performance," *Times of India*, December 22, 1888.

71. Many other military units organized blackface minstrel troupes. The Colaba Royal Artillery in Bombay maintained a minstrel troupe in the 1890s complete with banjos that on at least one occasion brought "down the house with roars of laughter" ("Colaba Royal Artillery A.T.A. Minstrel Troupe," *Times of India*, January 28, 1892).

72. Hughes, *Gazetteer*, 351.

73. "Music at Morley Hall," *Times of India*, November 20, 1874.

74. "The Gaiety Theatre," *Times of India*, May 26, 1880.

75. "Entertainment at Lowjee Castle," *Times of India*, March 14, 1874.

76. "Calcutta," *Times of India*, July 21, 1884.

77. Ibid.

78. Sometimes ships at dock brought the latest numbers from overseas. In 1890 at the Bombay Dockyards, the Canning's Seedy Boys from the ship *I.M.S. Canning*, performed "banjo eccentricities," in addition to a number of contemporary popular songs such as "A Kiss in the Dark," and "Over the Garden Wall." ("The 'Canning' Entertainment," *Times of India*, September 12, 1890.)

79. "Entertainment at Bhosawul [*sic*]," *Times of India*, December 1, 1890.

80. Bryant, *Bryant's Songs*, 61–62.

81. "Entertainment at Bhosawul [*sic*]," *Times of India*, December 1, 1890.

82. According to Rydell and Kroes, "Sousa dipped into the participatory well of America and turned his performance into festive sing-alongs" (*Buffalo Bill in Bologna*, 89).

83. Burkholder, Grout, and Palisca, *History of Western Music*, 783, and Berlin, *Ragtime*, 99. The earliest pieces referred to as "ragtime" were written in the late 1800s, and included William Krell's "Mississippi Rag" (1897) and Scott Joplin's "Original Rags" and "Maple Leaf Rag" (both in 1899), which became defining songs of the genre.

84. Bierley, *John Philip Sousa*, 18.

85. Stecopoulos, *Reconstructing the World*, 68–69.

86. "Mr. Sousa Says . . . ," *Times of India*, November 14, 1903.

87. Stecopoulos, *Reconstructing the World*, 69.

88. Also during these years, dozens of new dances emerged in Europe and North America (Dannett and Rachel, *Down Memory Lane*, 76) that spread American popular culture, leading popular music scholar Sigmund Spaeth to assert that "the decade between 1910 and 1920 can be identified primarily as the period in which America went dance mad" (*History of Music in America*, 369).

89. See "Band at the Exhibition," *Times of India*, December 29, 1904; and "Band at the Victoria Gardens," *Times of India*, February 4, 1905.

90. "Black and White Minstrels: Successful First Night," *Times of India*, August 24, 1904.

91. White, *Ragging It*, 102, 151.

92. Berlin, *Ragtime*, 106.

93. "Black and White Minstrels: Successful First Night," *Times of India*, August 24, 1904.

94. Rydell and Kroes, *Buffalo Bill in Bologna*, 91.

95. Wetzel, *Globalization of Music*, 58.

96. See, for example, "Music—Banjo," *Enoch Pratt Free Library of Baltimore City Bulletin* 8, no. 2 (1902): 142.

97. See, for example, *New England Magazine* 1, no. 6 (1890), n.p.

98. See, for example, "Metropolitan Band Records," *Phonoscope: A Monthly Journal Devoted to Scientific and Amusement Inventions Appertaining to Sound and Sight* 2, no. 10 (1898): 3.

99. Berlin, *Ragtime*, 109.

100. "The Darkie's Dream," Edison Military Band, Edison Gold Moulded Record, 1905. Cylinder Preservation and Digitization Project, Donald C. Davidson Library, University of California, Santa Barbara, Special collections, Performing Arts, Cylinder 8990.

101. "Amusements," *Times of India*, May 8, 1908.

102. Bhaumik, "Cinematograph to Cinema," 51.

103. "The Empire Theatre, Opening Night," *Times of India*, February 20, 1908.

104. Johnson, *Writings of James Weldon Johnson*, 287. Major publishing companies were located in a number of large cities, including Cincinnati, Chicago, Indianapolis, and New York City (Wetzel, *Globalization of Music in History*, 58). These respectable publishing houses disseminated affordable sheet music across the states and around the world.

105. Johnson, *American Negro Poetry*, x. Quoted in Stecopoulos, *Reconstructing the World*, 68.

106. Dawidoff, *Making History Matter*, 113–14.

107. "The Bandman Farewell," *Times of India*, November 19, 1921.

108. "Engagements," *Times of India*, November 26, 1921.

109. Carson, *Stage Year Book*, 48. Ragtime was controversial. Some were appalled at the scandalous movements on the dance floor, including London socialite Mrs.

Rexford Parsons, who banned ragtime and other transatlantic dances at her dance party in New York in 1913; she asserted, "If the tango, the turkey trot, or any other transatlantic freak dances should be attempted, the . . . orchestra would immediately cease playing." *Washington Post*, May 24, 1913. Quoted in Knowles, *Wicked Waltz*, 93. (The turkey trot facilitated close contact between partners and occasional arms pumping at the side like a turkey.)

110. Stearns and Stearns, *Jazz Dance*, 96.
111. "Christmas Shows. Nicely, Thanks," *Times of India*, January 21, 1913.
112. Ibid.
113. By 1913, regimental bands regularly performed Irving Berlin's ragtime music, and the band of the B. B. and C. I. Railway volunteers in Bombay frequently performed the popular song "Alexander's Ragtime Band." See, for example, "Moonlight Band Performance," *Times of India*, October 15, 1913.
114. Hamm, *Irving Berlin*, 208.
115. Berlin traveled to London in 1910, which helped to secure the popularity of his music throughout England (Moore, *André Charlot*, 39).
116. Parsonage, *Evolution of Jazz*, 12.
117. Stone, *Century of Musical Comedy*, 23.
118. "Engagements," *Times of India*, November 15, 1913.
119. "Hullo, Rag-time!" *Times of India*, July 22, 1913.
120. "Engagements," *Times of India*, November 13, 1913.
121. Berlin's songs and live performances in London were reviewed in the *Times of India* in Bombay in July 1913.
122. "Hullo, Rag-time!," *Times of India*, July 22, 1913.
123. "Bombay Amusements, The Excelsior," *Times of India*, May 17, 1915.
124. "The Banvard Company," *Times of India*, December 2, 1919.
125. "Excelsior Theatre, The Banvard Company's Debut," *Times of India*, December 12, 1919.
126. Ibid.
127. Ibid.
128. See, for example, "Banvard Comedy Company," *Times of India*, December 30, 1919.
129. Sharrar, *Avery Hopwood*, 226.
130. This troupe performed a number of themed events, including a Hawaiian show titled "Hello, Hawaii." See, for example, "Excelsior Theatre," *Times of India*, December 17, 1919.
131. "The Bing Boys Are Here," *Times of India*, August 7, 1917.
132. "Olympia Cinema," *Times of India*, April 8, 1916.
133. "Empire Cinema," *Times of India*, April 23, 1917.
134. "Bombay Amusements," *Times of India*, March 4, 1916.
135. Advertisements for the Vaudeville Theatre promoted "American Cabarets" in 1916 (see, for example, "Engagements: Great War Sale," *Times of India*, November 25, 1916).
136. Kincaid, *British Social Life*, 308.
137. One review of a cabaret in 1925 at the Gymkhana [Social Club] in Poona claims that it was organized and decorated like a scene from "American film dramas described as 'stupendour, staggering, stupefying [*sic*]'" ("Poona Cabaret Dance," *Times of India*, October 26, 1925).

Chapter Two

1. This institution is now known as the Lawrence School in Sanawar.
2. Creighton Thompson, who performed spirituals in New York City before traveling to India, perhaps added legitimacy to the group.
3. "Plantation Gala at the Taj, 'A Night Down South,'" *Times of India*, November 9, 1934.
4. A motion picture screenplay of the novel was shown as early as 1909 in the America-India Cineograph in Calcutta.
5. Walker, *Understanding Sound Tracks*, 123.
6. "Plantation Gala at the Taj," *Times of India*, November 9, 1934.
7. Smith, *Oxford Companion*, 493.
8. McElya, *Clinging to Mammy*, 3, 1, 4.
9. Cox, *Dreaming of Dixie*, 38.
10. Stokes, *American History*, 39.
11. Chadwick, *Reel Civil War*, 8.
12. French, *South and Film*, 107.
13. Kirby, *Media-Made Dixie*, 67, 68.
14. Guerrero, *Framing Blackness*, 20.
15. "Mississippi at the Taj," *Times of India*, August 28, 1936. The advertisement for the opening night states, "Presented by Universal Pictures and the Globe Theatres Ltd."
16. "Mississippi at the Taj," *Times of India*, August 28, 1936.
17. Berry, *Screen Style*, 110.
18. Knight, *Disintegrating the Musical*, 7.
19. Decker, *Performing Race*, 134–35, 137.
20. "Westminster Glee Singers," *Times of India*, November 14, 1924.
21. Ibid.
22. "The Louisana [*sic*] Quartet," *Times of India*, July 2, 1921.
23. "Taj Tonight," *Times of India*, February 16, 1935.
24. Mouvet, *Maurice's Art of Dancing*, 35.
25. Geffin, "Chez Maurice," 30.
26. Ibid., 36.
27. Ibid., 30. According to Geffin, the Café de Paris in New York began to prosper after this performance.
28. Drake-Boyt, *Latin Dance*, 104.
29. Abel, *Ciné Goes to Town*, 231.
30. See, for example, "In Aid of Lepers: A Variety Entertainment," *Times of India*, April 19, 1926.
31. "Taj Ballroom Turned into Paris 'Dive'," *Times of India*, February 15, 1935.
32. Ibid.
33. Krasner, *A Beautiful Pageant*, 4.
34. For further discussion of music and entrepreneurship, see Coulson, "Collaborating in a Competitive World."
35. Fernandes, *Taj Mahal Foxtrot*; and Shope, "'They Treat Us White Folks Fine.'"
36. "The Jazz Dance," *Times of India*, April 22, 1919.
37. Crease, "Jazz and Dance," 72–73.
38. Williams, "Teeming Highway," 466.

39. Indian dance-band musician Hal Green remembers domestic dance bands performing ragtime, waltzes, and foxtrots as early as 1917 (Collet, "Thirty Years of Jazz").

40. An account of the cruise of the HMS *New Zealand* in 1919 mentions a "Jazz" dance in Delhi on March 20, 1919, a month before the Bombay performances (*Cruise of H.M.S. New Zealand*, 30). No further information about this performance is available.

41. "Plays and Pictures," *Times of India*, April 26, 1919.

42. "Plays and Pictures," *Times of India*, April 12, 1919.

43. "Plays and Pictures," *Times of India*, April 26, 1919.

44. "Plays and Pictures," *Times of India*, June 21, 1919.

45. Stearns and Stearns, "Jazz Dance," 109.

46. See, for example, "Engagements: The Excelsior," *Times of India*, September 26, 1919.

47. "'Come Inside,'" *Wanganui Chronicle*, June 8, 1918.

48. See, for example, "Engagements: The Excelsior," *Times of India*, May 14, 1920.

49. "Song & Dance Annuals Xmas—1919," *Times of India*, December 9, 1919.

50. "Maurice Bandman," *Madras Mail*, March 13, 1922.

51. "The Banvard Company's Debut," *Times of India*, December 12, 1919. At least one review of their music was somewhat negative.

52. See "The Banvard Company," *Times of India*, December 2, 1919.

53. "League of Mercy Dance," *Times of India*, March 4, 1922.

54. "The Poona Season: Dancing and Sport," *Times of India*, July 9, 1923.

55. The Bombay Jazz Club started as early as 1922 ("Bombay Jazz Club," *Times of India*, July 21, 1922).

56. "Music in Bombay, A Mournful Picture," *Times of India*, January 30, 1920.

57. "Judge on the 'Jazz,'" *Times of India*, July 1, 1919.

58. "Jazz Thoughts, and Some Older Ones," *Times of India*, July 10, 1919.

59. Gulliver, "Crickett Smith," 4.

60. This material is from a legal contract between Roy G. Butler and Joseph Ghisleri's Symphonians held at the Roy G. Butler Collection, Visual and Performing Arts Division, Chicago Public Library.

61. Leon Abbey invited African American trumpeter Bill Coleman to perform with his group in Bombay in late 1936. He paid Coleman fifty dollars a week plus room and board (Coleman, *Trumpet Story*). A fifty-dollar stipend was substantial, especially considering that the Taj Mahal Palace Hotel in Bombay, where he primarily performed, covered many of his living expenses. He and the other band members were initially housed in the Taj Mahal Palace Hotel, which had exclusive accommodations. They then moved into paid private apartments, complete with servants. Stories that Coleman and others narrate during this time suggest that they maintained a privileged lifestyle (*Trumpet Story*, 107–8).

62. Leon Abbey, "Leon Abbey's Swing Band Opens Smart Nitery in Bombay, India; Teddy Weatherford Joins Troupe," *Chicago Defender*, December 19, 1936.

63. Fernandes, *Taj Mahal Foxtrot*.

64. The quote is taken from a postcard from Galle Face Hotel, Colombo, Sri Lanka. Roy G. Butler Collection, Visual and Performing Arts Division, Chicago Public Library.

65. Little is known about these musicians after their stays in India. Roy Butler returned to the United States and worked in the Postal Service, performing jazz occasionally.

Teddy Weatherford died of cholera in 1945 while in residence at the Grand Hotel, yet I found no indication that he and his Indian wife, Pansy Hill, planned to move from India.

66. Gioia, "Jazz and the Primitivist Myth," 130.
67. See Petrine Archer-Straw ("Exoticism in Black and White," 27) and Partha Mitter ("Modern Global Art," 45–46) for further discussion of primitivism and exoticism.
68. Locke, "Broader View of Musical Exoticism," 483–84.
69. Scholarly discussions about the relationship between exoticism and cosmopolitanism in music have been going on for decades. As D. C. Parker wrote in 1917, "Proper appreciation of the value of exoticism in music depends upon that artistic cosmopolitanism, upon that urbanity of mind which alone can give us a perception of striking and unusual features" ("Exoticism in Music," 134).
70. See Shope, "'They Treat Us White Folks Fine,'" and "From Imperial Exclusivity to Global Receptivity." Jim Holloway wrote in *Down Beat* magazine in 1945 that Weatherford "was pretty well known in Chicago jazz circles where his piano playing rated high . . . [and he] had a good technical grounding" ("Weatherford Took Jazz to the Orient," 5).
71. See Hughes, *I Wonder as I Wander*.
72. Shope, "'They Treat Us White Folks Fine,'" 106.
73. Gulliver, "Crickett Smith," 4.
74. White, "Negro on the American Stage," 180.
75. In 1935 Walter White wrote that in the United States performers "usually earning a mere pittance, hardly sufficient to provide more than a most meager existence, could and did indulge in lusty and, at times, ribald humor, in penetrating and, at times, merciless satire at the foibles and shortcomings of himself" ("Negro on the American Stage," 180).
76. Sometimes the musicians were depicted in tuxes, as indicated on the front page of the program booklet from the *Show Boat* dance.
77. Rogers, "Jazz at Home," 665.
78. Cox, *Dreaming of Dixie*, 62.
79. Craig, *Fireside Politics*, 254.
80. Arthur, "Blackpool Goes All-Talkie," 30.
81. Frith, "Playing with Real Feeling," 49.
82. Parsonage, *Evolution of Jazz*. Hot jazz was associated with the spirited, improvisational music of musicians such as Louis Armstrong and other black musicians.
83. Conversation on the musical abilities of white and black musicians was ongoing (Bakari, "Exploding Silence"), and included discourse on the racial roots of jazz and the implications of white British musicians performing an African American art form (Moore, *Inside British Jazz*, 36).
84. Abravanel, *Americanizing Britain*, 54–55.
85. Moore, *Inside British Jazz*, 35.
86. Jazz during this decade in India was not solely associated with Europeans and Americans, nor was it only performed or appreciated by foreigners. A number of Indian jazz enthusiasts I interviewed in Lucknow, Delhi, and Calcutta who had listened to jazz in the late 1930s expressed to me their admiration for the success of black jazz musicians and sympathy for black struggles in the United States, which brought attention to jazz and its African American connotations (Sheila D'Costa interview with author, October 23, 2000; Dorothy McFarland,

interview with author, January 18, 2001; and James Perry, interview with author, August 22, 2008).

87. Buettner, "Problematic Spaces," 279–81.

88. Kincaid, *British Social Life*, 243. British participation in these urban entertainment economies was partially bolstered by increased migration to large cities beginning in the 1920s. James Heitzman suggests that this migration formed "new types of public institutions and performance . . . [from which] new types of mass audiences were coalescing around technological innovation" (*City in South Asia*, 160). The urban environment and its lively entertainment possibilities excited many young Europeans.

89. Kincaid, *British Social Life*, 289–90.

90. For studies on the early development and growth of radio broadcasting in India, see Awasthy, *Broadcasting in India*; Baruah, *All India Radio*; Gupta, *Radio and the Raj*; and Lelyveld, "Upon the Subdominant."

91. "The Thrills of Short Wave Reception," *Times of India*, January 23, 1934.

92. I owe some of these ideas to Goodman, *Radio's Civic Ambition*, 228.

93. Contemporary American philosopher Sidney Hook claimed that a crucial function of the radio was "the training of the radio audience in the powers of independent and critical reflection . . . in the play of ideas . . . and the quest for truth" (broadcast on WEVD, New York, November 11, 1938; quoted in Goodman, *Radio's Civic Ambition*, 219).

94. Partha Gupta reminds us that during World War II Germany broadcast Hindustani news bulletins from Berlin, which were often regarded as more accurate than English news (*Radio and the Raj*, 34). Lionel Fielden, the first controller of broadcasting, suggested that the broadcasts out of Berlin were "swallowed by the masses like a patent medicine advertisement"(*Radio and the Raj*, 35). The colonial administration initiated efforts to stop these transmissions because of their strong potential to incite unfavorable activity.

95. From a survey of the "Radio Broadcast" section of the *Pioneer*, Lucknow ed., 1934.

96. See, for example, the *Statesman*, Calcutta, January 4, 1930.

97. From Stooge, "25 years a Band Leader," 1. From personal collection of Pamela McCarthy.

98. See, for example, "Empire Broadcasting Programmes," *Times of India*, December 28, 1937.

99. See, for example, "Today's Broadcasting Programmes," *Times of India*, December 13, 1938.

100. "Entertainment at the Taj," *Times of India*, June 17, 1938.

101. "At the Taj, New Act by Mimi and Jose," *Times of India*, July 15, 1938.

102. Many hotels and clubs featured art deco representations of radio signals in their stage designs. See Eric Gordon, "Hugh Ferriss," for further discussion of art deco representations of radio waves.

103. Zivin, "'Bent,'" 196.

104. Ibid., 198.

105. Shope, "'They Treat Us White Folks Fine,'" 113. This group included banjo player Al Bowlly, who went on to become a celebrity crooner in England. He traveled to India with "Edgar Adeler and his Syncopaters." These are some of Bowlly's first recordings.

106. Gronow, "Record Industry," 281.

107. Collet, "Thirty Years of Jazz."

108. This recording (REX 7994-A) references the Taj Mahal shrine in Agra. The first two stanzas hint at admiration for the monument: "Where dome and minaret outline the sky / In the shadows of the golden hue / There what lovely breeze softly sighs / As you hear the lovers croon / Taj Mahal / Taj Mahal / India's mystic shrine." This work represents a rare attempt to integrate Indian themes into a jazz composition, and was used as a marketing tool for the Taj Mahal Palace Hotel.

109. Stooge, "25 years a Band Leader," 1.

110. Ibid.

111. Angwin, "Music in the Himalayan Foothills," 227.

112. Angwin, "Music in the Himalayan Foothills."

113. Stooge, "25 years a Band Leader," 2.

114. Ibid.

115. It is important to note that this was not the more elite Byculla Social Club, which was known throughout India as a more exclusive establishment.

116. Stooge, "25 years a Band Leader," 2.

117. Ibid., 3.

118. Weber, *Musician as Entrepreneur*, 3.

119. "The Bombayman's Diary: Music and Smiles," *Evening News,* July 17, 1954.

120. Kincaid, *British Social Life in India*, 273.

121. Ibid., 271–72.

122. From a pamphlet titled "Under Distinguished Patronage, 'Correas,' The 'Optimists' Swing Orchestra," in the personal collection of Micky Correa.

123. Micky Correa, interview with author, August 5, 2008.

124. From a pamphlet titled "'Swing Action' of Karachi's Popular Orchestra" in the personal collection of Micky Correa.

125. From a pamphlet titled "Under Distinguished Patronage, 'Correas,' The 'Optimists' Swing Orchestra," in the personal collection of Micky Correa.

126. See, for example, "Swing High! Swing Low!" in the personal collection of Micky Correa.

127. From a pamphlet titled "God Save the King, Correas 'Optimists' Band," in the personal collection of Micky Correa.

128. From an undated newspaper clipping titled "Karachi Saxophonist Invited to Bombay," in the personal collection of Micky Correa. No further citation information is available.

129. From an undated newspaper clipping titled "Karachi Saxophonist Invited to Bombay."

130. "Eros Ballroom and Restaurant Opens To-day," *Times of India*, October 1, 1938.

131. Correa interview, August 5, 2008.

132. Ibid.

133. "The Bombayman's Diary: Music and Smiles," *Evening News,* July 17, 1954.

134. In the case of the Taj Mahal Palace Hotel, the hotel management cited criteria for choosing groups and they claimed that they arranged collaborations between groups to offer improved entertainment. In a season brochure from 1941, the management describes the increased difficulty of booking new acts, and claims that "[they] shall endeavor to put together Programmes which [they] feel will meet with general approval." From the Roy Butler Collection, Visual and Performing Arts Division, Chicago Public Library.

135. Fernandes, *Taj Mahal Foxtrot*, 84.

136. Weber, *Musician as Entrepreneur*, 11. Weber is discussing eighteenth-century musicians in Europe, but his views on entrepreneurial activity are relevant to our discussion.
137. Correa interview, August 5, 2008.
138. Sebastiani, *Seconda Speditione all'Indie Orientali*, 105; translated by Coelho, "Connecting Histories," 131.
139. Coelho, "*Kapsberger's* Apotheosis," 43.
140. See Molz, "Cosmopolitanism and Consumption," 36, for further discussion of localized commodity consumption as a cosmopolitan experience. See Beck, "Rooted Cosmopolitanism," "Cosmopolitical Realism," and *Cosmopolitan Vision*, for further discussion of cosmopolitan encounters found in everyday life.

Chapter Three

1. Watson, Hoyler, and Mager, "Spaces and Networks of Musical Creativity in the City," 863. See also Andersson and Andersson, *Economics of Experiences*.
2. Gehrke, "Community at the End of the World," 131.
3. Khan, "Sex in an Imperial War Zone," 243.
4. Ibid. These numbers were in addition to an Indian army of about 2.5 million (ibid.).
5. Long, *Charisma and Commitment*, 295.
6. Bhattacharya, "An Official Policy," 49.
7. Long, *Charisma and Commitment*, 295.
8. Much of this information comes from, *Air Operations in China*.
9. Baade, *Victory through Harmony*, 176.
10. Ibid., 176–77.
11. Ibid. The arrival of American star performers in England during the months after D-Day in 1944 was met with enthusiasm. "British dance musicians," Christina Baade claims, "availed themselves of every opportunity to learn from their transatlantic allies . . . [and this] was a dream come true for dance music and jazz enthusiasts" (*Victory through Harmony*, 175).
12. In addition to VU2ZU, the AFN launched VU2ZY in New Delhi, VU2ZX in Karachi, and VU2ZW in Agra ("AFRS Still Has 113 Stations on Air," *Broadcasting: The Weekly Newsmagazine of Telecasting*, January 21, 1946).
13. Asthana, "Broadcasting, Space, and Sovereignty," 521–23.
14. "Station VU2ZU and Crew Coming to You," *Command Post*, May 26, 1944.
15. Morley, "*American Forces Network*," 73.
16. "VU2ZU Daily Radio Programs," *Command Post*, May 26, 1944.
17. "CBI Radio Productions Featured over Coast to Coast Network," *Command Post*, September 8, 1944.
18. Sterling, *Encyclopedia of American Radio*, 110.
19. "CBI Radio Productions Featured over Coast to Coast Network," *Command Post*, September 8, 1944.
20. Engelman, "'My Rhodes Scholarship,'" 117.
21. Ibid., 116–17.
22. "CBI Radio Productions Featured over Coast to Coast Network," *Command Post*, September 8, 1944.

23. "'Jive Bombers' Hit Symphonic Heights at India Air Base," *CBI Roundup*, October 29, 1943. I was unable to find their exact service location, but reviews of their performances in the *CBI Roundup* and other publications suggest that they traveled frequently.

24. From "Historical Report (January 1945) of the 578th Air Material Squadron of the 25th Air Service Group," accessed June 22, 2015, http://www.25thasg.org/jan-1945578thams.htm.

25. Another station, Radio SEAC (South-East Asian Command), broadcasted from Colombo, Sri Lanka between 1944 and 1949. It was established when the South-East Asia Command took over Radio Colombo.

26. Pfau and Hochfelder, "'Her Voice a Bullet,'" 56, 57, 60.

27. Report by Albert J. Roberts Jr. (February 1, 1946), File: 2/4, Item 4, Box 3, Records related to Criminal Case 31712, RG 118, National Archives Pacific Region. Quoted in Pfau and Hochfelder, "Her Voice a Bullet," 60.

28. Virginia C. Claudon Allen, Library of Congress Veterans History Project, accessed June 22, 2015, http://lcweb2.loc.gov/diglib/vhp-stories/loc.natlib.afc2001001.33674/.

29. Ibid.

30. Radio broadcasts were not always reliable or clear. In 1943, British naval petty officer Henry R. Coombs lamented the poor reception in India: "It has become clear to me that the broadcasting of good music to men in distant parts of the world is a futile waste of time. . . . No matter how good the receiving set . . . the reception is invariably grossly distorted . . . a meaningless jumble of sound" ("A Sailor on Jazz," 124).

31. Young and Young, *Music of World War II*, 101.

32. Ibid., 102.

33. Ibid.

34. Micky Correa, interview with author, August 5, 2008.

35. Bombay was also a center of jazz consumption and it retained key musicians. Before arriving in Calcutta in 1941, Weatherford returned to the Taj Mahal Palace Hotel in Bombay for a brief few months beginning January 12, 1940 ("Notes from the Taj," *Times of India*, January 3, 1940). That year, the hotel featured several types of performers, including the more classically oriented Melody Trio (made up of Mehli Mehta, Egido Verga, and Mario Pagliarin), the cabaret dance group Trio Sarter and the Danish Beauties, Latin American cabaret duo Doray and Chela, Tau Moe and the Hawaiian Trio, and the Rudenko Trio (a juggling act that promoted Mexican and Latin American themes). Dozens of additional jazz orchestras and variety groups resided at the hotel for brief periods through the end of the war. The demand for entertainment at the Taj Mahal Palace Hotel was always strong, and the hotel increased the frequency of performances during these years. Delhi venues also hosted US military, including the Astoria Ballroom, which Raj Chatterji, an executive in the Imperial Tobacco Company of England at the time, recalls was popular among US troops: "There was this famous place, the Astoria Ballroom [in Delhi], where you had a tea-dance on Wednesdays and a Saturday night dance as the normal run. . . . And of course, during the war, plenty of army people, until the day when places like the Astoria were completely taken over by the Yanks" (quoted in Masani, *Indian Tales*, 68). US servicemen increased the market base for paying customers as they targeted select venues in Delhi that accommodated their amusement needs.

36. Brooks, "Obituary."
37. Holloway, "Torrid India," 14.
38. Columbia FB 40067.
39. Columbia FB 40081.
40. Columbia FB 40187. Jazz writer Sinclair Traill, in Calcutta at the time with the Royal Air Force, organized a studio session with Weatherford in August 1942. They recorded "Basin Street Blues," "Memphis Blues," and "St. Louis Blues," which made use of Weatherford's early Chicago style.
41. See Kim, *Transnational Migration*, for further discussion of the appeal of global media in local markets.
42. *Calcutta Key*, Services of Supply Base Section Two, Information and Education Branch, United States Army Forces in India—Burma, n.p. The *Calcutta Key* also suggests that military personnel should "try at least one Indian movie . . . [though] you may not like them . . . long, slow moving, principally made in Hindustani, based mostly on modern Indian life glamorized" (*Calcutta Key*, n.p., n.d.).
43. Another advertisement in the *Statesman* on November 2, 1943, lists Teddy Weatherford's recordings "Three Dreams" and "Cabin in the Sky," both from the film *Cabin in the Sky* (1943), starring Louis Armstrong. The ad also features local Calcutta band Reuben Soloman and His Jive Boys and British and American stars Vera Lynn and Bing Crosby.
44. From an unpublished manuscript written by K. Peter Darke held in the Roy G. Butler Collection, Visual and Performing Arts Division, Chicago Public Library. For another version of this manuscript, see Darke, "Weatherford's Indian Recording Sessions."
45. Darke, "Weatherford's Indian Recording Sessions," 6.
46. *Debonair* (India), 56. From the personal collection of Micky Correa. No further citation information is available.
47. See Rovisco and Nowicka ("Introduction," 6) and Regev ("Cultural Uniqueness") for a discussion of the relationship between cosmopolitanism (or provincialism) and a feeling of belonging.
48. See Ford, *Racial Culture*, for further discussion of provincialism and cosmopolitanism.
49. Camp, *Lingering Fever*, 137, 138.
50. Khan, "Sex in an Imperial War Zone," 244.
51. "People in Calcutta: The Homeless Man," *Calcutta Key*, n.p., n.d.
52. Branson, *British Soldier in India*, 100.
53. Ibid., 107.
54. Dupee, *Traveling India*, 24. Branson was killed in action in 1944.
55. Ó hAllmhuráin, "The Great Famine," 104. Ó hAllmhuráin suggests that the famine influenced music in both Ireland and the United States: "With the onslaught of famine, disease, and panic-stricken emigration, the music maker too went the way of his audience—to the mass grave, the workhouse, and the coffin ship. In the resulting diaspora, his trade would find its way to the sidewalks of Brooklyn, the music halls of vaudeville, and the lace-curtain parlors of Irish America" ("The Great Famine," 117). To this day, the traditional music of Ireland in the west of the country still bears the cultural impact of rural depopulation and the profit economics of post-famine agriculture ("The Great Famine," 105). A time of great shame for some, the Irish famine reduced the population from over eight million to less than

half that number (Williams, *Focus*, 62). It brought about a shift in the context and function of music because of economic, social, and political changes during and after the famine in Ireland. Many chose to emigrate to North America, and among those who stayed, "Culture moved indoors where it was kept under watchful eyes" of priests and prominent community members (Dowling, *Traditional Music and Irish Society*, 49).

56. Dowling, *Traditional Music and Irish Society*, 50.

57. Group cohesiveness among families and small communities, a necessary element of surviving the famine and avoiding future tragedies, meant new norms in performances that prevented conflict and promoted group stability. These changes included maintaining outward hip placement to avoid physical contact during couples dancing.

58. Merriam, *Anthropology of Music*, 213.

59. To be sure, military troops were not the only group living in Calcutta beyond the threat of the famine. Economist and Nobel Prize recipient Amartya Kumar Sen remembers the famine from his childhood: "One morning a very skinny man appeared in our school compound behaving in a deranged way, which—I would learn later—is a common sign of undergoing prolonged starvation. He had come in search of food from a distant village, wandering around hoping to get help. In the days that followed, came tens, then thousands then a procession of countless people—emaciated, hollow-cheeked, with dazed eyes, often carrying in their arms children made of skin and bones. . . . It is hard to forget the sight of thousands of shriveled people—begging feebly, suffering atrociously, and dying quietly" ("Individual Freedom," 54). Sen is describing people coming into Calcutta from villages and towns outside Calcutta. He laments the lack of attention to the famine by the political class and others, and mourns the sharp distinction between starving folks from rural areas and the residents of Calcutta.

60. Muehl, *American Sahib*, 209.

61. Interview conducted by G. Kurt Piehler and Darren Purtlebaugh in New Brunswick, New Jersey, in 1995. Transcript accessed via the Rutgers Oral History Archives, April 5, 2013, http://oralhistory.rutgers.edu/interviews.

62. The American Red Cross of the China, Burma, India Command, *A Guidebook to Calcutta, Agra, Delhi, Karachi, and Bombay*, 1943.

63. Webster, *Burma Road*, 128.

64. Kincaid, *British Social Life*, 308. Kincaid relates that Firpo's had the capacity to appeal to the older generation, which was a rare accomplishment.

65. Mathews, *Education of a Correspondent*, 384.

66. Many older English residents resisted listening to jazz and continued to enjoy members-only clubs. LaVonne Telshaw Camp stresses that senior members of British society "had established a rhythm of life that was easy to fall into. . . . Insulated from reality, theirs was a world of clubs, tennis, polo, and servants to wait upon them for almost every human activity" (*Lingering Fever*, 76).

67. From a survey of advertisements in the Calcutta *Statesman*. Firpo's also designed cabarets that featured Indian folk and classical music and dance, and was a rare venue in which these styles represented suitable entertainment among British and US patrons.

68. Blackford, *One Hell of a Life*, 13.

69. Bayly and Harper, *Forgotten Armies*, 297.

70. Heinemann, interview by Kurt Piehler and Rheka Gandhi, New Brunswick, New Jersey, August 1, 1995. Transcript accessed via the Rutgers Oral History Archives, April 9, 2015, http://oralhistory.rutgers.edu/interviews.
71. Muehl, *American Sahib*, 208–9.
72. A number of mid-twentieth-century writings directly place Firpo's in the context of the dynamic, difficult demographics of Calcutta. Seafaring navigator Tom McCulloch sarcastically called Calcutta around the time a "hellhole" (*Navigator to Hydrographer*, 20). Blackford called it a "cosmopolitan metropolis" (*One Hell of a Life*, 13). Calcutta itself was a contextualizing source that added to the rarity of Firpo's and the jazz performed inside.
73. The allure of jazz at Firpo's is also mentioned in Mircea Eliade's semiautobiographical novel *Bengal Nights*, which is set in 1930s Calcutta.
74. Quoted in McGuire, *Taps for a Jim Crow Army*, 227. The US civil-rights organization, the National Association for the Advancement of Colored People (NAACP), was formed in 1909.
75. Not everyone felt that dances were a good use of time, especially senior administrators or military personnel who viewed the war in a more serious light. The diaries of Sir Arthur Jules Dash in the late 1930s and early 1940s describe increasing pessimism as the war progressed. Dash, an ICS officer, traveled during the summer to Darjeeling, a hill station with frequent dances. Toward the outset of World War II, he began to write about social dances in Darjeeling and elsewhere in India with noticeable sarcasm. In early 1939, after returning to India from an extended holiday overseas, he notes with concern that dances in England were much more abbreviated and tempered than in India. (Arthur Jules Dash. British Library, India Office Section. MSS EUR C188/5, 1939.) By 1940, he takes on an increasingly negative tone that reflected the mounting seriousness of the war. He bemoans that in Darjeeling, "the silly life . . . went on as if the world had nothing left of interest to offer." With a strong sense of disdain he writes, "Dance floor [was] never more assiduously used" (1940). In a later entry, he claims dances represented an "irresponsible Darjeeling social scene," and scorns the leftover cigarettes and beer bottles that littered clubs after dances. By 1941 his tone is even more negative, and he describes dances with increasing whimsicality, asserting that "the social routine in Darjeeling seemed like the climate vegetation in the foothills. It seemed permanent and its permanence seemed more or less inevitable . . . in spite of a war that was going on against Germany" (1941).
76. Fauser, *Sounds of War*, 35.
77. Ibid., 36–37.
78. Andre Kostelanetz, letter to Ethel and Boris Kostelanetz, January 3, 1945 (quoted in Fauser, *Sounds of War*, 49).
79. Kendall is quoted in Isabel Morse Jones, "Place of Music in Global War Conditions Defined," *Los Angeles Times*, October 3, 1943.
80. Fauser, *Sounds of War*, 108.
81. Ibid.
82. Ibid., 106.
83. In September 1944, the USO arranged for a troupe of six Broadway showgirls to perform songs, dances, and skits from Broadway productions. This troupe travel across North India and performed three nights of shows at most venues, presenting a variety show on the first evening, a musical quiz show the second evening, and

the Broadway play *My Sister Eileen* on the third evening ("USO Troupe to Tour CBI-Land," *CBI Roundup*, September 14, 1944).

84. Ann Sheridan, "Short Circuit," *Time*, October 23, 1944, 69 (quoted in Matson, "Theatre for the Armed Forces," 3).

85. From a newspaper clipping titled, "'Rhythm and Blues' Finished Local Run." Roy Butler, Visual and Performing Arts Division, Chicago Public Library. Complete citation information unavailable.

86. Celia Nicolls, WW 2 People's War. WW2 People's War is an online archive of wartime memories contributed by members of the public and gathered by the BBC. The archive can be found at bbc.co.uk/ww2peopleswar.

87. Matson, "Theatre for the Armed Forces."

88. Ibid., 10.

89. Ibid.

90. Virginia Claudon Allen, *A Red Cross Volunteer in the China Burma India Theater, World War II*, 15. Virginia C. Claudon Allen, Library of Congress Veterans History Project, accessed September 4, 2015, http://lcweb2.loc.gov/diglib/vhp-stories/story/loc.natlib.afc2001001.33674/pageturner?ID=pm0001001.

91. Another unit, the Seventh Bombardment Group of the 10th Air Force, EAC (Eastern Air Command), maintained a dance band that regularly broadcast half-hour shows on a temporary radio station. In September 1944, they performed a concert of dance music for an orphanage near the base. The repertoire for the concert included "Stomping at the Savoy" and "Easy to Remember," both high-energy dance tunes. According to the article, the band members struggled to prevent the piano from being swept off the stage because of the monsoon rains ("10th A.F. Band Plays for Orphan Tots," *CBI Roundup*, September 21, 1944).

92. The Ledo Road, a road construction project whose goal was to connect Assam, India, to Kunming, China, boasted a music group called the Four Aces Quartet. In 1944 they performed vocal music that the *CBI Roundup* claimed regularly knocked "the cats out with solid jive" in hospitals, clubs, and other venues along the road ("Song Introduced by Four Aces," *CBI Roundup*, March 30, 1944.) They borrowed much of their repertoire from the famous American black vocal group the Ink Spots, but also composed original songs and entertained thousands of troops. A review in the *CBI Roundup* states that original songs were a significant component of their performance repertoire: "The Four Aces, Negro quartet . . . introduced a new song the other night at a performance for officers and men at an evacuation hospital entitled 'Jumping at the Hindu Hall.' Several months ago, the quartet introduced the song everybody is whistling on either side of the Burma-India border, 'Who's Taking My Place with Her Now?' The Four Aces, who have entertained more than 10,000 men in the past five months with a wide variety of tunes ranging from Ink Spots arrangements to their own sentimental style are available for performances" ("Song Introduced by Four Aces," *CBI Roundup*, March 30, 1944). They composed new tunes that drew from local material, as is evidenced by the title of their song "Jumping at the Hindu Hall."

93. One ad in July 1942 said, "R.A.F. Welfare Officer appeals for dance band musical instruments" ("Wanted," *Statesman*, July 4, 1942).

94. Braganza, interview with author, May 5, 2001. Mr. Braganza also supplied bands in Lucknow, Nainital, Simla, and other hill stations with instruments and music.

95. Online archive WW2 People's War. In this instance some members of the "Woodpecker" Squadron amateur jazz band performed between sets of a more serious jazz group.

96. Unruly behavior was not in short supply in the clubs. Dances organized for US troops were sometimes riotous. At the opening night of the India Air Task Force (IATF) Non-Commissioned Officer Club in August 1943, bartenders served spiked punch referred to as the "witches' brew." "The witches' brew . . . is designed to grow pink moss on the imbiber's chest and leave him barking like a jackal. Thus lubricated [with alcohol], the party, superfluous to say, was some soiree, and pronounced a big success (by those who could still pronounce) when the last jitterbug had been shooed home and the groaning sideboard unburdened" ("Clubs Sets 'Em Up at India Base," *CBI Roundup*, August 19, 1943). Dances were edgy and offered diversions from the gravity of the war effort.

97. Bayly and Harper, *Forgotten Armies*, 363–64. The American military promoted propaganda to reinforce their positive presence in India. An advertisement in the *Pioneer* newspaper in Lucknow titled "For the Future of Asia" says, "Today the United States has established a policy of free political and commercial association with all peoples of Asia. The Expeditionary Forces of the United States of America are in India today to defend the future of Asia and fight against Asia for the Japanese" (*Pioneer*, February 3, 1943).

98. Bayly and Harper, *Forgotten Armies*, 362.

99. William Fisher, "Yanks Make a Hit In India," *Life*, January 18, 1943, 14.

100. Koerner, *Piano Demon*, location 509 of 717.

101. Men and women in the US military also patronized private and military-sponsored clubs in cities and towns outside of Calcutta. Railway institutes in railway colonies throughout North India organized dances open to US troops during the war. Railway colonies were areas adjacent to railway stations and included worker housing and other essential services. Railway institutes in colonies offered entertainment for railway workers and their families, and typically included a stage and an area for dancing. They were a center of Anglo-Indian social life, and by the 1940s designated social directors were booking jazz. Mr. Sebastian, a social director at the railway institute in Allahabad during World War II, booked bands and told me once that American military personnel frequently attended his dances. The US military built a "secret" army station there sometime around 1942 (Bhattacharya, "British Military Information Management," 499), which populated the city with a small number of US troops. Sebastian's initial encounter with American foreigners was tense and confrontational; a group of Americans tried to attend a dance at the institute without wearing ties. He required formal dress at dances and placed a placard at the entrance that read, "Do not enter unless you have a tie" (Sebastian, interview with author, January 27, 2001). He was adamant that such rules were followed. He was strict when it came to maintaining formalities at dances, and told them that if the sign was "good enough for me, it's good enough for you." They continued to resist, but he calmed the tense encounter and brought them to his home to give them ties. Sebastian later admitted to me, "people coming from abroad shouldn't be given any liberties." In this instance, Americans were considered pushy, but Sebastian told me that most were well behaved and that they increased the frequency and liveliness of dances.

102. *Anglo-Indian Review*, September 1944, quoted in Blunt, *Domicile and Diaspora*, 67.

103. *Anglo-Indian Review*, December 1944, quoted in Blunt, *Domicile and Diaspora*, 67.
104. Khan, "Sex in an Imperial War Zone."
105. Blunt, *Domicile and Diaspora*, 67.
106. Braganza interview, May 5, 2001.
107. I owe some of these ideas to Malene Freudendal-Pedersen's discussion of unfree-dom in *Mobility in Daily Life*. See Cohen, "Urban Musicscapes" and "Paying One's Dues," and Cohen, Lashua, and Schofield, "Introduction," for discussions of musical meaning associated with place or location in urban centers. See Finnegan, *Hidden Musicians*, for a discussion of how urban space can give meaning to musicianship.

Chapter Four

1. Social and military clubs, private residences, and for-profit venues featured jazz in the 1920s, though much more rarely.
2. Perry, interview with author, February 21, 2001.
3. Perry, interview with author, October 24, 2010.
4. For further discussion of the global influence of jazz, see Prouty, *Knowing Jazz*, 151. Atkins, *Jazz Planet*, xx.
5. For further discussion of these narratives, see Austerlitz, *Jazz Consciousness*.
6. Deveaux, "Constructing the Jazz Tradition," 529. Sandke, *Where the Dark and the Light Folks Meet*, 2–3.
7. Barbara Antunis, interview with author, January 13, 2001.
8. Ibid.
9. Ibid. The distribution of gramophone discs was not nearly as efficient as in the 1930s when their dissemination piggybacked film distribution mechanisms, but interested individuals had at least some access in Lucknow.
10. Westmacott Papers (Mss. Eur. F86, Oriental and India Office Collections, British Library), 154. Quoted in Collingham, *Imperial Bodies*, 153. A number of memoirs reference Lucknow during Civil Service week in similar terms. It was deemed popular and it brought many European tourists to the city. Francis Yeats-Brown once complained profusely that he could not attend Civil Service week because of required military exercises in another city (*Bengal Lancer*, 35). For a discussion of the "Victorian" character of ICS week, see Hunt and Harrison, *District Officer in India*, 128.
11. Gundevia, *Districts of the Raj*, 93, 94, 94–95.
12. "Indian Civil Service Week: Constant Round of Gaiety," *Pioneer*, Lucknow ed., February 2, 1934.
13. This is illustrated in a photo of the enclosure at Lucknow Racecourse in the *Pioneer*, Lucknow edition, February 11, 1935.
14. "Indian Civil Service Week: Constant Round of Gaiety," *Pioneer*, Lucknow edition, February 2, 1934.
15. Ibid.
16. Ibid.
17. "Government House Dance," *Pioneer*, Lucknow ed., February 4, 1934.
18. "Civil Service Week Ends: Good Crowds at All Functions," *Pioneer*, Lucknow ed., February 5, 1934.
19. "Valerio's Lucknow," *Pioneer*, Lucknow ed., January 25, 1935.

20. This venue featured ballroom music and dance as well, hosting the Uttar Pradesh. Amateur Dancing Championship in October that year.

21. According to the *Pioneer*, the yearly Hog Hunter's Ball and band concerts at the Mahomed Bagh Club were produced, but a lack of attendance put a damper on the gaiety. However, the Government House Ball boasted seven hundred attendees ("Government House Ball," *Pioneer*, Lucknow ed., February 5, 1938).

22. "Civil Service 'Week,'" *Pioneer*, Lucknow ed., January 30, 1938.

23. *Pioneer*, Lucknow ed., December 30, 1933.

24. Lord Clive initiated the policy of building cantonments in 1765, but the practice of segregating troops from cities and towns began in the early eighteenth century (Jacob, *Cantonments in India*, 19). The aim of these cantonments, according to Veena Talwar Oldenburg, was to "create a small European cosmos at the edge of the city . . . [and] also to provide European soldiers with adequate recreational facilities so they would be less tempted to taste the pleasures the city had to offer" (Oldenburg, *Making of Colonial Lucknow*, 53).

25. "New Year Parade at Lucknow," *Pioneer*, Lucknow ed., January 4, 1934.

26. The Band of the 10th Hussars was in demand because it was also highly regarded for its athletic prowess in polo and other sports ("Rich and Varied Programme," *Pioneer*, Lucknow ed., February 6, 1935).

27. Hamilton, *East Indian Gazetteer*, 131.

28. Heber, *Narrative of a Journey*, 383, 386. Heber is likely referring to Strawberry Gothic style.

29. *Jitterbug* is a term that describes a style popularized in Cab Calloway's recording "Call of the Jitterbug" and in the short film *Cab Calloway's Jitterbug Party* (1935).

30. Advertisement for Agabeg's, *Pioneer*, Lucknow ed., January 19, 1934.

31. "Valerio's Lucknow," *Pioneer*, Lucknow ed., January 25, 1935.

32. Advertisement for Blue Room, *Pioneer*, Lucknow ed., October 15, 1934.

33. Moreover, the origin of the idea of the "Blue Room" stretches back to the Hotel de Rambouillet of Paris, where a salon constructed in 1610 was attended by literary figures (and others) to engage in stimulating and controversial conversation (Vincent, *Hotel de Rambouillet*, 17–36). The salon, referred to as the Blue Room, was a demarcated a space where men and women from diverse social classes could meet, a practice that would otherwise have been unheard of in seventeenth-century France. Evoking the name "Blue Room" at the Prince of Wales Theatre was a strategy used to market the venue as an appropriate social space for an innovative style of music and a new type of consumer.

34. A June 28, 1919, edition of the Madras *Anglo-Indian* claims that "Anglo-Indians are too fond of dancing and spend too much of their time and money at local dancing halls" (Caplan, *Children of Colonialism*, 221).

35. See, for example, "Lucknow Club Dance," *Pioneer*, Lucknow ed., July 6, 1935.

36. Dignam, interview with author, November 28, 2000.

37. Park, "Human Migration," 881. According to Park, a curious effect of marginality was that it encouraged migration to a cosmopolitan urban center, considered more accepting and sophisticated (892).

38. Stonequist, "Problem of the Marginal Man," 5.

39. Hedin, "Anglo-Indian Community," 176.

40. Gbah Bear, "Miscegenations of Modernity," 539.

41. Cottrell, "Today's Asian-Western Couples are Not Anglo-Indians," 354.

42. For a discussion on the etymology of his ideas about race, see Dover, "The Snail Regrets." For a discussion of his ideas about cultural affinities between members of minority communities or people of color, see Dover, "The Black Knight" and "The Black Knight: Part II." For further discussion of the "marginal man" theory, see Green, "A Re-Examination."
43. Dover, "Notes on Coloured Writing," 244.
44. For further discussions on attitudes toward the Anglo-Indian community, see Gbah Bear, "Miscegenations of Modernity"; Caplan, "Iconographies of Anglo-Indian Women"; Spear, *The Nabobs*; and Younger, *Anglo-Indians*. For a history of interracial unions between Indians and British, and later between Anglo-Indians and British, see Caplan, *Children of Colonialism*.
45. Advertisement for Federal Talkies, *Pioneer*, Lucknow ed., January 1, 1934.
46. This is illustrated in an advertisement for *Flying Down to Rio* at the Plaza Talkies in the *Pioneer*, Lucknow ed., January 13, 1935.
47. "The Latest New Song and Dance Albums," *Pioneer*, Lucknow ed., January 18, 1934. "As." denoted the now obsolete currency unit anna, which was 1/16 of a rupee.
48. This is illustrated in an advertisement for Sirdar Gramophone Company in the *Pioneer*, Lucknow ed., December 16, 1933.
49. Advani, interview with author, March 14, 2001.
50. Head, "British Colonial Broadcasting Policies," 39.
51. See, for example, "Broadcasting Programmes: Calcutta Wavelength," *Pioneer*, January 12, 1934.
52. Office of the Controller of Broadcasting, *Progress of Broadcasting*, 6.
53. One newspaper cartoon in the *Pioneer*, Lucknow ed., on January 26, 1935, titled "Chandu the Chowkidar," laments that the listeners can only hear "music from Java," which Chandu claims is much less preferred than the "atmospherics," or static sound.
54. "Radio Station at Lucknow: Results of University Test Broadcast," *Pioneer*, Lucknow ed., February 12, 1934. The article then suggests that the residents of Lucknow take matters into their own hands and launch an amateur radio club using a transmitter at the University of Lucknow for the growing number of "listeners in and around Lucknow who possess powerful receivers and are keen on radio reception."
55. Gupta, *Radio and the Raj*, xi–xiv.
56. Advani, "The New Radio Station, 'Modern to the Minute,'" *Pioneer*, Lucknow ed., February 1, 1938.
57. Gupta, *Radio and the Raj*, 184.
58. Office of the Controller of Broadcasting, *Progress of Broadcasting*, 25.
59. Classical music was transmitted as well. Performances of Belgian jazz musician-composer Jules Craen were popular. Jules Craen led the Bombay Symphony Orchestra.
60. "Indian Broadcast Programmes," *Pioneer*, Lucknow ed., February 1, 1938.
61. "Indian Broadcast Programmes," *Pioneer*, Lucknow ed., January 7, 1938.
62. "Indian Broadcast Programmes," *Pioneer*, Lucknow ed., January 3, 1939.
63. Perry, interview with author, August 15, 2009, and Shepard, interview with author, August 21, 2009.
64. He also maintains with pride that they owned a gramophone player and bought disks pressed by Columbia and HMV.
65. Perry, interview with author, February 21, 2001.
66. Ibid.

67. See, for example, "On the Air India: Lucknow," *Pioneer*, Lucknow ed., January 8, 1940.

68. *Pioneer*, Lucknow ed., January–February 1940.

69. D'Costa, interview with author, October 21, 2001.

70. McFarland, interview with author, January 18, 2001.

71. D'Costa, interview with author, October 23, 2000.

72. D'Costa, interview with author, August 15, 2008.

73. "Boomps, Yips," *Time*, July 10, 1939, 31.

74. Dance club patrons did the Lambeth Walk and the Palais Glide in elite venues throughout India. Cabaret dancers at the Taj Mahal Palace Hotel in Bombay during the 1938–39 winter season taught patrons both dances. The program booklet of the Taj Mahal Hotel, 1938–39, states that the "Lambeth Walk shot from Park Lane to Park Avenue, and now its slated for the Taj." From the Roy G. Butler Collection, Visual and Performing Arts Division, Chicago Public Library.

75. See, for example, "At Last! Tonight! The Funniest Film! For the Mayfair Opening," *Pioneer*, January 28, 1939.

76. Advani, "Personalities of Hazratganj," 73.

77. Much of this material is from a personal interview with Barbara Antunis, Peter Antunis's daughter, on January 13, 2001.

78. See, for example, an advertisement for the Savoy Hotel on January 26, 1935, in the *Pioneer*, Lucknow edition, which boasted its "running hot and cold water and modern sanitation." For another example of the focus on the modern amenities of the hotel, see the advertisement for the Savoy Hotel in the Calcutta edition of the *Statesman*, December 7, 1941.

79. Dignam, interview with author, October 21, 2000.

80. Bhattacharya, *Propaganda and Information*, 1.

81. Ibid., 19–20.

82. Ibid., 49.

83. Perry, interview with author, January 22, 2001.

84. Peter Antunis, interview with author, January 14, 2001. Antunis Jr. claims that Italian priests took responsibility for the restricted movement of the prisoners.

85. Interview on September 12, 2005. Accessed April 4, 2008, http://www.bbc.co.uk/history/ww2peopleswar/stories/23/a5705723.shtml.

86. Advani, "Personalities of Hazratganj," 73.

87. Peter Antunis, interview with author, January 14, 2001.

88. D'Costa, interview with author, August 15, 2008.

89. Dignam, interview with author, October 21, 2000.

90. Dignam directly attributes the viability of performing jazz in Lucknow to Goans and claims that "in India at that time we had live bands. The Goans have a lot of music from Goa. Very musically minded. They used to do it really well" (October 21, 2000).

91. Frank, interview with author, October 24, 2000.

92. Frank also directed the Lucknow Christian Choir. They sang for the Allied forces each Wednesday at the request of the military leadership. A boys' choir of twenty-five to thirty participants, they sang Christian songs in both English and Hindustani.

93. Barbara Antunis, interview with author, January 13, 2001.

94. Frank, interview with author, October 24, 2000.

95. Abbott and Daniell, *International Directory*, 141.

96. Perry, interview with author, February 21, 2001.
97. Ibid.
98. Perry, interview with author, August 19, 2009.
99. Ibid.
100. Ibid.
101. Sharar, *Lucknow*, 139.
102. Singh, interview with author, October 6, 2000.
103. See Attia Hosain's novel, *Sunlight on a Broken Column*, for an interesting account of the relationship between Anglo-Indians and Europeans in Lucknow.
104. Advani, interview with author, March 14, 2001.
105. Misra, *Lucknow Fire of Grace*, 229–30.
106. McFarland, interview with author, January 18, 2001; Dignam, interview with author, October 21, 2000; and D'Costa, interview with author, October 23, 2000.
107. D'Costa, interview with author, October 23, 2000.
108. Dignam, interview with author, October 21, 2000.
109. Advani, interview with author, March 14, 2001.
110. Singh, interview with author, October 6, 2000.
111. Advertisement for Mayfair Ballroom, *Pioneer*, Lucknow ed., February 10, 1940.
112. Advertisement for Mayfair Ballroom, *Pioneer*, Lucknow ed., January 22, 1942.
113. Advertisement for Plaza Cinema, *Pioneer*, Lucknow ed., January 1, 1942.
114. "A Real Hawaiian Night," *Pioneer*, Lucknow ed., January 2, 1942.
115. Frank, interview with author, October 6, 2000.
116. Advertisement for Ambassador, *Pioneer*, Lucknow ed., October 29, 1944.
117. Advertisements for the Ambassador, *Pioneer*, Lucknow ed., December 10–16, 1944.
118. "Lucknow's Feast of Good Things," *Pioneer*, Lucknow ed., November 27, 1944.
119. "General Forces Programme," *Pioneer*, Lucknow ed. July 1, 1944.
120. Advertisement for Mayfair Ballroom, *Pioneer*, Lucknow ed., February 23, 1945.
121. "Mayfair Ballroom: Grand Opening Night of the All American Swing Band," *Pioneer*, Lucknow ed., May 4, 1945.
122. See, for example, "Mayfair Ballroom: Victory at Last," *Pioneer*, Lucknow ed., May 9, 1945.
123. "Ambassador Cocktail Dance," *Pioneer*, Lucknow ed., March 9, 1945.
124. "Ambassador Presents Unrivaled Triple Attraction," *Pioneer*, Lucknow ed., May 16, 1945.
125. McFarland, interview with author, January 18, 2001.
126. "Victory Celebrations in Lucknow," *Pioneer*, Lucknow ed., August 20, 1945.
127. "Ambassador New Year's Eve Ball," *Pioneer*, Lucknow ed., December 30, 1947.
128. Peter Antunis, interview with author, January 14, 2001.
129. See Bhabha ("Unsatisfied," 195–96) for a similar discussion of cosmopolitan capital.
130. McFarland, interview with author, January 18, 2001.
131. Schulz, "A City of Picture Palaces," 58–60.

Chapter Five

1.   See Jayson Beaster-Jones, "Film Song and Its Other," for additional discussion of this stylistic continuity. Gregory Booth's "Moment of Historical Conjuncture" informs some of my approach to this chapter.

2.   Beaster-Jones, *Bollywood Sounds*, 11.
3.   Ibid., 10.
4.   Quoted in Gilling, "Colour of Music," 36.
5.   See J. P. Singh (*Globalized Arts*, xxiv) for a more complete discussion of this value chain in films.
6.   Cooke, *Hollywood Film Music Reader*, viii–ix.
7.   Quoted in Sullivan, *Hitchcock's Music*, xix.
8.   As film music scholar George Burt has stated, "If the music draws away or diverts from the dramatic shape, line or impulse, it doesn't fit the film" (*Art of Film Music*, 5).
9.   See Turino, *Music as Social Life*, for further dicussion of of continuity and change in music.
10. For additional discussion of the dynamic nature of film music, see Shuker, *Understanding Popular Music Culture.*
11. See Arora, "Popular Songs in Hindi Films"; Gopal and Moorti, *Global Bollywood*; and Morcom, *Hindi Film Songs.*
12. See Barnouw and Krishnaswamy, *Indian Film*; Baskaran, *Eye of the Serpent*; and Chandavarkar, "Great Film Song Controversy" and "Tradition of Music."
13. In "Popular Songs in Hindi Films," Arora observes that plays popularized by traveling theater groups were even included in films by the immensely famous actor Raj Kapoor beginning with *Aag* in 1948.
14. In discussing stylistic continuity and compositional approach, Leonard Meyer suggests that when music "is no longer compatible with the ideological/aesthetic values of the culture, then there will be a search, often by trial and error, for greater stability," and this search frequently results in innovation (*Style and Music*, 109). He also points out that when stylistic attributes are compatible with prevalent aesthetic-cultural ideals, innovation is modest but productivity is often high (109–10).
15. Nayar, "Values of Fantasy," 75. Similarly, according to Alison Arnold, "Generally speaking, the broader the musical sources a composer used, the less regional and more national was his musical appeal" (*Hindi Filmi Geet*, 200). Musically evoking the "uniformity of the West" was deliberate and calculated, part of a process of innovation that expanded compositional stylistics beyond Indian dramatic genres. Ravi Vasudevan also argues that Western musical elements created a "mobility to the spectator's imaginary identity" that offered audiences an appealing glimpse beyond their cultural or linguistic environs ("Shifting Codes, Dissolving Identities," 99).
16. Perhaps somewhat ancillary to our discussion but nonetheless interesting to note is that Hollywood affected audiences with content that was by some measures problematic in India. According to the Indian Cinematograph Committee (ICC) Report, the summary of a comprehensive study of the state of cinema in India, films sometimes included potentially harmful misrepresentations of Western life: "[Audiences are] amazed and shocked by such commonplaces of Western life as the emancipation of women, their free social intercourse with men, their spirits, their dances and even their dress . . . which lower Western, especially European, civilization in the minds of Indians" (122). The cinema lured audiences away from the usual perceptions of their surroundings to perceptions of adjacent environments that were eclectic in nature, transnational in scope, and transgressive in content.

17. For additional discussion of "stylistic plateau" in music, see Washabaugh, *Flamenco Music and National Identity*, 45–46.
18. Brown, *Cosmopolitan Criticism*, 30.
19. Arnold, "Popular Film Song in India" and *Hindi Filmi Git.*
20. See Wachsmann ("Ethnomusicology in Africa," 133) and Rycroft ("Evidence of Stylistic Continuity in Zulu 'Town' Music," 216) for further discussion of musical borrowing.
21. Composers embraced musicians from a diversity of backgrounds. It has been comprehensively documented that Goan musicians increasingly worked as arrangers, musicians, and consultants in the industry beginning in the 1930s. Music director Madhulal Damodar Master asserts that Goan musicians were first employed as film studio orchestra musicians as early as 1932 for the film *Navchetan* (Arnold, *Hindi Filmi Git*, 91), and because of their ability to read staff notation, were later found to be essential to orchestras. Music director Keshavrao Bhole remembers that when players from Bombay were not available during this period, he depended on musicians from Goa to read music notation and effectively cover the parts (ibid., 53).
22. Booth, "Moment of Historical Conjuncture"; Fernandes, *Taj Mahal Foxtrot*; and Shope, "'They Treat Us White Folks Fine'" and "Latin American Music."
23. "Film Studio News," *Federation of Musicians* (India), June 4, 1949, 3.
24. Fernandes, *Taj Mahal Foxtrot*, 115.
25. His first job was at the Majestic Hotel with Italian pianist Beppo di Siati.
26. "The Show Is On, Frank Fernand Excels," *Federation of Musicians* (India), October 27, 1948, 5.
27. Taj Mahal Palace Hotel, *All Star Band Presents Swing Concert*. Described as an "Indian theme" song, it received last place in a composer's competition on September 28, 1948, at the Taj Mahal Palace Hotel.
28. Relationships between dance band musicians and film composers began in the 1930s, and some of the earliest collaborations was represented by a trio of musicians referred to as "A-R-P." The acronym stood for the trio of Alphonso Albuquerque on cello, Ram Singh on saxophone, and Peter Sequiera on violin and guitar (Booth, *Behind the Curtain*, and "Moment of Historical Conjuncture"). Dance band musician Johnny Gomes and the more classically focused Anthony Gonsalves also worked in the film music industry around this time.
29. "New Band for Taj Hotel," *Times of India*, November 6, 1933.
30. Abby also played jazz standards.
31. "Taj Cabaret, New Russian Peasant Comedy," *Times of India*, March 6, 1936.
32. "Variety at the Taj," *Times of India*, February 7, 1936.
33. See Segel, *Turn-of-the-Century Cabaret*, for additional discussion of the cabaret industry of the early twentieth century.
34. Gulzar, Chatterjee, and Nihalani, *Encyclopedia of Hindi Cinema*, 475. Khan claims that "screenwriters and film directors strained the storylines at the seams to include a cabaret number" (Khubchandani, "Song Picturization and Choreography," 203).
35. In style and approach, cabarets in India were also somewhat similar to those seen in Shanghai, New Zealand, Australia, and Singapore. Cabarets in India benefited from the availability of traveling groups from these metropolises. Wong Yunn Chii and Tan Kar Lin observe that Singapore cabarets featured dance orchestras and choruses ("Emergence of Cosmopolitan Space," 298–99) that sometimes travelled to India through the Singapore circuit.

36. "Swing Concert," *Federation of Musicians* (India), June 4, 1949, 7.

37. "Bombay Swing Club," *Federation of Musicians* (India), June 4, 1949, 4.

38. From the 1948–49 winter program booklet of the Taj Mahal Hotel, Bombay.

39. Taj Mahal Palace Hotel, *Grand Gala at the Taj Bombay*. The October 27, 1948, edition of the Federation of Musicians publication states that the hotel spent Rs. 100,000 to obtain these musicians, a considerable sum at the time.

40. Taj Mahal Palace Hotel, *Cabaret: "A Breath of Spain."*

41. Advertisement for Taj Mahal Palace Hotel, *Times of India*, November 3, 1951.

42. Taj Mahal Palace Hotel, *May the New Year Bring You Joy and Happiness Is the Warmest Wish of the Taj Bombay*.

43. The Solovox was an amplified instrument manufactured in the 1940s by the Hammond Organ Company. It was attached underneath the keyboard of a piano and produced a variety of string-, woodwind- and organ-type sounds.

44. Taj Mahal Palace Hotel, *Grand Gala Dance: "Place Pigalle."*

45. Taj Mahal Palace Hotel, *Quatorze Juillet a Montparnasse: Grand Gala Dance*.

46. Advertisement for Ambassador's Starlet Roof Garden, *Times of India*, December 11, 1951.

47. Taj Mahal Palace Hotel, *South Sea Rhapsody* (Bombay: Taj Mahal Palace Hotel, 1949).

48. Hawaiian and island themes are found in a number of song-dance sequences in Hindi films at the time, including *Albela* (1951).

49. Taj Mahal Palace Hotel, *Cabaret: "A Breath of Spain"* (Bombay: Taj Mahal Palace Hotel, date unknown).

50. Taj Mahal Palace Hotel, *Taj Dinner/Dance*.

51. Taj Mahal Palace Hotel, *Singing Debut of Nutan, Indian's Beauty Queen 1951 and Starlet*. Presenting contestants from beauty contests was common at the time at the hotel.

52. Taj Mahal Palace Hotel, *The Indian Republic Day: 26th January*, 1–2.

53. Rishi, "Bless You Bollywood!" 116.

54. Booth, *Behind the Curtain*, 34.

55. Ibid., 40.

56. Arnold, *Hindi Filmi Git*, 134.

57. Ibid., 137.

58. To affirm that jazz virtuosity still existed in India, head musicians organized star orchestras or all-star performances in Bombay to showcase the best musicians and the newest repertoire. Some of the most highly publicized all-star jazz events occurred in 1948, the year after Independence. Both musicians and dance hall proprietors organized these events, and included the latest jazz standards. For example, an All Star Band composed of key Bombay musicians (many from Micky Correa's orchestra at the Taj Mahal Palace Hotel) performed a concert on September 15 that included twenty-eight songs such as "Flying Home," "Apple Honey," "Bach Bit'in," "Swanee Bebop," and the "Laughing Samba" (Taj Mahal Palace Hotel, *All Star Swing Band Presents: Swing Concert*).

59. "The Writing on the Wall," *Federation of Musicians* (India), October 27, 1948, 1.

60. Jazz in Calcutta after Independence was also somewhat diminished. The October 27, 1948, edition of the Federation of Musicians (India) newsletter contains a brief article titled "Calcutta Comments," which claims that "the standard of the Musicians [in Calcutta] is very much below the average, they are not even mediocre. . . . They

somehow or other eke out an existence and are gigging, though they do not earn enough to keep body and soul together" (4). This article reports that the listening public in Calcutta had become disillusioned by the poor quality of performances, and laments that audiences did not demand higher quality musicianship. The article asserts that "the Calcutta public had been dosed so much with 'crap' music from lousy hands that any outstanding polished combination that plays the real McCoy does not make sense—so the gig jobs are executed by those awful instrumentalists" (4).

61. "The Writing on the Wall," *Federation of Musicians* (India), October 27, 1948, 1.
62. Ibid.
63. Hartman De Souza, drawing from interviews with a number of Goan musicians who played during this time, claims that three realities were possible for jazz musicians: "To play their own music and starve, to play bad music at the hotels and the films and live, or, to give up music altogether, making it into a hobby instead of a visionary quest" ("Swing Hadn't Really Stopped," 17).
64. Darke and Gulliver, "Teddy Weatherford," 187.
65. Quoted in Booth, *Behind the Curtain*, 145.
66. Collet, "Thirty Years of Jazz."
67. See, for example, YMCA, *75th Anniversary Bombay Y.M.C.A. Swing Concert*, and "Gala Swing Concert," *Times of India*, June 15, 1950.
68. Innovation in the area of orchestration and instrumentation was apparent from the beginning of film production. Orchestras that accompanied American and European silent films influenced some of the first music composers such as Keshavrao Bhole and Naushad Ali. Bhole attended silent films in theaters with full-scale orchestra pits and large resident orchestras between 1919 and 1930. He fondly remembers that "their combination, sometimes so soft and then so grand, evok[ed] such sentiments" (Ranade, "Keshavrao Bhole," 50–51). More extensive experimentation with orchestration and Western instruments began as early as the mid-1930s in Hindi films. Large orchestras at the time appealed to audiences and became a status symbol for large-budget films. According to an interview with Naushad Ali in 1999, these orchestras were linked to ideas about grandiosity and lavishness (Naushad Ali, interview with Morcom, April 20, 1999; quoted in Morcom, *Hindi Film Songs*, 148–49).
69. Dwyer, *100 Bollywood Films*, 23.
70. "Film Studio News," *Federation of Musicians* (India), June 4, 1949, 3.
71. Booth, *Behind the Curtain*, 239.
72. A review of one of his compositions performed on March 13, 1949, at Sunderbai Hall in Bombay claims that the piece covered "the entire field of Jazz or Swing Moods," including be-bop. ("Swing Concert," *Federation of Musicians* (India), June 4, 1949, 7).
73. Some film music scholars suggest that the use of Western music was the product of technological development in sound production, not so much an embraceing of Hollywood films or other Western sources (Chanavarkar, "Great Film Song Controversy" 72).
74. Booth, "Moment of Historical Conjuncture," 31.
75. Kaur and Sinha, *Bollyworld*, 12–13.
76. See Manuel, "Popular Music in India," 161 for further discussion of meaning in cabaret scenes in films.

77. Fernandes, *Taj Mahal Foxtrot*, 124.

78. See, for example, Collet, "Thirty Years of Jazz."

79. Sollo Jacobs performed in Lucknow in the 1930s and 1940s and was referred to as the "Teddy Wilson of India" (Collet, "Thirty Years of Jazz"). Wilson was a jazz pianist from the United States.

80. Booth, *Behind the Curtain*, 140.

81. Shope, "Latin American Music," 213.

82. See, for example, "Tonight at the West End Hotel," *Times of India*, November 10, 1951.

83. Lewis, "Beyond the Reef."

84. See, for example, "Ambassador Roof Garden Tonight: Hawaiian Madness," *Times of India*, February 25, 1950.

85. Many of my thoughts on stylistic continuity here are informed by Leonard Meyer, *Style and Music*, 108–16.

Afterword

1. Perry, interview with author, January 22, 2001.

2. Fraser, "Recognition without Ethics?" 24.

3. Pinckney, "Jazz in India," 39. Ved Mehta observes that Bombay was open to jazz in the 1960s, especially in club Venice, and that some bands played "morning to night, whether or not anyone [was] dancing, or even listening" (*Portrait in India*, 66).

4. Booth, "Beat Comes to India," 217.

5. Ibid., 218.

6. Blacking, "*A Commonsense View.*"

Bibliography

Abbas, Khwaja Ahmad. *I Write as I Feel.* Bombay: Hind Kitabs, 1948.

Abbott, Frank and C. A. Daniell. *The International Directory of Music Industries.* Chicago: Presto Publishing, 1911.

Abel, Richard. *The Ciné Goes to Town: French Cinema, 1896–1914.* Berkeley: University of California Press, 1998.

Abravanel, Genevieve. *Americanizing Britain: The Rise of Modernism in the Age of Entertainment Empire.* New York: Oxford University Press, 2012.

Advani, Ram. "Personalities of Hazratganj." In *Hazratganj: A Journey through the Times,* edited by Rosie Llewellyn-Jones, 72–74. Lucknow: Bennett, Coleman, 2011.

Air Operations in China, Burma, India, World War II: The United States Strategic Bombing Survey. Washington, DC: Military Analysis Division, 1947.

All Star Band Presents Swing Concert. Bombay: Taj Mahal Palace Hotel, 1948.

All Star Swing Band Presents: Swing Concert. Bombay: Taj Mahal Palace Hotel, 1948.

Allen, Charles, and Michael Mason. *Plain Tales from the Raj: Images of British India in the Twentieth Century.* New York: St. Martin's Press, 1976.

Allen, Ray, and Lois Wilcken. *Island Sounds in the Global City: Caribbean Popular Music and Identity in New York.* New York: New York Folklore Society and the Institute for Studies in American Music, 1998.

Andersson, A. E., and D. E. Andersson. *The Economics of Experiences: The Arts and Entertainment.* Northhampton, MA: Edward Elgar, 2006.

Angwin, Benjamin Easterbrook. "Music in the Himalayan Foothills." *Musical Times* 77, no. 1117 (1936): 226–30.

Anthony, Frank. *Britain's Betrayal in India: The Story of the Anglo-Indian Community.* Bombay: Allied Publishers, 1969.

Appadurai, Arjun. "Grassroots Globalization and the Research Imagination." In *Globalization,* edited by Arjun Appadurai, 1–21. Durham, NC: Duke University Press, 2001.

Appelrouth, Scott. "Body and Soul: Jazz in the 1920s." *American Behavioral Scientist* 48, no. 11 (2005): 1496–509.

Archer-Straw, Petrine. "Exoticism in Black and White." *Nka: Journal of Contemporary African Art* 21 (2007): 24–33.

Arnold, Alison. "Aspects of Production and Consumption in the Popular Hindi Film Song Industry." *Asian Music* 24, no. 1 (1992–93): 122–36.

———. *Hindi Filmi Git: On The History of Commercial Indian Popular Cinema.* PhD diss., University of Illinois, 1991.

———. "Popular Film Song in India: A Case of Mass Market Musical Eclecticism." *Popular Music* 7, no. 2 (1988): 177–88.

Arora, Poonam. "'Imperiling the Prestige of the White Woman': Colonial Anxiety and Film Censorship in British India." *Visual Anthropology Review* 11, no. 2 (1995): 36–50.

Arora, V. N. "Popular Songs in Hindi Films." *Journal of Popular Culture* 20, no. 2 (1986): 143–66.

Arthur, Sue. "Blackpool Goes All-Talkie: Cinema and Society at the Seaside in Thirties Britain." *Historical Journal of Film, Radio and Television* 29, no. 1 (2009): 27–39.

A.S.C. "Calcutta Cathedral and Its New Organ." *Musical Times* 56, no. 872 (1915): 600–603.

Asthana, Sanjay. "Broadcasting, Space, and Sovereignty in India." *Media Culture Society* 35, no. 4 (2013): 516–34.

Athique, Adrian. "From Cinema Hall to Multiplex: A Public History." *South Asian Popular Culture* 9, no. 2 (2011): 147–60.

Atkins, E. Taylor. *Jazz Planet.* Jackson: University of Mississippi Press, 2003.

Auerbach, Jeffery. "Imperial Boredom." *Common Knowledge* 11, no. 2 (2005): 283–305.

Austerlitz, Paul. *Jazz Consciousness: Music, Race and Humanity.* Middletown, CT: Wesleyan University Press, 2005.

Awasthy, G. C. *Broadcasting in India.* Bombay: Allied Publishers Private, 1965.

Baade, Christina. *Victory through Harmony: The BBC and Popular Music in World War II.* Oxford: Oxford University Press, 2012.

Bacon, Thomas. *First Impressions and Studies from Nature in Hindostan: Embracing an Outline of the Voyage To Calcutta, and Five Years' Residence in Bengal and the Doáb, from 1831–1836.* Vol. 2. London: William H. Allen, 1837.

Badger, R. Reid. "James Reese Europe and the Prehistory of Jazz." *American Music* 7, no. 1 (1989): 48–67.

Bakhle, Janaki. *Two Men and Music: Nationalism in the Making of an Indian Classical Tradition.* New York: Oxford University Press, 2005.

Bakari, Imruh. "Exploding Silence: African-Caribbean and African American Music in British Culture towards 2000." In *Living Through Pop,* edited by Andrew Blake, 98–111. New York: Routledge, 1999.

Baker, Charles. *The Gentleman's Companion.* New York: Crown, 1946.

Bandmann, Daniel. *An Actor's Tour.* Boston: Cupples, Upham, 1885.

Barkawi, Tarak. *Globalization and War.* Lanham, MD: Rowman and Littlefield, 2006.

Barnouw, Erik, and S. Krishnaswamy. *Indian Film.* New York: Columbia University Press, 1963.

Baruah, U. L. *This Is All India Radio: A Handbook of Radio Broadcasting in India.* New Delhi: Publications Division, Ministry of Information and Broadcasting, Government of India, 1983.

Baskaran, Sundararaj Theodore. *The Eye of the Serpent: An Introduction to Tamil Cinema.* Madras: East West Books, 1996.

Bayly, Christopher, and Tim Harper. *Forgotten Armies: The Fall of British Asia, 1941–1945.* Cambridge, MA: Belknap Press of Harvard University Press, 2005.

Bear, Laura. *Lines of the Nation: Indian Railway Workers, Bureaucracy and the Intimate Historical Self.* New York: Columbia University Press, 2007.

Beaster-Jones, Jayson. *Bollywood Sounds: The Cosmopolitan Mediation of Hindi Film Song*. New York: Oxford University Press, 2015.

———. "Evergreens to Remixes: Hindi Film Songs and India's Popular Music Heritage." *Ethnomusicology* 53, no. 3 (2009): 425–48.

———. "Film Song and Its Other: Stylistic Mediation and the Hindi Film Song Genre." In Booth and Shope, *More Than Bollywood*, 97–113.

Beck, Ulrich. "Cosmopolitical Realism: On the Distinction between Cosmopolitanism in Philosophy and the Social Sciences." *Global Networks* 4, no. 2 (2004): 131–56.

———. *Cosmopolitan Vision*. Cambridge: Polity Press, 2006.

———. "Rooted Cosmopolitanism: Emerging from a Rivalry of Distinctions." In *Global America? The Cultural Consequences of Globalization*, edited by Ulrich Beck, Natan Sznaider, and Rainer Winter, 15–29. Liverpool: Liverpool University Press, 2003.

Beck, Ulrich, and Natan Sznaider. "Unpacking Cosmopolitanism for the Social Sciences: A Research Agenda." *British Journal of Sociology* 57, no. 1 (2006): 381–403.

Bennett, Andy. "Consolidating the Music Scenes Perspective." *Poetics* 32 (2004): 223–34.

Berlin, Edward. *Ragtime: A Musical and Cultural History*. Berkeley: University of California Press, 1984.

Berry, Sarah. *Screen Style: Fashion and Femininity in 1930s Hollywood*. Minneapolis: University of Minnesota Press, 2000.

Bhabha, Homi. "Unsatisfied: Notes on Vernacular Cosmopolitanism." In *Text and Nation*, edited by Laura Garcia-Moreno and Peter C. Pfeifer, 191–207. Columbia, SC: Camden House, 1996.

Bhabha, Homi K., Carol A. Breckenridge, Dipesh Chakrabarty, and Sheldon Pollock. "Cosmopolitanisms." *Public Culture* 12, no. 3 (2000): 577–89.

Bhattacharya, Sanjoy. "British Military Information Management Techniques and the South Asian Soldier: Eastern India during the Second World War." *Modern Asian Studies* 34, no. 2 (2000): 483–510.

———. "An Official Policy That Went Awry: The Colonial State's Second World War Propaganda Campaign against the Indian National Congress." *International Institute of Asian Studies Newsletter* 13 (1997): n.p.

———. *Propaganda and Information in Eastern India, 1939–1945: A Necessary Weapon of War*. Richmond, UK: Curzon Press, 2001.

Bhaumik, Kaushik. "Cinematograph to Cinema: Bombay 1896–1928." *Bioscope: South Asian Screen Studies* 2, no. 1 (2011): 41–67.

Bierley, Paul E. *John Philip Sousa: American Phenomenon*. Miami: Warner Brothers, 2001.

Bill, Katina. "Attitudes towards Women's Trousers: Britain in the 1930s." *Journal of Design History* 6, no. 1 (1993): 45–54.

Blackford, Stan. *One Hell of a Life: An Anglo-Indian Wallah's Memoire from the Last Decades of the Raj*. Fulham Gardens, SA: S. T. Blackford, 2000.

Blacking, John. *'A Commonsense View of All Music': Reflections on Percy Grainger's Contribution to Ethnomusicology and Music Education*. Cambridge: Cambridge University Press, 1987.

Blunt, Alison. *Domicile and Diaspora: Anglo-Indian Women and the Spatial Politics of Home.* Oxford: Blackwell, 2005.

Bolles, Albert. *Industrial History of the United States from the Earliest Settlements.* Norwich, CT: Henry Bill Publishing, 1878.

Booth, Gregory. "The Beat Comes to India: The Incorporation of Rock Music into the Indian Soundscape." In Booth and Shope, *More Than Bollywood,* 216–37.

———. *Behind the Curtain.* New York: Oxford University Press, 2008.

———. *Brass Baja: Stories from the World of Indian Wedding Bands.* New York: Oxford University Press, 2005.

———. "Brass Bands: Tradition, Change and Mass Media in Indian Wedding Music." *Ethnomusicology* 34, no. 2 (1990): 245–62.

———. "The Madras Corporations Band: A Story of Social Change and Indigenization." *Asian Music* 28 no. 1 (1996–97): 61–86.

———. "A Moment of Historical Conjuncture in Mumbai: Playback Singers, Music Directors, and Arrangers and the Creation of Hindi Song (1948–1952)." In Booth and Shope, *More Than Bollywood,* 21–37.

———. "Religion, Gossip, Narrative Conventions and the Construction of Meaning in Hindi Film Songs." *Popular Music* 19, no. 2 (2000): 125–45.

Booth, Gregory, and Bradley Shope, eds. *Beyond Bollywood: Studies in Indian Popular Music.* New York: Oxford University Press, 2014.

Bowman, LeRoy E., and Maria Ward Lambin. "Evidences of Social Relations as seen in Types of New York City Dance Halls." *Journal of Social Forces* 3, no. 2 (1925): 286–91.

Braddon, Edward. *Life in India: A Series of Sketches Showing Something of the Anglo-Indian—The Land He Lives In—And the People Among Whom He Lives.* London: Longmans, Green, 1872.

Branson, Clive. *British Soldier in India: The Letters of Clive Branson.* London: Communist Party, 1945.

Brooks, Deton J. "Obituary." *Chicago Defender,* May 26, 1945.

Brown, Claude. *The Ordinary Man's India.* London: Palmer, 1927.

Brown, Julia Prewitt. *Cosmopolitan Criticism: Oscar Wilde's Philosophy of Art.* Charlottesville: University Press of Virginia, 1997.

Brown, T. Allston. "Early History of Negro Minstrelsy." *New York Clipper,* May 18, 1912.

Brown, Garrett Wallace, and David Held. *The Cosmopolitan Reader.* Cambridge: Polity, 2010.

Bryant, Daniel. *Bryant's Songs from Dixieland Containing All the New, Laughable, Humorous, Comic and Fashionable Songs and Melodies of That Popular Band of Ethiopian Performers, The Bryant Brothers.* New York: Robert M. De Witt, 1861.

Buettner, Elizabeth. "Problematic Spaces, Problematic Races: Defining 'Europeans' in Late Colonial India." *Women's History Review* 9, no. 2 (2000): 277–98.

Burkholder, J. Peter, Donald Jay Grout, and Claude Palisca. *A History of Western Music.* New York: Norton, 2010.

Burt, George. *The Art of Film Music: Special Emphasis on Hugo Friedhofer, Alex North, David Raskin, and Leonard Rosenman.* Boston: Northeastern University Press, 1995.

Busteed, Henry Elmsley. *Echoes from Old Calcutta: Being Chiefly Reminiscences of the Days of Warren Hastings, Francis, and Impey*. London: W. Thacker, 1888.

Cabaret: "A Breath of Spain." Bombay: Taj Mahal Palace Hotel, 1950.

Cabral e Sá, Mário. *Winds of Fire: The Music and Musicians of Goa*. New Delhi: Promilla, 1997.

Camp, La Vonne Telshaw. *Lingering Fever: A World War II Nurse's Memoir*. Jefferson, NC: McFarland, 2012.

Caplan, Lionel. *Children of Colonialism: Anglo-Indians in a Post-Colonial World*. Oxford: Berg, 2001.

———. "Iconographies of Anglo-Indian Women: Gender Constructs and Contrasts in a Changing Society." *Modern Asian Studies* 34, no. 4 (2000): 863–92.

Capwell, Charles. *The Music of the Bauls of Bengal*. Kent, OH: Kent State University Press, 1986.

Carson, Lionel. *The Stage Year Book with Which Is Included the Stage Provincial Guide*. London: Carson and Comerford, 1914.

Castle, Terry. "Eros and Liberty at the English Masquerade, 1710–1790." *Eighteenth-Century Studies* 17 (1983–84): 156–76.

———. *Masquerade and Civilization: The Carnivalesque in Eighteenth-Century English Culture and Fiction*. Stanford, CA: Stanford University Press, 1986.

Chabot, Sean. "Framing, Transnational Diffusion, and African American Intellectuals in the Land of Gandhi." *International Review of Social History* 49, Supplement S12 (2004): 19–40.

Chadwick, Bruce. *The Reel Civil War: Mythmaking in American Film*. New York: Vintage Books, 2001.

Chakrabarty, Dipesh. "Minority Histories, Subaltern Pasts." *Postcolonial Studies* 1, no. 1 (1998): 15–29.

———. "Postcoloniality and the Artifice of History: Who Speaks for 'Indian' Pasts?" *Representations* 37 (1992): 1–26.

Chakravarti, Mahadev. *Administration Report of Tripura State since 1902: Volume 4*. New Delhi: Gyan Publication House, 1994.

Chakravarty, Rangan. "The Imagined Community of *Maa Tujhe Salaam*: The Global and the Local in the Postcolonial." In *Refashioning Pop Music in Asia: Cosmopolitan Flows, Political Tempos, and Aesthetic Industries*, edited by Allen Chun, Ned Rossiter, and Brian Shoesmith, 63–74. London: RoutledgeCurzon, 2004.

Chakravarty, Sumita S. *National Identity in Indian Popular Cinema 1947–1987*. Austin: University of Texas Press, 1993.

Chanda, Nayan. *Bound Together: How Traders, Preachers, Adventurers, and Warriors Shaped Globalization*. New Haven, CT: Yale University Press, 2008.

Chandavarkar, Bhaskar. "The Great Film Song Controversy." *Cinema Vision India* 1, no. 4 (1980): 66–75.

———. "The Tradition of Music in Indian Cinema: Birth of the Film Song." *Cinema in India* 1, no. 2 (1987): 7–11.

Choudhury, Ranabir. *Early Calcutta Advertisements, 1875–1925: A Selection from the Statesman*. Bombay: Nachiketa, 1992.

Chii, Wong Yunn, and Tan Kar Lin. "Emergence of a Cosmopolitan Space for Culture and Consumption: The New World Amusement Park-Singapore (1923–70) in the Inter-war Years." *Inter-Asia Cultural Studies* 5, no. 2 (2004): 279–304.

Chinitz, David. "Rejuvenation through Joy: Langston Hughes, Primitivism, and Jazz." *American Literary History* 9, no. 1 (1997): 60–78.

Chun, Allen, and Ned Rossiter. "Introduction." In *Refashioning Pop Music in Asia: Cosmopolitan Flows, Political Tempos, and Aesthetic Industries*, edited by Allen Chun, Ned Rossiter, and Brian Shoesmith, 1–14. London: RoutledgeCurzon, 2004.

Clark, Hyde. "The English Stations in the Hill Regions of India: Their Value and Importance, with Some Statistics of Their Products and Trade." *Journal of the Statistical Society* 44, no. 3 (1881): 528–73.

Clayton, Martin. "Rock to Raga: The Many Lives of the Indian Guitar." In *Guitar Cultures*, edited by Andy Bennett and Kevin Dawe, 179–208. New York: Berg, 2001.

Coelho, Victor Anand. "Connecting Histories: Portuguese Music in Renaissance Goa." In *Goa and Portugal: Their Cultural Links*, edited by Charles Borges and Helmut Feldmann, 131–47. New Delhi: Concept Publishing, 1997.

———. "Kapsberger's *Apotheosis* . . . of Francis Xavier (1622) and the Conquering of India." In *The Work of Opera: Genre, Nationhood, and Sexual Difference*, edited by Richard Dellamora and Daniel Fischlin, 27–48. New York: Columbia University Press, 1997.

Cohen, Sara. "Paying One's Dues: The Music Business, the City and Urban Regeneration." In *The Business of Music*, edited by Michael Talbot, 263–91. Liverpool: Liverpool University Press, 2002.

———. "'Rock Landmark at Risk': Popular Music, Urban Regeneration, and the Built Environment." *Journal of Popular Music Studies* 19, no. 1 (2007): 3–25.

———. "Sounding Out the City: Music and the Sensuous Production of Place." *Transactions of the Institute of British Geographers* 20, no. 4 (1995): 434–46.

———. "Urban Musicscapes: Mapping Music-Making in Liverpool." In *Mapping Cultures: Place, Practice, Performance*, edited by Les Roberts, 123–43. Basingstoke: Palgrave Macmillan, 2012.

Cohen, Sara, Brett Lashua, and John Schofield. "Introduction to the Special Issue: Music Characterization and Urban Space." *Popular Music History* 4, no. 2 (2010): 105–10.

Coleman, Bill. *Trumpet Story*. Boston: Northeastern University Press, 1991.

Collet, H. J. "Thirty Years of Jazz in India: Our Top Bands Can Swing It with the Best." *Illustrated Weekly of India*, August 22, 1948.

Collingham, E. M. *Imperial Bodies: The Physical Experience of the Raj, c. 1800–1947*. Cambridge: Polity, 2001.

Conrad, Gerhard. "Trevor Mac: An Investigation by Gerhard Conrad." *Der Jazzfreund* 43 (1998): n.p.

Cook, Nilla Cram. *My Road to India*. New York: L. Furman, 1939.

Cooke, Mervyn. *The Hollywood Film Music Reader*. Oxford: Oxford University Press, 2010.

Coombs, Henry R. "A Sailor on Jazz." *Musical Times* 84, no. 4 (1943): 124.

Cooper, Frederick, and Ann Stoler. "Introduction: Tensions of Empire: Colonial Control and Visions of Rule." *American Ethnologist* 16, no. 4 (1989): 609–21.

Cottrell, Ann Baker. "Today's Asian-Western Couples Are Not Anglo-Indians." *Phylon* 40, no. 4 (1979): 351–61.

Coulson, Susan. "Collaborating in a Competitive World: Musicians' Working Lives and Understandings of Entrepreneurship." *Work, Employment, and Society* 26, no. 2 (2012): 246–61.

Cousins, Margaret. *The Music of the Orient and Occident: Essays towards Mutual Understandings.* Madras: B. G. Paul, 1935.

Cox, Karen. *Dreaming of Dixie: How the South Was Created in American Popular Culture.* Chapel Hill: University of North Carolina Press, 2011.

Craig, Douglas. *Fireside Politics: Radio and Political Culture in the United States, 1920–1940.* Baltimore: Johns Hopkins University Press, 2006.

Crease, Robert. "Jazz and Dance." In *The Cambridge Companion to Jazz*, edited by Mervyn Cooke and David Horn, 69–82. Cambridge: Cambridge University Press, 2002.

Cressey, Paul. "The Anglo-Indians: A Disorganized Marginal Group." *Social Forces* 14, no. 2 (1935): 263–68.

The Cruise of H.M.S. New Zealand. Ottawa: Simmons Print Co., 1919.

Dannett, Sylvia, and Frank Rachel. *Down Memory Lane: Arthur Murray's Picture Story of Social Dancing.* New York: Greenberg, 1954.

Darke, Peter. "Teddy Weatherford's Indian Recording Sessions 1941–1945." *Matrix* 107/108 (1975): 3–6.

Darke, Peter, and Ralph Gulliver. "Roy Butler's Story." *Storyville* 71 (1977): 178–90.

_____. "Teddy Weatherford." *Storyville* 65 (1976): 175–90.

Dawidoff, Robert. *Making History Matter.* Philadelphia: Temple University Press, 2000.

Dejung, Christof. "Bridges to the East: European Merchants and Business Practices in India and China." In *Commerce and Culture: Nineteenth Century Business Elites*, edited by Robert Lee, 93–116. Burlington: Ashgate, 2011.

Decker, Todd. *Performing Race in an American Musical.* New York: Oxford University Press, 2013.

Delanty, Gerard. "The Cosmopolitan Imagination: Critical Cosmopolitanism and Social Theory." *British Journal of Sociology* 57, no. 1 (2006): 25–47.

DeNora, Tia. *After Adorno: Rethinking Music Sociology.* Cambridge: Cambridge University Press, 2003.

De Souza, Hartman. "Swing Hadn't Really Stopped Then." *Debonair*, Special Feature (March 1982): 14–17.

Deveaux, Scott. "Constructing the Jazz Tradition: Jazz Historiography." *Black American Literature Forum* 25, no. 3 (1991): 525–60.

Dinerstein, Joel. *Swinging the Machine: Modernity, Technology, and African American Culture between the World Wars.* Amherst: University of Massachusetts Press, 2003.

Dobson, Andrew. "Thick Cosmopolitanism." *Political Studies* 54, no. 1 (2006): 165–84.

Dover, Cedric. "The Black Knight." *Phylon* 15, no. 1 (1954a): 41–57.

———. "The Black Knight: Part II." *Phylon* 15, no. 2 (1954b): 177–89.
———. *Cimmerii? or Eurasians and their Future.* Calcutta: Modern Art Press, 1929.
———. "Notes on Coloured Writing." *Phylon* 8, no. 3 (1947): 213–24.
———. "The Snail Regrets." *Phylon* 12, no. 4 (1951): 347–56.
Dowling, Martin. *Traditional Music and Irish Society: Historical Perspectives.* Burlington, VT: Ashgate, 2014.
Drake-Boyt, Elizabeth. *Latin Dance.* Santa Barbara, CA: Greenwood, 2011.
Duff, William E. *A Time for Spies: Theodore Stephanovich Mally and the Era of the Great Illegals.* Nashville, TN: Vanderbilt University Press, 1999.
Dupee, Jeffery N. *Traveling India in the Age of Gandhi.* Lanham, MD: University Press of America, 2008.
Dwyer, Rachel. *100 Bollywood Films.* New Delhi: Roli Books, 2005.
Dwyer, Rachel, and Divia Patel. *Cinema India: The Visual Culture of Hindi Film.* New Brunswick, NJ: Rutgers University Press, 2002.
Eliade, Mircea. *Bengal Nights.* Chicago: University of Chicago Press, 1995.
Elliott, Lorraine. "Cosmopolitan Militaries, Cosmopolitan Force." In *Fault Lines of International Legitimacy,* edited by Hilary Charlesworth and Jean-Marc Coicaud, 279–302. Cambridge: Cambridge University Press, 2010.
Encyclopaedia Britannica (India) Pvt. Ltd. *Encyclopaedia of Hindi Cinema.* New Delhi, 2003.
Engelman, Ralph. "'My Rhodes Scholarship: Fred Friendly as an Information Officer in World War II." *Journalism History* 30, no. 3 (2004): 114–22.
Erskine, Toni. "'Citizen of Nowhere' or 'The Point Where Circles Intersect'? Impartialist and Embedded Cosmopolitanisms." *Review of International Studies* 28, no. 3 (2002): 457–77.
"Farewell Ball at the Town Hall, Calcutta." In *Speeches by the Marquis of Lansdowne: Viceroy and Governor General of India Vol. II,* 653–54. Calcutta: Office of the Superintendent of Government Printing, India, 1894.
Farrell, Gerry. "The Early Days of the Gramophone Industry in India: Historical, Social and Musical Perspectives." *British Journal of Ethnomusicology* 2 (1993): 31–53.
———. *Indian Music and the West.* Oxford: Oxford University Press, 1999.
Fauser, Annegret. *Sounds of War: Music in the United States during World War II.* New York: Oxford University Press, 2013.
Fielden, Lionel. Letter to F. W. Ogilvie on December 5, 1939. BBC Archives E1/896/3, 1939.
Fernandes, Naresh. "Remembering Anthony Gonsalves." 2004. Accessed February 26, 2006. http://www.india-seminar.com/2004/543/543%20naresh%20fernandes.htm.
———. *Taj Mahal Foxtrot.* New Delhi: Roli Books, 2012.
———. "Tomb Raider: Looking for St. Francis Xavier." *Transition* 9, no. 4 (2000): 4–19.
Ferrell, Gerry. *Indian Music and the West.* Oxford: Oxford University Press, 2000.
Finnegan, Ruth. *The Hidden Musicians: Music-Making in an English Town.* Cambridge: Cambridge University Press, 1989.
Ford, Richard. *Racial Culture: A Critique.* Princeton, NJ: Princeton University Press, 2005.

Fraser, Nancy. "Recognition without Ethics?" *Theory, Culture and Society* 18, nos. 2–3 (2001): 21–42.

French, Warren. *The South and Films.* Hattiesburg: University of Southern Mississippi, 1981.

Freudendal-Pedersen, Malene. *Mobility in Daily Life: Between Freedom and Unfreedom.* Burlington, VT: Ashgate, 2009.

Friedman, Susan Stanford. "Definitional Excursions: The Meanings of Modern/ Modernity/Modernism." *Modernism/Modernity* 8, no. 3 (2001): 493–513.

Frith, Simon. "Playing with Real Feeling—Jazz and Suburbia." In *Music for Pleasure: Essays in the Sociology of Pop,* edited by Simon Frith, 45–63. New York: Routledge, 1988.

Gaisberg, Frederick W. *The Music Goes Round: An Autobiography.* New York: Macmillan, 1942.

Gay, J. Drew. *The Prince of Wales in India.* Detroit, MI: Craig and Taylor, 1877.

Gbah Bear, Laura. "Miscegenations of Modernity: Constructing European Respectability and Race in the Indian Railway Colony, 1857–1931." *Women's History Review* 3, no. 4 (1994): 531–48.

Geffin, Yetta. "Chez Maurice." *Theatre Magazine* 21 (1915): 30, 37–40.

Gehrke, Pat J. "Community at the End of the World." In *Communication Ethics: Between Cosmopolitanism and Provincialism,* edited by Kathleen Roberts and Ronald Arnett, 121–38. New York: Peter Lang, 2008.

Ghosh, Arabinda. "Industrial Concentration by the Managing Agency System in India, 1948–1968." *Economic and Political Weekly* 8, no. 23 (1973): 57, 59–63.

Gilling, Ted. "The Colour of Music: An Interview with Bernard Herrmann." *Sight and Sound* 41 (1971–72): 36–39.

Gilmore, Paul. "'De Genewine Artekil': William Wells Brown, Blackface Minstrelsy, and Abolitionism." *American Literature* 69, no. 4 (1997): 743–80.

Gioia, Ted. "Jazz and the Primitivist Myth." *Musical Quarterly* 73, no. 1 (1989): 130–43.

Gist, Noel P. "Cultural Versus Social Marginality: The Anglo-Indian Case." *Phylon* 28, no. 4 (1967): 361–75.

Goldberg, Milton M. "A Qualification of the Marginal Man Theory." *American Sociological Review* 6, no. 1 (1941): 52–58.

Goodlad, Lauren M. E. "Cosmopolitanism's Actually Existing Beyond: Toward a Victorian Geopolitical Aesthetic." *Victorian Literature and Culture* 38, no. 2 (2010): 399–411.

Goodman, David. *Radio's Civic Ambition: American Broadcasting and Democracy in the 1930s.* New York: Oxford University Press, 2011.

Gopal, Sangita, and Sujata Moorti. *Global Bollywood: Travels of Hindi Song and Dance.* Minneapolis: University of Minnesota Press, 2008.

Gordon, Eric. "Hugh Ferriss, Rockefeller Center, and the 'Invisible Empire of the Air.'" *Space and Culture* 9, no. 3 (2005): 247–68.

Grand Gala Dance: "Place Pigalle." Bombay: Taj Mahal Palace Hotel, 1949.

Grand Gala at the Taj Bombay. Bombay: Taj Mahal Palace Hotel, 1948.

Green, Arnold. "A Re-Examination of the Marginal Man Concept." *Social Forces* 26, no. 2 (1947): 167–71.

Greene, Paul. "Mixed Messages: Unsettled Cosmopolitanisms in Nepali Pop." *Popular Music* 20, no. 2 (2001): 169–87.

———. "Musical Media and Cosmopolitanisms in Nepal's Popular Music, 1950–2006." In *South Asian Media Cultures: Audiences, Representations, Contexts*, edited by Shakuntala Banaji, 91–108. London: Anthem Press, 2011.

Grenier, Line, and Jocelyne Guilbault. "'Authority' Revisited: The 'Other' in Anthropology and Popular Music Studies." *Ethnomusicology* 34, no. 3 (1990): 381–97.

Grijp, Paul van der. "A Cultural Search for Authenticity: Questioning Primitivism and Exotic Art." In *Debating Authenticity: Concepts of Modernity in Anthropological Perspective*, edited by Thomas Fillitz and A. Jamie Saris, 128–41. New York: Berghahn Books, 2013.

Gronow, Pekka. "The Record Industry Comes to the Orient." *Ethnomusicology* 25, no. 2 (1981): 251–84.

Guerrero, Ed. *Framing Blackness: The African American Image in Film*. Philadelphia: Temple University Press, 1993.

Gulliver, Ralph. "Crickett Smith." *International Association of Jazz Record Collectors Journal* 3, no. 3 (1979): 3–5.

Gulzar, Saibal Chatterjee, and Gobind Nihalani. *Encyclopedia of Hindi Cinema*. New Delhi: Oxford University Press, 2003.

Gundevia, Y. D. *In the Districts of the Raj*. London: Sangam, 1992.

Gupta, Partha Sarathi. *Radio and the Raj, 1921–47*. Calcutta: K. P. Bagchi, 1995.

Hamilton, Walter. *East Indian Gazetteer*. Vol. 2. London: Wm. H. Allen, 1828.

Hamm, Charles. *Irving Berlin*. New York: Oxford University Press, 1997.

Hannerz, Ulf. "Cosmopolitans and Locals in World Culture." *Theory, Culture and Society* 7 (1990): 237–51.

Hansen, Kathryn. "Language, Community, and the Theatrical Public: Linguistic Pluralism and Change in the Nineteenth-Century Parsi Theatre." In *India's Literary History: Essays on the Nineteenth Century*, edited by Stuart Blackburn and Vasudha Dalmia, 60–86. Delhi: Permanent Black, 2004.

———. "Languages on the Stage: Linguistic Pluralism and Community Formation in the Nineteenth-Century Parsi Theatre." *Modern Asian Studies* 37, no. 2 (2003): 381–406.

———. "Parsi Theatre and the City: Locations, Patrons, Audiences." In *Sarai Reader 2002: The Cities of Everyday Life*, edited by Ravi Vasudevan et al., 40–49. Delhi: Sarai, CSDS and Society for Old and New Media, 2002.

Hastie, W. "The Bengalee Baboo." In *Hindus As They Are: A Description of the Manners, Customs and Inner Life of Hindoo Society in Bengal*, edited by Shib Chunder Bose, 191–209. Calcutta: W. Newman, 1881.

Hayes, M. Horace. *Indian Racing Reminiscences*. London: W. Thacker, 1883.

Head, Raymond. "Corelli in Calcutta: Colonial Music-Making in India During the 17th and 18th Centuries." *Early Music* 13, no. 4 (1985): 548–53.

Head, Sydney W. "British Colonial Broadcasting Policies: The Case of the Gold Coast." *African Studies Review* 22, no. 2 (1979): 39–47.

Heathcote, T. A. "The Army of British India." In The *Oxford History of the British Army*, edited by David G. Chandler and Ian Beckett, 362–84. Oxford: Oxford University Press, 1994.

Heber, Reginald. *Narrative of a Journey through the Upper Provinces of India, from Calcutta to Bombay, 1824–1825 (with Notes upon Ceylon)*. London: John Murray, Albemarle Street, 1849.

Hedge, R., and R. Shome. "Critical Communication and the Challenge of Globalization." *Critical Studies in Mass Communication* 19, no. 2 (2002): 172–89.

Hedin, Elmer. "The Anglo-Indian Community." *American Journal of Sociology* 40, no. 2 (1934): 165–79.

Heitzman, James. *The City in South Asia*. New York: Routledge, 2008.

Herbert, Trevor, and Helen Barlow. *Music and the British Military in the Long Nineteenth Century*. New York: Oxford University Press, 2013.

Herbert, Trevor, and Margaret Sarkissian. "Victorian Bands and Their Dissemination in the Colonies." *Popular Music* 16, no. 2 (1997): 165–79.

Hill, Errol, and James Hatch. *A History of the African American Theatre*. Cambridge: Cambridge University Press, 2004.

Holloway, Jim. "Torrid India Lacks Jazz Appreciation." *Down Beat*, May 20, 1945, 14.

———. "Weatherford Took Jazz to the Orient." *Down Beat*, July 15, 1945.

Horne, Gerald. *The End of Empires: African Americans and India*. Philadelphia: Temple University Press, 2008.

Hosain, Attia. *Sunlight on a Broken Column*. New York: Penguin Books-Virago Press, 1989.

Hughes, A. W. *A Gazetteer of the Province of Sindh*. London: George Bell, 1874.

Hughes, Langston. *I Wonder as I Wander*. New York: Rinehart, 1956.

Hughes, Stephen. "Film Genre, Exhibition and Audiences in Colonial South India." In *Explorations in New Cinema History: Approaches and Case Studies*, edited by Richard Maltby et al., 295–309. London: Wiley-Blackwell, 2011.

———. "House Full: Silent Film Genre, Exhibition and Audiences in South India." *Indian Economic and Social History Review* 43, no. 1 (2006): 31–62.

———. "The Lost Decade of Film History in India." *Journal of the Moving Image* 9 (2010): 72–93.

———. "The 'Music Boom' in Tamil South India: Gramophone, Radio, and the Making of Mass Culture." *Historical Journal of Film, Radio and Television* 22, no. 4 (2002): 445–73.

———. "Music in the Age of Mechanical Reproduction: Drama, Gramophone, and the Beginnings of Tamil Cinema." *Journal of Asian Studies* 66, no. 1 (2007): 3–34.

———. "Play It Again Saraswathi: Gramophone, Religion, and Devotional Music in Colonial South India." In *Beyond Bollywood: Studies in Indian Popular Music*, edited by Gregory Booth and Bradley Shope, 114–41. New York: Oxford Univeristy Press, 2014.

———. "When Film Came to Madras." *BioScope: South Asian Screen Studies* 1, no. 2 (2010): 147–68.

Hunt, Roland, and John Harrison. *The District Officer in India*. London: Scholar Press, 1980.

"India: A Market Whose Value is Beginning to Be Appreciated by American Manufacturers and Merchants." *American Trade with India*. Philadelphia: Commercial Museum, 1898.

Indian Cinematograph Committee, 1927–1928. Calcutta: Government of India Central Publication Branch, 1928.

The Indian Republic Day: 26th January. Bombay: Taj Mahal Palace Hotel, 1952.

Jackson, Jeffrey. *Making Jazz French: Music and Modern Life in Interwar Paris.* Durham, NC: Duke University Press, 2003.

Jacobs, J. M. *Edge of Empire: Postcolonialism and the City.* London: Routledge, 1996.

Jacob, T. *Cantonments in India: Evolution and Growth.* New Delhi: Reliance Publishing, 1994.

Jarman-Ivens, Freya. *Oh Boy! Masculinities and Popular Music.* New York: Routledge, 2007.

Jha, Shweta Sachdeva. "Eurasian Women as *Tawa'if* Singers and Recording Artists: Entertainment and Identity-Making in Colonial India." *African and Asian Studies* 8, no. 3 (2009): 268–87.

Johnson, Alan. "Club Members? Reading John Masters's *Bowani Junction*." *Journal of Commonwealth Literature* 35, no. 3 (2000): 3–26.

Johnson, James Weldon. *The Book of American Negro Poetry Chosen and Edited with an Essay on the Negro's Creative Genius.* New York: Harcourt, Brace, 1922.

Jones, Andrew F. "Black Internationale: Notes on the Chinese Jazz Age." In *Jazz Planet,* edited by E. Taylor Atkins, 225-43. Jackson: University of Mississippi Press, 2003.

———. *Yellow Music: Media, Culture, and Global Modernity in the Chinese Jazz Age.* Durham, NC: Duke University Press, 2001.

Joshi, G. V. "Our Shipping and Ship Building." In *The Modern Review III(1),* edited by Ramananda Chatterjee, 170–86. Calcutta: Modern Review Office, 1908.

Juluri, Vamsee. "Music Television and the Invention of Youth Culture in India." *Television and New Media* 3, no. 4 (2002): 367–86.

Kaminksy, Arnold P. "'The Imaginative Use of the Art of Communication': Propaganda and the Raj During World War II." In *Charisma and Commitment in South Asian History: Essays Presented to Stanley Wolpert,* edited by Roger Long, 294–331. New Delhi: Orient Longman, 2004.

Kantaris, Elia Geoffrey. "The Last Snapshots of Modernity: Argentine Cinema after the 'Process.'" *Bulletin of Hispanic Studies,* 73 (1996): 219–44.

Kanwar, Pamela. "The Change in the Profile of the Summer Capital of British India: Simla 1864–1947." *Modern Asian Studies* 18, no. 2 (1984): 215–36.

Kaur, Raminder, and Ajay Sinha. *Bollywood: Popular Indian Cinema through a Transnational Lens.* New Delhi: Sage, 2005.

Kendall, Patricia. *Come with Me to India! A Quest for Truth among Peoples and Problems.* London: Scribner's Sons, 1931.

Kenny, Judith. "Climate, Race and Imperial Authority: The Symbolic Landscape of the British Hill Station in India." *Annals of the Association of American Geographers* 85, no. 4 (1995): 694–714.

Khan, Yasmin. "Sex in an Imperial War Zone: Transnational Encounters in Second World War India." *History Workshop Journal* 73, no. 1 (2012): 240–58.

Khubchandani, Lata. "Song Picturization and Choreography." In *Encyclopedia of Hindi Cinema,* edited by Gulazara, Govind Nihalani, and Saibal Chatterjee, 197–208. New Delhi: Encyclopedia Britannica (India), 2003.

Kim, Youna. *Transnational Migration, Media and Identity of Asian Women: Diasporic Daughters.* New York: Routledge, 2011.

Kincaid, Dennis. *British Social Life in India: 1608–1937.* London: Routledge, 1938.

Kinnear, Michael. *The Gramophone Company's First Indian Recordings, 1899–1908.* Bombay: Popular Prakashan, 1994.

Kippen, James. *The Tabla of Lucknow: A Cultural Analysis of a Musical Tradition.* Cambridge: Cambridge University Press, 1988.

Kirby, Jack. *Media-Made Dixie: The South in the American Imagination.* Athens: University of Georgia Press, 1986.

Kling, Blair. *Blue Mutiny: The Indigo Disturbances in Bengal 1859–1862.* Philadelphia: University of Pennsylvania Press, 1966.

Klintberg, Bengt af. "Folksagner i dag." *Fataburen* (1976): 269–96.

Knight, Arthur. *Disintegrating the Musical: Black Performance and American Musical Film.* Durham, NC: Duke University Press, 2002.

Knowles, Mark. *The Wicked Waltz and Other Scandalous Dances: Outrage at Couple Dancing in 19th and Early 20th Centuries.* Jefferson, NC: McFarland, 2009.

Koerner, Brendan I. *Piano Demon: The Globetrotting, Gin-Soaked, Too-Short Life of Teddy Weatherford, the Chicago Jazzman Who Conquered Asia* (Kindle Single) (Kindle Locations 715–17). The Atavist. Kindle Edition, 2011.

Koshiro, Yukiko. "Beyond an Alliance of Color: The African American Impact on Modern Japan." *Positions* 11, no. 1 (2003): 183–215.

Krasner, David. *A Beautiful Pageant.* New York: Palgrave Macmillan, 2002.

Kruty, Paul, and Paul Sprague. *Two American Architects in India: Walter B. Griffin and Marion M. Griffin, 1935–1937.* Urbana: University of Illinois School of Architecture, 1997.

Kumar, Nand. *Indian English Drama: A Study in Myths.* New Delhi: Sarup, 2003.

Kumar, Shanti, and Michael Curtin. "'Made in India': In between Music Television and Patriarchy." *Television and New Media* 3, no. 4 (2002): 345–66.

Kvetko, Peter. "Can the Indian Tune Go Global?" *TDR* 48, no. 4 (2004): 183–91.

———. "Indipop: Producing Global Sounds and Local Meanings in Bombay." PhD diss., University of Texas at Austin, 2005.

LaFont, Jean Marie. *Indika: Essays in Indo-French Relations, 1630–1976.* New Delhi: Manohar-Centre de sciences humaines, 2000.

Lal, Vijay. "Ethnographies of the Popular and the Public Sphere in India." *South Asian Popular Culture* 5, no. 2 (2007): 87–95.

Laird, Ross. "A Draft Discography of Jazz and Western Style Dance Bands and English Popular Vocals Recorded in India 1926–1954." Accessed March 1, 2005. http://scarcesounds.com/files/discfile3.pdf.

Largey, Mchael. *Vodou Nation.* Chicago: University of Chicago Press, 2006.

Laubenstein, Paul. "Jazz-Debt and Credit." *Musical Quarterly* 15, no. 4 (1929): 606–24.

Lee, Leo Ou-fan. *Shanghai Modern: The Flowering of a New Urban Culture in China, 1930–1945.* Cambridge, MA: Harvard University Press, 1999.

Lee, Robert. *Commerce and Culture: Nineteenth-Century Business Elites.* Burlington, VT: Ashgate, 2011.

Lelyveld, David. "Upon the Subdominant: Administering Music on All-India Radio." *Social Text* 39 (1994): 111–27.

Lewis, George. "Beyond the Reef: Cultural Constructions of Hawaii in Mainland America, Australia and Japan." *Journal of Popular Culture* 30, no. 2 (1996): 123–35.

Lewis, Su Lin. "Cosmopolitanism and the Modern Girl: A Cross-Cultural Discourse in 1930s Penang." *Modern Asian Studies* 43, no. 6 (2009): 1385–419.

Llewellyn-Jones, Rosie. *A Fatal Friendship: The Nawabs, the British and the City of Lucknow.* New York: Oxford University Press, 1985.

———. *Engaging Scoundrels: True Tales of Old Lucknow.* New York: Oxford University Press, 2000.

———. *A Very Ingenious Man: Claude Martin in Early Colonial India.* New York: Oxford University Press, 1992.

Locke, Ralph. "A Broader View of Musical Exoticism." *Journal of Musicology* 24, no. 4 (2007): 477–521.

Londré, Felicia Hardison, and Daniel J. Watermeier. *The History of the North American Theater: From Pre-Columbian Times to the Present.* New York: Continuum, 1998.

Long, Roger. *Charisma and Commitment in South Asian History: Essays Presented to Stanley Wolpert.* New Delhi: Orient Longman, 2004.

Lotz, Rainer. Liner notes to *Jazz and Hot Dance in India-1926–1944.* Harlequin, HQ, 1984.

Low, Rachael. *History of British Film (Volume 4): The History of the British Film 1918–1929.* London: Allen and Unwin, 2013.

Lukose, Ritty. "Consuming Globalization: Youth and Gender in Karala, India." *Journal of Social History* 38, no. 4 (2005): 915–35.

Magaldi, Cristina. "Cosmopolitanism and World Music in Rio De Janeiro at the Turn of the Twentieth Century." *Musical Quarterly* 92, nos. 3–4 (2009): 329–64.

Magee, Gary, and Andrew Thompson. *Empire and Globalization: Networks of People, Goods, and Capital in the British World, 1850–1914.* Cambridge: Cambridge University Press, 2010.

Mahadevan, Sudhir. "Traveling Showmen, Makeshift Cinemas." *Bioscope: South Asian Screen Studies* 1, no. 1 (2010): 27–47.

Malm, Krister. "Music on the Move: Traditions and Mass Media." *Ethnomusicology* 37, no. 3 (1993): 339–52.

Manuel, Peter. *Cassette Culture: Popular Music and Technology in North India.* Chicago: University of Chicago Press, 1993.

———. "The Cassette Industry and Popular Music in North India." *Popular Music* 10, no. 2 (1991): 189–204.

———. "Popular Music in India: 1901–1986." *Popular Music* 7, no. 2 (1988): 157–76.

———. *Popular Musics of the Non-Western World: An Introductory Survey.* New York: Oxford University Press, 1988.

Marsden, Magnus. "Muslim Cosmopolitans? Transnational Life in Northern Pakistan." *Journal of Asian Studies* 67, no. 1 (2008): 213–47.

Masani, Zareer. *Indian Tales of the Raj.* Berkeley: University of California Press, 1987.

Mason, Philip. *Kipling: The Glass, the Shadow, and the Fire.* New York: Harper and Row, 1975.

Mathews, Herbert. *The Education of a Correspondent.* New York: Harcourt, 1946.

Matson, Lowell. "Theatre for the Armed Forces in World War II." *Educational Theatre Journal* 6, no. 1 (1954): 1–11.

May the New Year Bring You Joy and Happiness Is the Warmest Wish of the Taj Bombay. Bombay: Taj Mahal Palace Hotel, 1951.

McCulloch, Thomas. *Navigator to Hydrographer.* Victoria, BC: Trafford, 2005.

McElya, Micki. *Clinging to Mammy: The Faithful Slave in Twentieth-Century America.* Cambridge, MA: Harvard University Press, 2007.

McGuire, Phillip. *Taps for a Jim Crow Army.* Santa Barbara, CA: ABC-Clio, 1983.

McPherson, Kenneth. "Port Cities as Nodal Points of Change, 1890s–1920s." In *Modernity and Culture: From the Mediterranean to the Indian Ocean,* edited by Leila Fawaz, Robert Ilbert, and C. A. Bayly, 75–95. New York: Columbia University Press, 2002.

Meer, Sarah. *Uncle Tom Mania: Slavery, Minstrelsy and Transatlantic Culture in the 1850s.* Athens: University of Georgia Press, 2005.

Mehta, Ved. *A Portrait of India.* Harmondsworth: Penguin, 1973.

Merriam, Alan. *The Anthropology of Music.* Evanston, IL: Northwestern University Press, 1964.

Meyer, Leonard. *Style and Music: Theory, History, and Ideology.* Chicago: University of Chicago Press, 1996.

Middleton, Richard. "Mum's the Word: Men's Singing and Maternal Law." In *Oh Boy! Masculinities and Popular Music,* edited by Freya Jarmin-Ivens, 103–24. New York: Routledge, 2007.

Mignolo, Walter D. *Local Histories/Global Designs: Coloniality, Subaltern Knowledges, and Border Thinking.* Princeton, NJ: Princeton University Press, 2012.

Miner, Harry. *American Dramatic Directory: Route Around the World.* New York: Wolf and Palmer Dramatic Publishing, 1884.

Misra, Amaresh. *Lucknow Fire of Grace: The Story of Its Revolution, Renaissance, and the Aftermath.* New Delhi: HarperCollins, 1998.

Misra, Maria. *Business, Race, and Politics in British India c. 1850–1960.* Oxford: Oxford University Press, 1999.

Mitter, Partha. "Modern Global Art and Its Discontents." *Avant Garde Critical Studies* 30 (2014): 35–54.

Molz, Jennie Germann. "Cosmopolitanism and Consumption." In *The Ashgate Research Companion to Cosmopolitanism,* edited by Magdalena Nowicka and Maria Rovisco, 33–52. Burlington, VT: Ashgate, 2011.

Moore, Hilary. *Inside British Jazz: Crossing Borders of Race, Nation, and Class.* Burlington, VT: Ashgate, 2008.

Moore, James. *André Charlot: The Genius of Intimate Musical Revue.* Jefferson, NC: McFarland, 2005.

Morcom, Anna. "An Understanding between Bollywood and Hollywood? The Meaning of Hollywood-Style Music in Hindi Films." *British Journal of Ethnomusicology* 10, no. 1 (2001): 63–84.

———. *Hindi Film Songs and the Cinema.* Hampshire: Ashgate, 2007.

Morley, Patrick. *"This Is the American Forces Network": The Anglo-American Battle of the Air Waves in World War II.* Westport, CT: Praeger, 2001.

Morris, Jan. *Stones of Empire: The Buildings of the Raj.* Oxford: Oxford University Press, 1983.

Mouvet, Maurice. *Maurice's Art of Dancing.* New York: Schirmer, 1915.

Muehl, John Frederick. *American Sahib.* New York: John Day, 1946.

Nayar, Sheila. "The Values of Fantasy: Indian Popular Cinema through Western Scripts." *Journal of Popular Culture* 31, no. 1 (1997): 73–90.

Nexica, Irene J. "Music Marketing: Tropes of Hybrids, Crossovers, and Cultural Dialogue through Music." *Popular Music and Society* 21, no. 3 (1997): 61–82.

Notar, Beth. "Producing Cosmopolitanism at the Borderlands: Lonely Planeteers and 'Local' Cosmopolitans in Southwest China." *Anthropological Quarterly* 81, no. 3 (2008): 615–50.

O'Conner, Barbara. "Sexing the Nation: Discourses of the Dance Hall in Ireland in the 1930s." *Journal of Gender Studies* 14, no. 2 (2005): 89–105.

Office of the Controller of Broadcasting. *Report on the Progress of Broadcasting in India up to the 31st March 1939.* Simla: Manager of Publications, 1940.

Ó hAllmhuráin, Gearóid. "The Great Famine: A Catalyst in Irish Traditional Music Making." In *The Great Famine and the Irish Diaspora in America,* edited by Arthur Gribben, 104–32. Amherst: University of Massachusetts Press, 1999.

Olaniyan, Tejumola. "The Cosmopolitan Nativist: Fela Anikulapo-Kuti and the Antinomies of Postcolonial Modernity." *Research in African Literature* 32, no. 2 (2001): 76–89.

Oldenburg, Veena Talwar. *The Making of Colonial Lucknow, 1856–1877.* Princeton, NJ: Princeton University Press, 1984.

Oliver, Paul. "Twixt Midnight and Day: Binarism, Blues and Black Culture." *Popular Music* 2 (1982): 179–200.

Osella, Filippo, and Caroline Osella. "'I Am Gulf': The Production of Cosmopolitanism in Kozhikode, Kerala, India." In *Struggling with History: Islam and Cosmopolitanism in the Western Indian Ocean,* edited by Simpson and Kresse, 323–55. New York: Columbia University Press, 2007.

Park, Robert. "Human Migration and the Marginal Man." *American Journal of Sociology* 3, no. 6 (1928): 881–93.

Parker, D. C. "Exoticism in Music in Retrospect." *Musical Quarterly* 3, no. 1 (1917): 134–61.

Parkhurst, Jessie W. "The Role of the Black Mammy in the Plantation Household." *Journal of Negro History* 23, no. 3 (1938): 349–69.

Parkinson, J. C. *The Ocean Telegraph to India: A Narrative and Diary.* Edinburgh: W. Blackwood, 1870.

Parsonage, Catherine. *The Evolution of Jazz in Britain: 1880–1935.* Aldershot: Ashgate, 2005.

Pearson, Robert. *Eastern Interlude: A Social History of the European Community in Calcutta.* Calcutta: Thacker, Spink, 1954.

Pennell, Elizabeth. *Charles Godfrey Leland.* Boston: Houghton, Mifflin, 1906.

Peters, John Durham. "The Uncanniness of Mass Communication in Interwar Social Thought." *Journal of Communication* 46, no. 3 (1996): 108–23.

Peterson, Richard, and Andy Bennett. *Music Scenes: Local, Translocal, and Virtual.* Nashville, TN: Vanderbilt University Press, 2004.

Pfau, Ann Elizabeth, and David Hochfelder. "'Her Voice a Bullet': Imaginary Propaganda and the Legendary Broadcasters of World War II." In *Sound in the*

Age of Mechanical Reproduction, edited by David Suisman and Susan Strasser, 47–68. Philadelphia: University of Pennsylvania Press, 2010.

Pieris, Ralph. "Bilingualism and Cultural Marginality." *British Journal of Sociology* 2, no. 4 (1951): 328–39.

Pieterse, Jan N. "Emancipatory Cosmopolitanism: Towards and Agenda." *Development and Change* 37, no. 6 (2006): 1247–57.

Pinckney, Warren. "Jazz in India: Perspectives on Historical Development and Musical Acculturation." *Asian Music* 21, no. 1 (1989–90): 35–77.

Pollock, Shledon, Homi K. Bhabha, Carol Breckenridge, and Dipesh Chakrabarty. "Cosmopolitanism." *Public Culture* 12, no. 3 (2000): 577–89.

Procida, Mary A. "Good Sports and Right Sorts: Guns, Gender, and Imperialism in British India." *Journal of British Studies* 40, no. 4 (2001): 454–88.

Prouty, Ken. *Knowing Jazz: Community, Pedagogy, and Canon in the Information Age.* Jackson: University Press of Mississippi, 2012.

Quatorze Juillet à Montparnasse: Grand Gala Dance. Bombay: Taj Mahal Palace Hotel, 1949.

Qureshi, Regula. "His Master's Voice? Exploring *Qawwali* and 'Gramophone Culture' in South Asia." *Popular Music* 18, no. 1 (1999): 63–98.

Radano, Ronald. *Lying Up a Nation: Race and Black Music.* Chicago: University of Chicago Press, 2003.

———. *New Musical Figurations: Anthony Braxton's Cultural Critique.* Chicago: University of Chicago Press, 1994.

Radano, Ronald, and Philip Bohlman. *Music and the Racial Imagination.* Chicago: University of Chicago Press, 2000.

Rai, Amit. *Untimely Bollywood: Globalization and India's New Media Assemblage.* Durham, NC: Duke University Press, 2009.

Ranade, Ashok. "Keshavrao Bhole: Excerpts from his *Mazhe Sangeet*." *Journal of Sangeet Natak Akademi* 100 (1991): 49–63.

———. *Stage Music of Maharashtra.* New Delhi: Sangeet Natak Akademi, 1986.

Rangoonwalla, Firoze. *Satyajit Ray's Art.* Ann Arbor, MI: Clarion, 1980.

Regev, Motti. "Cultural Uniqueness and Aesthetic Cosmopolitanism." *European Journal of Social Theory* 10, no. 1 (2007): 123–38.

———. *Pop-Rock Music: Aesthetic Cosmopolitanism in Late Modernity.* Hoboken, NJ: Wiley, 2013.

Renford, Raymond K. *The Non-Official British in India to 1920.* New Delhi: Oxford University Press, 1987.

Rice, Edward. *Monarchs of Minstrelsy: From "Daddy" to Date.* New York: Kenny Publishing, 1911.

Richards, Jeffrey. *Imperialism and Music: Britain 1876–1953.* Manchester: Manchester University Press, 2001.

Rinzler, Paul. *The Contradictions of Jazz.* Plymouth: Scarecrow Press, 2008.

Rishi, Tilak. *Bless You Bollywood! A Tribute to Hindi Cinema on Completing 100 Years.* Bloomington, IN: Trafford On Demand Pub, 2012.

Roberts, Kathleen, and Ronald Arnett, eds. *Communication Ethics: Between Cosmopolitanism and Provinciality.* New York: Peter Lang, 2008.

Rogan, J. Mackenzie. "Regimental Bands: Their History and Role of Usefulness." *Musical Times* 54, no. 839 (1913): 28–30.

Rogers, Joel A. "Jazz at Home." *Survey Graphic* 6, no. 6 (1925): 665–67, 712.

Rogin, Michael. "'Democracy and Burnt Cork': The End of Blackface, the Beginning of Civil Rights." *Representations* 46 (1994): 1–34.

Roudometof, Victor. "Transnationalism, Cosmopolitanism and Glocalization." *Current Sociology* 53, no. 1 (2005): 113–35.

Rovisco, Maria, and Magdalena Nowicka. "Introduction: Making Sense of Cosmopolitanism." In *Cosmopolitanism in Practice*, edited by Maria Rovisco and Magdalena Nowicka, 1–16. Burlington, VT: Ashgate, 2012.

Rungta, Radhe Shyam. *The Rise of Business Corporations in India 1851–1900.* Cambridge: Cambridge University Press, 1970.

Russell, George W. E. *Portraits of the Seventies.* New York: C. Scribner's, 1916.

Rycroft, David. "Evidence of Stylistic Continuity in Zulu 'Town' Music." In *Essays for a Humanist: An Offering to Klaus Wachsmann*, edited by Nono Pirrotta, 216–61. New York: Town House Press, 1977.

Rydell, Robert W., and Robert Kroes. *Buffalo Bill in Bologna: The Americanization of the World, 1869–1922.* Chicago: University of Chicago Press, 2005.

Sahay, Keshari. *Visual Anthropology in India and Its Development.* New Delhi: Gyan Books, 1993.

Said, Edward. *Orientalism.* New York: Vintage Books, 1979.

Saldanha, Arun. "Music, Space, Identity: Geographies of Youth Culture in Bangalore." *Cultural Studies* 16, no. 3 (2002): 337–50.

Sandeman, High David. *Selections from the Calcutta Gazettes of the Years 1806 to 1815 Inclusive, Showing the Political and Social Condition of the English in India Upwards of Fifty Years Ago.* Calcutta: Office of Superintendent Government Printing, 1868.

Sandke, Randall. *Where the Dark and the Light Folks Meet: Race and the Mythology, Politics, and Business of Jazz.* Lanham, MD: Scarecrow Press, 2010.

Sanjek, David. "One Size Does Not Fit All: The Precarious Position of the African American Entrepreneur in Post WW2 American Popular Music." *American Music* 15, no. 4 (1997): 535–62.

Sarkar, Kobita. *Indian Cinema Today: An Analysis.* New Delhi: Sterling, 1975.

Saxton, Alexander. "Blackface Minstrelsy and Jacksonian Ideology." *American Quarterly* 27, no. 1 (1975): 3–28.

Schulz, Suzanne. "A City of Picture Palaces." In *Hazratganj: A Journey through the Times*, edited by Rosie Llewellyn-Jones, 58–60. Lucknow: Bennett, Coleman, 2011.

Scott, Clement. "The Rise and Fall of the Calcutta Stage." *The Theatre: A Monthly Review, Vol. 4.* London: Charles Dickens & Evans, 1881.

Scott, Derek. *Sounds of the Metropolis: The Nineteenth-Century Popular Music Revolution in London.* New York: Oxford University Press, 2008.

Scriver, Peter, and Vikramaditya Prakash. *Colonial Modernities: Building, Dwelling, and Architecture in British India and Ceylon.* New York: Routledge, 2007.

Sebastiani, Giuseppe. *Seconda Speditione all'Indie Orientali.* Venice, 1683.

Segel, Harold. *Turn-of-the-Century Cabaret: Paris, Barcelona, Berlin, Munich, Vienna, Cracow, Moscow, St. Petersburg, Zurich.* New York: Columbia University Press, 1987.

Sen, Amartya Kumar. "Individual Freedom as Social Commitment." *India International Centre Quarterly* 25, no. 4 and 26, no. 1 (Winter 1998/Spring 1999): 53–69.

Sharar, Abdul Halim. *Lucknow: The Last Phase of an Oriental Culture*. London: Elek, 1975.

Sharma, Miriam. "Censoring India: Cinema and the Tentacles of Empire in the Early Years." *South Asia Research* 29, no. 1 (2009): 41–73.

Sharrar, Jack. *Avery Hopwood: His Life and Plays*. Ann Arbor: University of Michigan Press, 1989.

Sheppard, Samuel. *The Byculla Club: 1833–1916, A History*. Bombay: Bennett, Coleman, 1916.

Shope, Bradley. "Anglo Indian Identity, Knowledge and Power: Western Ballroom Music in Lucknow." *Drama Review* 48, no. 4 (2004): 167–82.

———. "From Imperial Exclusivity to Global Receptivity: Change in the Consumption of Western Music in Colonial North India." *South Asia: Journal of South Asian Studies* 31, no. 2 (2008): 271–89.

———. "Latin American Music in Moving Pictures and Jazzy Cabarets in Mumbai, 1930s to 1950s." In *More Than Bollywood: Studies in Indian Popular Music*, edited by Gregory Booth and Bradley Shope, 201–15. New York: Oxford University Press, 2014.

———. "Masquerading Cosmopolitanism: Fancy Dress Balls of Britain's Raj." *Journal of Imperial and Commonwealth History* 39, no. 3 (2011): 375–92.

———. "'They Treat Us White Folks Fine': African American Musicians and the Popular Music Terrain in Late Colonial India." *Journal of South Asian Popular Culture* 5, no. 2 (2007): 97–116.

Shuker, Roy. *Understanding Popular Music Culture*. New York: Routledge, 2013.

Singh, J. P. *Globalized Arts: The Entertainment Economy and Cultural Identity*. New York: Columbia University Press, 2011.

Singing Debut of Nutan, Indian's Beauty Queen 1951 and Starlet. Bombay: Taj Mahal Palace Hotel, 1951.

Sinha, Mrinalini. "Britishness, Clubbability, and the Colonial Public Sphere: The Genealogy of an Imperial Institution in Colonial India." *Journal of British Studies* 40, no. 4 (2001): 489–521.

———. *Colonial Masculinity: The "Manly Englishman" and the "Effeminate Bengali" in the late Nineteenth Century*. Manchester: Manchester University Press, 1995.

Sinha, Nitin. *Communication and Colonialism in Eastern India: Bihar, 1760s–1880s*. New York: Anthem Press, 2012.

Sircar, Ajanta. "Of 'Metaphorical' Politics: Bombay Films and Indian Society." *Modern Asian Studies* 29, no. 2 (1995): 325–35.

Skrbis, Zlatko, Gavin Kendall, and Ian Woodward. "Locating Cosmopolitanism: Between Humanist Ideal and Grounded Social Category." *Theory, Culture and Society* 21, no. 6 (2004): 115–36.

Slout, William. *Burnt Cork and Tambourines: A Source Books for Negro Minstrelsy*. Rockville, MD: Wildside Press, 2007.

Smith, Andrew. "The City of London, British Ethnic and National Identities, and Investment Decisions in the Anglophone New World, 1860–1914." In *Com-*

parative Responses to Globalization: Experiences of British and Japanese Enterprises, edited by Maki Umemura and Rika Fujioka, 71–98. New York: Palgrave Macmillan, 2013.

———. *The Oxford Companion to American Food and Drink*. Oxford: Oxford University Press, 2007.

Smith, William Hanbury Sanmarez. India Office Collection. British Library. MSS EUR D881.

South Sea Rhapsody. Bombay: Taj Mahal Palace Hotel, 1949.

Spaeth, Sigmund. *A History of Music in America*. New York: Random House, 1948.

Spear, Thomas George Percival. *The Nabobs: A Study of the Social Life of the English in Eighteenth Century India*. New Delhi: Oxford University Press, 1932.

Spencer, J. E., and W. L. Thomas. "The Hill Stations and Summer Resorts of the Orient." *Geographical Review* 38, no. 4 (1948): 637–51.

Stearns, Marshall Winslow, and Jean Stearns. *Jazz Dance: The Story of American Vernacular Dance*. New York: Da Capo Press, 1994.

Stecopoulos, Harry. *Reconstructing the World: Southern Fictions and U.S. Imperialisms, 1898–1976*. Ithaca, NY: Cornell University Press, 2008.

Sterling, Christopher. *The Concise Encyclopedia of American Radio*. New York: Routledge, 2010.

Stokes, Martin. "On Musical Cosmopolitanism." Macalester International Roundtable. Paper 3 (2007).

Stokes, Melvyn. *American History through Hollywood Film: From the Revolution to the 1960s*. London: Bloomsbury, 2013.

Stoler, Ann. *Race and the Identification of Desire*. Durham, NC: Duke University Press, 1995.

———. "Rethinking Colonial Categories: European Communities and Boundaries of Rule." *Comparative Studies in Society and History* 31, no. 1 (1989): 134–61.

Stone, Harry. *The Century of Musical Comedy and Revue*. Milton Keynes: AuthorsHouse, 2009.

Stonequist, Everett V. "The Problem of the Marginal Man." *American Journal of Sociology* 41, no. 1 (1935): 1–12.

Stooge. "25 Years a Band Leader: Ken Mac (1922–1947) Pioneer of European Dance Bands in India." Unpublished paper, 1947.

Stowe, Harriet Beecher. *Uncle Tom's Cabin*. London: John Cassell, 1852.

Strachey, Jane Maria. *Diary of Jane Maria Strachey*. London: British Library, MSS EUR Photo 038, 1863.

Strausbaugh, John. *Black Like You: Blackface, Whiteface, Insult and Imitation in American Popular Culture*. New York: Penguin, 2007.

Suisman, David, and Susan Strasser. *Sound in the Age of Mechanical Reproduction*. Philadelphia: University of Pennsylvania Press, 2010.

Sullivan, Jack. *Hitchcock's Music*. New Haven, CT: Yale University Press, 2006.

Sun-Young, Yoo. "Embodiment of American Modernity in Colonial Korea." *InterAsia Cultural Studies* 2, no. 3 (2001): 423–41.

Swanson, Philip. "Going Down on Good Neighbours: Imagining América in Hollywood Movies of the '30s and '40s (Flying Down to Rio and Down Argentine Way)." *Bulletin of Latin American Research* 29, no. 1 (2010): 71–84.

Szerszynski, Bronislaw, and John Urry. "Cultures of Cosmopolitanism." *Sociological Review* 50, no. 4 (2002): 461–81.

———. "Visuality, Mobility and the Cosmopolitan: Inhabiting the World from Afar." *British Journal of Sociology* 57 (2006): 113–31.

Taj Dinner/Dance. Bombay: Taj Mahal Palace Hotel, 1948.

Tan, Tai Yong, and Gyanesh Kudaisya. *The Aftermath of Partition in South Asia.* London: Routledge, 2000.

Tomlinson, John. *Globalization and Culture.* Chicago: University of Chicago Press, 1999.

———. "The Political Economy of the Raj: The Decline of Colonialism." *Journal of Economic History* 42, no. 1 (1982): 133–37.

Travis, Dempsey J. "Chicago's Jazz Trail, 1893–1950." *Black Music Research Journal* 10, no. 1 (1990): 82–85.

Trivedi, Poonam. "Performing the Nation: Dave Carson and the Bengali Babu." In *The Nation across the World,* edited by Harish Trivedi, Meenakshi Mukherjee, C. Vijayasree, and T. Vijay Kumar, 246–69. New York: Oxford University Press, 2007.

Tucker, Joshua. "Music Radio and Global Mediation." *Cultural Studies* 24, no. 4 (2010): 553–79.

Tunner, William. *Over the Hump.* New York: Duell, Sloan and Pearce, 1964.

Turino, Thomas. *Music as Social Life: The Politics of Participation.* Chicago: University of Chicago Press, 2008.

———. *Nationalists, Cosmopolitans, and Popular Music in Zimbabwe.* Chicago: University of Chicago Press, 2000.

Van der Meer, Wim. *Hindustani Music in the 20th Century.* The Hague: M. Nijhoff, 1980.

Van der Veer, Peter. "Cosmopolitan Options." *Ethnográfica* 6, no. 1 (2002): 15–26.

Vasudevan, Ravi. "Shifting Codes, Dissolving Identities: The Hindi Social Film of the 1950s as Popular Culture." In *Making Meaning in Indian Cinema,* edited by Ravi S. Vasudevan, 99–121. New Delhi: Oxford University Press, 2000.

Vincent, Leon Henry. *Hotel de Rambouillet and the Precieuses.* Boston: Houghton, Mifflin, 1900.

Von Eschen, Penny M. *Race Against the Empire: Black Americans and Anticolonialism, 1937–1957.* Ithaca, NY: Cornell University Press, 1997.

Wacha, Dinshaw Edulji. *Shells from the Sands of Bombay: Being My Recollections and Reminiscences, 1860–1875.* Bombay: KT Anklesaria, 1920.

Wachsmann, Klaus. "Ethnomusicology in Africa." In *African Experience,* edited by John Paden and Edward Soja, 128–51. Evanston, IL: Northwestern University Press, 1970.

Walker, Elsie. *Understanding Sound Tracks through Film Theory.* New York: Oxford University Press, 2015.

Walkowitz, Judith. *Nights Out: Life in Cosmopolitan London.* London: Yale University Press, 2012.

Washabaugh, William. *Flamenco Music and National Identity in Spain.* Burlington, VT: Ashgate Publishing, Ltd, 2010.

Watson, Allan, Michael Hoyler, and Christoph Mager. "Spaces and Networks of Musical Creativity in the City." *Geography Compass* 3, no. 2 (2009): 856–78.

Weber, William. *The Musician as Entrepreneur, 1700–1914: Managers, Charlatans, and Idealists*. Bloomington: Indiana University Press, 2004.

Webster, Donovan. *The Burma Road: The Epic Story of the China-Burma-India Theater in World War II*. New York: Farrar, Straus and Giroux, 2005.

Weidman, Amanda. "Guru and Gramophone: Fantasies of Fidelity and Modern Technologies of the Real." *Public Culture* 15, no. 3 (2003): 453–76.

Welter, Volker M. "Arcades for Lucknow: Patrick Geddes, Charles Rennie Mackintosh and the Reconstruction of the City." *Architectural History* 42 (1999): 316–32.

Wetzel, Richard. *The Globalization of Music in History*. New York: Routledge, 2012.

White, H. Loring. *Ragging It: Getting Ragtime into History*. New York: IUniverse, 2005.

White, Walter. "The Negro on the American Stage." *English Journal* 24, no. 3 (1935): 179–88.

Wilberforce-Bell, Sir Harold. India Office Collection. British Library. MSS EUR G 57/11.

Williams, Maynard Owen. "A Teeming Highway Extending for Fifteen Hundred Miles, from the Khyber Pass to Calcutta." *National Geographic Magazine* 40, no. 5 (1921): 433–67.

Williams, Sean. *Focus: Irish traditional Music*. Oxford: Routledge, 2010.

Wilson, Sheryl. "Politicizing Dance in Late-Victorian Women's Poetry." *Victorian Poetry* 46, no. 2 (2008): 191–205.

Windover, Michael. *Art Deco: A Mode of Mobility*. Quebec: Presses de l'Université du Québec, 2012.

Wittman, Matthew. "Empire of Culture: U.S. Entertainers and the Making of the Pacific Circuit, 1850–1890." PhD. diss., University of Michigan, 2010.

Woodfield, Ian. "Collecting Indian Songs in Late 18th-Century Lucknow: Problems of Transcription." *British Journal of Ethnomusicology* 3 (1994): 73–88.

———. *Music of the Raj: A Social and Economic History of Music in Late Eighteenth Century Anglo-Indian Society*. New York: Oxford University Press, 2000.

Woodward, Ian, and Zlatko Skrbis. "Performing Cosmopolitanism." In *Routledge Handbook of Cosmopolitan Studies*, edited by Gerard Delanty, 127–37. New York: Routledge, 2012.

Wright, Susan, and Roy Dean Wright. "A Plea for a Further Refinement of the Marginal Man Theory." *Phylon* 33, no. 4 (1972): 361–68.

Yagnik, Achyut, and Suchitra Sheth. *The Shaping of Modern Gujarat: Plurality, Hindutva and Beyond*. New Delhi: Penguin Books, 2005.

Yeats-Brown, Francis. *Bengal Lancer*. London: V. Gollancz, 1930.

———. *Lancer at Large*. New York: Viking Press, 1937.

Yeoh, Brenda. "Postcolonial Cities." *Progress in Human Geography* 25, no. 3 (2001): 456–68.

YMCA. *75th Anniversary Bombay Y.M.C.A. Swing Concert*. Bombay, 1949.

Young, Craig, Marina Diep, and Stephanie Drabble. "Living with Difference? The 'Cosmopolitan City' and Urban Reimagining in Manchester, UK." *Urban Studies* 43 (2006): 1687–714.

Young, William H., and Nancy K. Young. *Music of the World War II Era*. Westport, CT: Greenwood Press, 2008.

Younger, Coralie. *Anglo-Indians: Neglected Children of the Raj*. Delhi: B. R. Publishing, 1987.

Zivin, Joselyn. "'Bent': A Colonial Subversive and Indian Broadcasting." *Past and Present* 162 (1999): 195–220.

Filmography and Discography

Filmography

Aag. Directed by Raj Kapoor. Produced by R. K. Films, 1948.

Aar Paar. Directed by Guru Dutt. Produced by Guru Dutt Films Pvt. Ltd., 1954.

Albela. Directed by Master Bhagwan. Produced by Bhagwan Art Productions, 1951.

Andaaz. Directed by Mehboob. Produced by Mehboob Productions, 1949.

Anmol Ghadi. Directed by Mehboob. Produced by Mehboob Productions, 1946.

Awaara. Directed by Raj Kapoor. Produced by R. K. Films, 1951.

Barsaat. Directed by Raj Kapoor. Produced by R. K. Films, 1949.

Cab Calloway's Jitterbug Party. Directed by Fred Waller. Produced by Paramount Pictures, 1935.

Copacabana. Directed by Alfred E. Green. Produced by Beacon Productions, Inc., 1947.

Down Argentine Way. Directed by Irving Cummings. Produced by Twentieth Century Fox Film Corporation, 1940.

Dulari. Directed by Kardar. Produced by Kardar Productions, 1949.

Five Pennies. Directed by Melville Shavelson. Produced by Dena Productions, 1959.

Greenwich Village. Directed by Walter Lang. Produced by Twentieth Century Fox Film Corporation, 1944.

Hamari Beti. Directed by Shobhna Samarth. Produced by Shobhna Pictures, 1950.

Hello Dolly. Directed by Gene Kelly. Produced by Chenault Productions Inc., 1969.

High Society. Directed by Charles Walters. Produced by Bing Crosby Productions, 1956.

Hum Log. Directed by Zia Sarhady. Produced by Ranjit Studios, 1951.

If I'm Lucky. Directed by Lewis Seiler. Produced by Twentieth Century Fox Film Corporation, 1946.

Kanoon. Directed by Abdul Rashid Kardar. Produced by Kardar Productions, 1943.

Moonlight in Havana. Directed by Anthony Mann. Produced by Universal Pictures, 1942.

Nagina. Directed by Ravindra Dave. Produced by Pancholi Productions, 1951.

Namoona. Directed by Hira Singh. Produced by M. & T. Films, 1949.

Nirala. Directed by Devendra Mukherji. Produced by M. & T. Films, 1950.

Patanga. Directed by Harnam Singh Rawail. Produced by Varma Films, 1949.

Sargam. Directed by Santoshi. Produced by Filmistan, 1950.

Shehnai. Directed by Santoshi. Produced by Filmistan, 1947.

Showboat. Directed by James Whale. Produced by Universal Pictures, 1936.

Shree 420. Directed by Raj Kapoor. Produced by R. K. Films, 1955.

That Night in Rio. Directed by Irving Cummings. Produced by Twentieth Century Fox Film Corporation, 1941.

Tin Pan Alley. Directed by Walter Lang, Produced by Twentieth Century Fox Film Corporation, 1941.

Discography

All Star Swing Band. 1942. Columbia (FB 40221, 40226, 40229 and 40230).

Chic & His Music Makers. 1943–45. Columbia (FB 40324, 40337, 40338, 40390, 40393, 40394, 40406, 40407, 40409, and 40446).

Crickett Smith and His Symphonians. 1936. Rex (7994-A).

Jazz and Hot Dance in India: 1926–1944. 1985. Harlequin (HQ 2013).

Jimmy Lequime's Grand Hotel Orchestra. 1926. HMV (P 7094).

John Abriani's Taj Mahal Hotel Orchestra. 1933. The Twin (FT 1500).

Julies Craen and His Quintette. 1936. Rex (ME 7994).

Paquita and Zarate with Teddy Weatherford and His Boys. 1941. Columbia (FB 40081 and FB 40099).

Reuben Solomon and His Jive Boys. 1942–44. Columbia (FB 40231, 40270, 40269, 40303, 40308, 40309, 40345, 40378, 40379, 40391, 40392, and 40405).

Taj Mahal Hotel Dance Orchestra. 1942. Columbia (FB 40175).

Teddy Weatherford. 1943. Columbia (FB 40316).

Teddy Weatherford and His Band. 1942. Columbia (FB 40174).

Teddy Weatherford at the Piano. 1941. Columbia (FB 40067).

Teddy Weatherford at the Piano. 1942. Columbia (FB 40154, 40164, 40220, and 40225).

Index

British Raj, 3, 51, 72, 113, 169, 173n3
Broadway, 45, 50, 64, 66, 102–3, 191n83
Broadway Boy's Jazz Band, 66
Brown, A. Claude, 27
Brubeck, Dave, 170
Bryant's Songs from Dixieland, 41. *See also* printed music
Burrell, Eric, 127. *See also* Lucknow
businesspeople, 1, 6, 8, 9, 19, 21, 26–27, 82, 178n34
Butler, Roy, 13, 14–16, 54, 67–71, 81, 90, 115, 144, 154, 183n65

cabaret: design of, 21, 51, 54, 57, 59–62, 66, 81, 97, 117, 133–37, 146, 148, 150–51, 167, 1181n135, 181n137, 188n35, 190n67, 200n35; in films, 13, 19, 50–51, 92, 153, 155, 157, 159–65, 167–68, 200n34; music in, 2, 13, 19, 48, 50–51, 64, 66, 115, 130, 133, 139–41, 143, 145–46; at the Taj Mahal Palace Hotel, 14, 54, 59–62, 145–46, 148–52, 197n74
cabasa, 143
Café de Paris, 6, 182n27. *See also* apache dance
cakewalk, 42–45. *See also* ragtime
Calcutta Key, 92, 95, 99–101. *See also* troops
Camberley High Street, 114. *See also* Hazratganj; Lucknow
Camp, LaVonne Telshaw, 94, 190n66. *See also* troops
cantonment, 29, 111–12, 114–16, 130–31, 137, 195n24
Cardoza's Band, 134
Carlton Hotel, 117–18, 124, 128, 135, 137. *See also* Lucknow
Carr, Tagore, and Company, 26, 27
Carson, Dave, 1, 2, 3, 4, 9, 19, 27, 31–32, 35– 41, 45, 65, 169, 173n2, 173n9. *See also* blackface; Town Hall
Carson, Lionel, 45. *See also* ragtime
castanets, 158–59
Catholic educational institution, 77, 111

Cavalry School, 53, 75–76. *See also* Mac, Ken
Chasers, The, 45. *See also* ragtime
Chattar Manzil (Lucknow), 115. *See also* social clubs
Chicago, 14, 23, 42, 55, 69, 91, 100, 180n104, 184n70, 189n40. *See also* Weatherford, Teddy
China-Burma-India (CBI), 20, 86, 88–89, 100, 103, 134, 188n23, 192n91, 192n92. *See also* World War II
Chinese: jazz, 176n58; troops, 100; restaurant, 128
Chocolate, Chic, 13, 82, 144, 163–64
chorus girls, 50. *See also* cabaret
chronophone, 13
cinématographe, 13
cinematography, 158
clave, 143–44, 155–57, 160, 162–64, 166–67
"Coal Black Mammy," 3. *See also* blackface; St. Helier, Ivy
cocktail, 79, 98–99, 113, 133–34, 148
Coelho Brothers, 112. *See also* Britannia Restaurant; Goa
Coleman, Bill, 14, 68, 164, 183n61
collaboration: in Allied military, 20; in business, 27, 178n34; in Indian film industry, 140, 160, 163, 200n28; among jazz musicians, 144; in live cabarets, 57, 146, 186n134
collections: of gramophone discs, 125; of printed music, 29–30, 34, 41
College of Saint Paul, 22, 83. *See also* Goa
Collet, H. J., 154
Colombo, 69, 183n64, 188n25
Coloured Opera Troupe, 39–40. *See also* blackface
Columbia Records, 74, 90–92, 164
comedy, 25, 48, 66, 70, 125
commerce, 4–6, 9, 19–20, 28, 51, 75, 78, 106, 110, 171
commercial network, 6, 8, 26
commodity, 6, 9, 26–27, 79, 110, 140, 174n36, 187n140

Entertainment Production Unit (EPU),
103. *See also* World War II
Entertainments National Service
Association (ENSA), 17, 102–3, 106.
See also World War II
entrepreneur, 5, 8, 19, 26, 44, 53, 55,
82–83, 97–98, 109, 111, 178n34. *See
also* Correa, Micky; Mac, Ken
Eros Cinema and Ballroom, 14, 79, 81.
See also Correa, Micky
Ethiopian Serenaders, 32. *See also*
blackface
exaggerated: blackface, 70; chord
movement, 156; dance, 36; dialect,
71; differences, 37; image, 3; lips,
15, 70
Excelsior Theatre, 48–51, 64. *See also*
Bandman, Maurice, ragtime
exoticism, 13–14, 26, 33, 53, 55, 58,
67–72, 82, 175n49, 184n69

fairyland, 66. *See also* ballroom dance
fanfare: on trumpet, 156, 160, 163,
166
fantasy: American South, 34; theme at
dances, 66, 99
Federal Talkies, 119. *See also* Lucknow
Federation of Musicians (publication),
146, 158, 201n60
Federation of Musicians, India
(organization), 146, 153, 154, 158
Fernand, Frank, 94, 144, 158
Fielden, Lionel, 73, 185n94. *See also*
radio
Firpo's Restaurant and Bar, 17, 50–51,
64, 73, 86, 94, 97–99, 101, 190n64,
190n67, 191n72, 191n73. *See also*
Bengal Famine
Flemming, Herb, 67–68, 121. *See also*
Grand Hotel
Flying Down to Rio (1933), 119, 120
Folies Bergère, 145. *See also* cabaret
foreignness in film, 143
formulaic, 156, 163, 166
Foster, Stephen, 34, 55
foxtrot, 72, 78, 115, 154, 183n39

Frank, Archie, 129, 134. *See also*
Lucknow; Mayfair Cinema
Frank Fernand and His All Star Band,
144
Fred Little's Rhythm Aces, 115. *See also*
Hazratganj; Lucknow; Valerio's
freelancing, 152
Frith, Simon, 8, 71. *See also* blackface

Gadimbas Band, 146
Gaiety Theatre, 9, 33, 39, 43–45,
176n69, 178n35. *See also* blackface;
Carson, Dave
Gaisberg, Frederick W., 12, 213. *See also*
Gramophone Company Ltd.
Galle Face Hotel, 70–71, 183n64. *See
also* Colombo
"ganjing," 127–28. *See also* Hazratganj;
Lucknow
Garrison Theatre, 91, 102. *See also*
World War II
ghazal, 131
Ghisleri, Joseph, 67, 145
GI Jill, 88–89. See also radio; troops,
World War II
GI-Jive, 88. See also radio; troops,
VU2ZU; World War II
Gloucestershire Regiment Crow
Minstrels, 39. *See also* blackface
Goa, 22, 77, 82–83, 94, 106, 109, 111,
112, 130, 137–38, 144, 163, 166,
175n53, 197n90, 200n2, 202n63
"God Save the King," 43, 78, 81,
186n127. *See also* Correa, Alex;
Correa, Micky
Godfrey's Band, 117. See also Agabeg's
Amusement Hall
Godfrey, Charles, 31
Gold Diggers of 1933 (1933), 119
Goody Seervai and His Orchestra, 146
Gothic: building, 39; style, 117, 195n28
Government House: Karachi, 77–78;
Lucknow, 114
Government of India Act (1935), 23
Governor's Ball, 114–15. *See also* Indian
Civil Service (ICS) Week

Gramophone Company Ltd., 10–12,
48, 217
Grand Hotel, 12, 67, 74, 90–92, 94, 101,
105, 110, 121, 184n65
Grant Road Theatre, 9, 36–37. *See also*
blackface; Carson, Dave
Great American Broadcast (1941), 92
great depression, 56
Great Eastern Hotel, 102
Green's Hotel, 51, 73, 76, 81, 164
grito, 166
guitar, 18, 104, 110, 120, 122, 142, 155–
60, 162, 165, 169, 171
Gujarat, 8, 21
Gundevia, Y. D., 113–15. *See also* Indian
Civil Service (ICS) Week
Gymkhana, 28, 66, 76–77, 112,
181n137. *See also* social club

hairstyle: American, 132; European,
132
Hallelujah (1929), 57
Hamari Beti (1950), 148
Handel, George Frideric, 22
Harlem Is Heaven (1932), 57
Hasting's Air Base, 104. *See also*
Monswooners
Hazratganj, 20, 109–17, 120, 123, 125–
28, 136–38. *See also* Ambasador Club;
Lucknow; Mayfair Cinema; Valerio's
Hearts in Dixie (1929), 57
Heinemann, George T., 17, 98–99. *See
also* Bengal Famine
Hellzapoppin' (1941), 125
Herman, Woody, 92
Herrmann, Bernard, 140–41
hill station, 76, 126, 164, 175n50,
191n75, 192n94
Himalayas, 3
Hippodrome, 6, 47. *See also Hullo,
Ragtime!*
His Master's Voice (HMV), 12, 48, 74,
90, 92, 196n64
history: of America, 2; of black
America, 25–26, 111; of blackface
minstrels in India, 5; of domination

of subcontinent, 21, 86; of India, 23,
95, 170; of Indian film, 141, 155–56;
personal, 22–23, 109, 112, 128, 169;
of stage performance, 61
HMS New Zealand, 64, 183n40. *See also*
Maurice Bandman
Hog-Hunter's Ball, 114. *See also* Indian
Civil Service (ICS) Week
Holloway, Jim, 91, 184n70. *See also*
Weatherford, Teddy
Hollywood: availability in India, 90–92,
132; cabarets scenes, 2, 59, 168;
excitement about, 119–20, 134; film
music, 2, 13, 18–19, 53–54, 56–57,
60, 69, 82, 90–92, 129–30, 138–44,
155–56, 164, 167–68, 199n16,
202n73; globalization of, 69, 74,
119–20, 130; representations of, 2,
13, 53–60, 82
Hullo Ragtime!, 6–7, 47–48. *See also*
ragtime
Hum Log (1951), 148
Hunter, Alberta, 102. *See also* USO;
World War II

iconographies, 13–14, 45, 60, 69–72
imagination, 4, 18, 54, 140, 173n11
imperial, 8, 20–21, 95
imported: alcohol, 145; gramophone
discs, 53, 74, 90, 92; instruments,
104
improvisation, 48, 110, 123, 143, 156–
59, 163, 166, 184n82
Indian Civil Service (ICS) Week, 109,
113–19. *See also* Lucknow
Indian Independence, 88, 137, 154, 168
Indian Rebellion, 23, 26
Indian State Broadcasting Service, 120–
21. *See also* All India Radio (AIR)
innovation: business, 32, 178n34; in
composition, 164, 167, 202n68; in
popular music, 73, 142, 199n14;
technological, 6
instrumental break, 157
Interlocutor, Mr., 3, 33, 41, 43, 179n50.
See also blackface